COMMUNICOLOGY

• • •

Sensing Media

Aesthetics, Philosophy, and Cultures of Media

EDITED BY WENDY HUI KYONG CHUN AND SHANE DENSON

COMMUNICOLOGY

Mutations in Human Relations?

VILÉM FLUSSER

EDITED BY RODRIGO MALTEZ NOVAES
WITH A FOREWORD BY N. KATHERINE HAYLES

STANFORD UNIVERSITY PRESS
Stanford, California

STANFORD UNIVERSITY PRESS
Stanford, California

Printed in the United States of America on acid-free, archival-quality paper

Library of Congress Cataloging-in-Publication Data

Names: Flusser, Vilém, 1920–1991, author. | Novaes, Rodrigo Maltez, editor, translator.
Title: Communicology : mutations in human relations? / Vilém Flusser ; edited by Rodrigo Maltez Novaes.
Other titles: Kommunikologie. English | Sensing media (Series)
Description: Stanford, California : Stanford University Press, 2022. | Series: Sensing media: aesthetics, philosophy, and cultures of media | Translation of: Kommunikologie. | Includes bibliographical references.
Identifiers: LCCN 2022012332 (print) | LCCN 2022012333 (ebook) | ISBN 9781503633261 (cloth) | ISBN 9781503634480 (paperback) | ISBN 9781503634497 (ebook)
Subjects: LCSH: Communication—Philosophy.
Classification: LCC P90 .F62513 2022 (print) | LCC P90 (ebook) | DDC 302.2—dc23/eng/20220318
LC record available at https://lccn.loc.gov/2022012332
LC ebook record available at https://lccn.loc.gov/2022012333

Cover designer: Michel Vrana
Cover photo: ralph hinterkeuser | www.architekturfoto.de

CONTENTS

FOREWORD

by N. Katherine Hayles

Writing in 2004, Sean Cubitt lamented the absence of Vilém Flusser's books in English, likening it to a situation in which we would have only snippets of Marshall McLuhan or fragments of Walter Benjamin. Even in 2010, when Flusser's *Into the Universe of Technical Images* was published as part of the Electronic Mediations Series by the University of Minnesota Press, Mark Poster in his foreword decried the absence of media theory in the major theorists of deconstruction, including Jacques Derrida, Gilles Deleuze, and Judith Butler, an absence he hoped Flusser's book would correct. Perhaps it is now safe to say that Flusser's writings have emerged as a major locus for media theory within the English-speaking world. With *Communicology: Mutations in Human Relations?* translator Rodrigo Maltez Novaes, working with Stanford University Press, aims to bring into English Flusser's original thesis on technical images and the technical imagination, the fountain from which flowed many of his later works, including *Post-History* (1979), *Towards a Philosophy of Photography* (1982), and *The Universe of Technical Images* (1983).

Flusser believes that humans are driven to communicate in a desperate search for meaning in the face of death's inevitability. This text makes clear that for Flusser, communication is thus a matter of social relations. Technologies, from oral transmissions to manuscripts to print, help mediate the transmissions, but technology itself is not the primary force driving social and psychological change. Thus, he begins his discussion with sketches illustrating the different kinds of communication situations and the social relations they embody. The premise undergirding these sketches is scarcely original, although Flusser makes it more explicit than did many of the earlier theorists working along similar lines. The premise is this: the modes of communication that a society uses have profound effects on shaping the consciousness of its members, or as Flusser frequently puts it, media "program us." We can locate similar ideas in the writings of Marshall McLuhan and, more recently, in the work of Bernard Stiegler, Mark Hansen, and Erich Hörl, among others. Moving much farther back in time, we may even see hints of it in Plato's banishing of poets from his *Republic* because (as Eric Havelock has argued) he feared that the poetic emphasis on emotion and rhetoric would undermine the rationality he valued above all else.

For Flusser, a central implication is his crucial insight that we are on the cusp of leaving one kind of consciousness and entering another. Flusser emphasizes that the consciousness of modern people living today (or at least in 1978 when he wrote this work) has been formed by the ideologies of print, even as the modes associated with technical images erupt within our world through photography, TV, radio, and so forth. The inevitable results, he writes, are social crises and internal conflicts.

Print culture, he argues, is associated with linearity and its social correlates, including historical consciousness, rationality, temporal progress, and nationalism (because print culture facilitated the displacement of local dialects by the "paper languages" of English, French, German, etc.). That he puts technologies of print production in second place makes his work distinctively different from that of Friedrich Kittler, who in analyzing a similar shift from one kind of network discourse to another put primary emphasis on the technologies (this may explain why Kittler chose to downplay the significance of Flusser's contribution, arguing that many books such as the Bible were not read in the linear order that Flusser associates with print texts).

What then are the communication modes characteristic of the new epoch, the technical image and the technical imagination? His most salient example of a technical image is the photograph, amplified in *Towards a Philosophy of Photography.* He contrasts the photograph with a painting, arguing that in one sense "photographs are more *objective* than paintings because the object impresses itself upon the surface, while in the painting there is a *subject* (the painter) who interferes in the image making." In another sense, they are less objective because "the interference of the *apparatus-operator* complex [camera and photographer] is far more intricate than is the interference of the painter in the process of image making." The passage may seem to suggest that his argument hinges on the presence of an apparatus-operator complex, but this would be a misreading: the main point is not how technical images are produced but rather "the meaning of the image." In print media ecology, Flusser argues, an image means a scene, described in linear fashion and implying a temporality that progresses from past to future. However, in the ecology of technical images, an image means a concept. "Behind a painting stands a painter who tries to imagine a scene," he writes. By contrast, "behind a photograph stands a text of optics, of chemistry, etc., a *theory* that tries to conceive a process." A particularly clear example is an astronomer who takes a photograph of a star. The image, highly mediated through telescopes, filters, light-gathering apparatus, and so forth, means to the specialist a concept of a star and the processes it signifies; as an elite communicator, the scientist consciously recognizes this status. Similarly, TV and video images also mean concepts, although this implication is often obscured for non-specialist viewers, who nevertheless unconsciously absorb the concepts through their "radiation" by mass media.

Since for Flusser the issue of meaning is central to the status of an image, it should come as no surprise that the force he sees propelling the transition from one media epoch to another is not so much technology (for example, the invention of the printing press) as a loss of meaning in a previous epoch's modes of communication. He repeatedly proclaims his impatience with discussions that focus on which came first, a technology or a change of perceptions. For Flusser, Einstein's theory of relativity did not, as Linda Henderson among others maintains, influence artists such as Pablo Picasso and Marcel Duchamp; from Flusser's point of view, one could just as easily argue that the fin-de-siècle artistic revolutions influenced Einstein. Such reasoning is apparent in this passage when he notes the post-historical entwinement of space and time. Flusser writes that in the new epoch, "the concept *space* can be imagined as a synchronization of time, and the concept *time*, as a diachronization of space." This sounds very Einsteinian, but Flusser denies the obvious connection: "The scientific *advance* cannot be the cause of this type of technical imagination; on the contrary, it is the result of technical imagination. . . . Any question of precedence is, of course, nonsense. It is of no consequence whether *modern humanity invented printing* or *printed books made modern humanity possible*; or whether *the Industrial Revolution introduced the public educational system* or *that system opened the field for the Industrial Revolution*. The difference of formulation is a question of points of view on the same phenomenon and of a subsequent different use of terms." Printing emerged not because movable type revolutionized print production, Flusser suggests, but because people had become overwhelmed by the plenitude of ritualistic practices associated with oral cultures. "People decided to explain images by texts and thus impoverish the meaning of images through clearness and distinction when meaning became intolerably compact. Conceptual thinking was, and is, the effort to save oneself from the cancerous growth of imagination." Now a new transition is energized for a related but opposite reason: not an over-fullness of meaning but a lack of it. "We no longer even pretend to believe in *theories*, *ideologies*, *discoveries*, and *progress*, if we are honest. We are no longer as literate as they were [participants in print culture]. In our program, *reason* is again challenged by a different code, such as the one before printing was invented. But the challenge is a new one: no longer must we translate from image to letter but from letter to a new type of image." In the transitions he traces, Flusser repeatedly emphasizes a kind of self-devouring logic that he claims is also true of our contemporary moment. The elite of primarily oral cultures, who knew how to write, "used the code of linear writing, which was to result in historical consciousness and historical action, as a method to sustain imaginary sacredness and a magical, ritual acting. It seems as if those early writers did not know what they were doing (that they were illiterate in spite of their technical skill in producing written texts), and certainly they had no inkling of the revolution they were provoking. In this, very probably, they were not unlike the present programmers." They wanted to "freeze a form of existence rendered meaningless by a new form of communication," and in this attempt to shore up something that was passing, they inadvertently accelerated its demise.

By analogy, our present programmers try to shore up our belief in texts by creating images that emerge from them, but in this endeavor they are inadvertently creating a new mode of communication—and of existence—that ironically has the effect of vaulting us out of linear, rational, historical consciousness and into technical imagination. If, as Mark Poster argued, the major theorists of deconstruction ignored media theory in general and Flusser in particular, Flusser for his part shows his disdain for the textual methods of deconstructive analysis. "The less one believes in texts, the more one criticizes them, and the more one criticizes them, the less one believes in them. The less one imagines what they mean, the less they mean, and the less they mean, the less one imagines their meaning. And this self-reinforcing circle must result in an involution of reason." Thus, from Flusser's perspective deconstruction itself can be seen as a symptom of a pending revolution already afoot, although its practitioners had little or no grasp of the nature and dynamics of what they were helping bring about.

It is not only the print era that is passing, Flusser argues, but writing in general. In *Does Writing Have a Future?* Flusser's answer to the titular question is a definitive "no." In our text he anticipates this later book in his remarks comparing traditional images to technical images. "Traditional images are mediations between humanity and the world. Technical images are mediations between humanity and texts. Traditional images imagine scenes and technical images imagine texts. Technical image codes mean texts; they are post-alphabetic, both in the sense that they no longer function like texts and in the sense that they could not have been invented without alphabetic writing." Emerging from alphabetic writing and texts created by it, technical images at once render the prior epoch obsolete and inaugurate the new.

Flusser creates a sketch showing this relationship, which he describes as follows: "The sketch shows that the *apparatus-operator* complex is one that devours texts and spits out technical images, one that devours history and spits out post-history. History flows into the complex in the form of texts (scientific, political, and artistic discourses) and is there recodified into post-historical programs (amphitheatrically radiated films, posters, TV programs)." These "programs" are in the process of transforming the consciousness of us, the readers of Flusser's text, who grew up with print but are now inundated daily by the technical images that slowly but surely are initiating us into the technical imagination. He sums up the process with this memorable aphorism: "The ultimate aim of history is to become a TV program."

The irony of our situation, according to Flusser, is that even those who program us, ignorant of the implications of their actions, are also being programmed. "The producers are not fully aware of what they are doing," he writes, "and the receivers do not want to know the meaning of their program. This is why technical images work as they do: toward totalitarian alienation." Even the elite specialists, such as the astronomer who knows very well the meaning of his photographs as concepts, slip into unawareness when they turn over their products to the mass media (think Carl Sagan intoning, "The Cosmos is all that is or ever was or ever will be"). "How did technical images *slip* from the elite into mass communication?" Flusser asks. The answer, he maintains, is "now obvious." "They were sucked into the *apparatus-operator* complex during the process of sucking in technical discourse. Cathode tubes became TV boxes, and photographs became posters, not because the scientists and the artists (the elite) handed them over to the manipulators of mass media but because the scientists and artists (the whole elite) were devoured by the apparatus and became operators. In other words, their own creature devoured them." This passage illustrates that the "totalitarian" aspect that Flusser emphasizes is invariably linked with what he calls the "massification" of media. We might reasonably wonder, then, how relevant his analysis is today, more than four decades later when the media landscape has changed almost beyond recognition. Broadcast TV, Flusser's usual target, has been largely replaced by the internet; movie theaters, which he likens to cathedrals and ritual spaces, have given way to streaming services; and the nightly news has been taken over by information (and misinformation) promulgated through social media.

To his credit, he anticipated some of these developments, although he failed to realize that they too could become programming media in their own right. Because these events work against "massification," he was able to imagine them only as liberatory strategies. "No technical difficulties prevent the TV set becoming a two-way channel like a telephone," he wrote as if channeling this possibility from the future. "And if thus changed, it would become a powerful tool for *democracy* and thus be far more revolutionary than are public meetings (let alone political elections). But such a change would require a new vision of politics, of decision-making, of action; it would involve the abandonment of concepts like *nation* or *class*, and it would involve the abandonment of the present, highly satisfactory use of television. It would require a technical imagination that nobody is willing and able to mobilize, neither those who manipulate current TV nor those who are its victims." What he failed to envision is how, with the breakup of media "massification," the public discourse on which democracy depends is now subject to alternative facts, conspiracy theories, and routine lies that try to transform actual events, which everyone saw with their own eyes and heard with their own ears, were actually something else. In this respect, George Orwell is a more accurate prognosticator of our present situation than Flusser.

But Flusser was not entirely wrong, either. The problem, in Flusserian terms, is that the media transformations came about without an accompanying awareness of what the technical imagination could be in its utopian possibilities. Technical images, in this aspect, have the possibility to "consolidate a new level of consciousness and of existence, to create a new mode of communication and therefore a new society and a new human. In sum, the function of technical images is to serve technical imagination." And it is by accepting and cultivating technical imagination that we might be able to escape from the horns of our dilemma, in which we are caught between the old codes that programmed us for print ideology and the new codes emerging from technical images.

This prospect cuts to the heart of Flusser's intervention. "The purpose of this book," he writes, is to enable us to see that technical imagination involves "a radical mutation of human relations, a radical change of the agreement between humans concerning the meaning of life in the world." This kind of technical imagination would be "fully awake," aware that an older order has passed away and a new order has arrived. "It is no easy decision," he warns, "because although totalitarian apparatus are certainly a horrible prospect, so is the *new human*." Accepting the transformation will involve realizing that the meanings of terms central to our way of life, from truth to objectivity to space and time to meaning itself, have changed into something we can now only vaguely grasp.

No doubt Flusser, in trying to limn the outline of these changes, has made many errors of interpretation and anticipation. Indeed, it would be miraculous if he were right in every instance; after all, he stands upon the same ground as we do, peering through the "fogs that surround us" into a still unknown future. But if he is correct enough—that is, if he is more or less accurate in describing the kind of transition that is occurring in human relations, understandings, and meanings—then this is an immensely important text with which we should all grapple. We are fortunate indeed to have this text now available to the English-speaking world to ponder, to agree and disagree with, and most important, to stimulate new conversations.

Works Cited

Cubitt, Sean. 2004. Review of *The Shape of Things: A Philosophy of Design*, and *Towards a Philosophy of Photography*, and *Writings*, and *The Freedom of the Migrant: Objections to Nationalism*. *Leonardo* 3, no. 5 (October): 403–5, esp. 403.

Flusser, Vilém. (1979) 2013. *Post-History*. Translated by Rodrigo Maltez Novaes. Reprint, Minneapolis: Univocal Publishing/University of Minnesota Press.

Flusser, Vilém. (1982) 2000. *Towards a Philosophy of Photography*. Introduction by Hubertus Von Amelunxen. Translated by Anthony Matthews. Reprint, London: Reaktion Books.

Flusser, Vilém. (1983) 2011. *Into the Universe of Technical Images*. Translated by Nancy Ann Roth. Electronic Mediations Series. Reprint, Minneapolis: University of Minnesota Press.

Flusser, Vilém. 2011. *Does Writing Have a Future?* Electronic Mediations Series. Minneapolis: University of Minnesota Press.

Hansen, Mark. 2015. *Feed-Forward: On the Future of Twenty-First-Century Media*. Chicago: University of Chicago Press.

Havelock, Eric. 1963. *Preface to Plato (History of the Greek Mind)*. Cambridge, MA: Belknap Press/Harvard University Press.

Henderson, Linda. 1998. *Duchamp in Context: Science and Technology in the Large Glass and Related Works*. Princeton, NJ: Princeton University Press.

Henderson, Linda. 2014. *The Fourth Dimension and Non-Euclidean Geometry in Modern Art*. Princeton, NJ: Princeton University Press.

Hörl, Erich, ed. 2017. *General Ecology: The New Ecological Paradigm*. London:

Bloomsbury Academic.
Kittler, Friedrich. 1990. *Discourse Networks: 1800/1900*. Stanford, CA: Stanford University Press.
Kittler, Friedrich. 2001. "Perspective and the Book." *Grey Room* 5:38–53.
McLuhan, Marshall. 1994. *Understanding Media: Extensions of Man*. Cambridge, MA: MIT Press.
Poster, Mark. 2011. "An Introduction to Vilém Flusser's *Into the Universe of Technical Images* and *Does Writing Have a Future?*" In *Into the Universe of Technical Images*, by Vilém Flusser, translated Nancy Ann Roth, Electronic Mediations Series, ix–xxvii. Minneapolis: University of Minnesota Press. Stiegler, Bernard. 2010. *Taking Care of Youth and the Generations*. Stanford, CA: Stanford University Press.

EDITOR'S NOTE

by Rodrigo Maltez Novaes

It is a pleasure to be able to introduce this work by Vilém Flusser to an anglophone audience more than forty years after it was originally written. Today the ideas and concepts in this book, in our post-internet age, may feel surprisingly familiar to any media theory reader. Particularly if read alongside the books Flusser wrote in the 1980s, *Communicology* emerges as a true work of our times.

Flusser was a polyglot, writing and self-translating most of his books between Portuguese, German, English, and French, using the translation process to gain different insights into his own work, sometimes translating a book more than once. In the case of *Communicology*, he wrote three full versions—in English, German, and French—during the winter of 1977–78 in France. From his correspondence it seems he wrote the complete English version first, then translated it to German, and then French.[1] He had only recently immigrated back to Europe after thirty-two years in Brazil. In fact, Flusser initially intended *Communicology* for publication first in the United States, with the clear intention of sending it to MIT Press. Because the press had included his paper "Two Approaches to the Phenomenon, Television" in its publication *The New Television: A Public/Private Art*,[2] he thought he would have an opening with the editors. However, despite *Communicology*'s forward-looking and prescient nature in a pre-internet age, it was rejected by MIT in 1979, with editors suggesting that although they were initially intrigued and excited by the concepts in the work, stylistic and language problems posed too great a barrier for publication. Correspondence between Flusser and the editors shows the efforts he made to defend his style (something that I am very familiar with through my work of editing and translation of his books). In a letter on June 21, 1978, he writes:

> For instance, my terminology is not the one used in your country, and terms like *discourse* and *symbol* would have to be either explained or adjusted for an American reader. (Some terms I have coined myself, however, like *technical-imagination*, and it is necessary to maintain them.) Also, I purposely abstain from quoting literature. . . . As for the ideas advanced in the manuscript, I do not think they should be manipulated very much, but left as they are: as hypotheses and suggestions, not as definitive statements.

And on April 26, 1979, he further argues:

> You say that the problem with publishing my manuscript *Mutation in Human Relations?* is its language and style. I believe it is more the style than the language. Although my English needs some polishing, it is good enough for me to have published several papers in English. As to style, this has more to do with the way one thinks and lives than with the way one speaks. I must confess that my style is rather unusual in all the languages I write, including Portuguese and German, which are closest to me. My stylistic particularities have earned me the epithet of "a baroque thinker" in a Brazilian encyclopaedia. Of course: my style is both the result of my natural inclination and of my deliberate effort to accentuate this.

A final note from MIT in October 1979 expresses the challenges the press had in obtaining sufficient reviews of *Communicology*; when this push for publication failed, Flusser simply archived the book.

Eventually, the book was published posthumously in German by Stefan Bollmann.[3] This first edition by Bollmann also has additional essays, added at the end of the book by the editors, selected from the many loose texts Flusser wrote on the theme of technical images throughout the 1980s. However, my intention with this first English edition is to restore the work to Flusser's original manuscript, following the approach I have been taking with the complete works series being edited in Portuguese.[4] For this reason, this book does not follow the editorial decisions of the first German edition but honors what I understand to be Flusser's original intentions for the project.

Fortunately, today the world seems to have become accustomed to Flusser's particular style, and, as the reader will soon experience, the work no longer needs the explanations it did in the 1970s. Still, it is worth spending some time here discussing some aspects of the development of Flusser's communication (media) theory and the emergence of the concepts of *technical images* and *technical imagination* in his work, which will hopefully help contextualize *Communicology* for a contemporary reader.

In 1974, when Flusser traveled to the United States to deliver the paper "Two Approaches to the Phenomenon, Television" as a lecture, he had the opportunity to meet several artists and intellectuals of the New York scene. Nam Jun Paik, an artist who was at the time director of the Kitchen and working with the medium of video art, left a strong impression on Flusser.[5] Even though Flusser had not yet formulated the terms *technical image* or *technical imagination*, perhaps the seed was sown in his mind during that trip. Also, during the late 1960s prior to his move back to Europe in 1972, he had been developing a course on communication theory for the School of Communication and Humanities at the A. A. Penteado Foundation in São Paulo. Despite having already developed his "apparatus theory," which he explored extensively in *The Last Judgement: Generations* (1966),[6] the concepts of *technical image* and *technical imagination* were not yet present in his published work. The development of the apparatus theory was a seminal moment in his overall philosophical project. However, it was not complete until the emergence of the concepts of *technical image* and *technical imagination* in the mid-1970s.

The first instance of the term *technical imagination* may have been in 1976 in a proposal for a lecture titled "L'irruption du techno-imaginaire" at the École Nationale des Beaux Arts de Dijon. The lecture was eventually delivered in Paris in 1977,[7] and he then expanded it into a course on communication theory, which he delivered at the Département de Communication Visuelle et Audio-Visuelle de l'École Supérieure d'Art et d'Architecture de Marseille–Luminy the same year, later expanding it further to become *Communicology*. I also propose this date because in 1975 Flusser delivered a series of twelve lectures in France titled *Les phénomènes de la communication* in which he did not use the terms *technical image* or *technical imagination.*[8] Therefore, the two concepts emerge around 1976 as complementary formulations to his apparatus theory, which he continued developing in the late 1970s and throughout the 1980s. Notably, despite the time line just suggested, Flusser began laying the foundations for what would emerge in the mid-1970s as this book during his course on communication theory at the A. A. Penteado Foundation during the harshest years of military dictatorship in Brazil. It is worth reproducing here two excerpts from his autobiography *Groundless*, which may further help us situate *Communicology* in the chronological development of his thought:

> The programme is "open" due to the following: (1) the theory's scope is not pre-established; (2) the theory's methods are not pre-established; (3) the praxis for the manipulation of phenomena is not pre-established. The programme's premises are the following: (a) the scope of the theory must be a field that is already part of the scope of other established disciplines; (b) the methods must be borrowed from these disciplines; and (c) the praxis for the manipulation must be original. In sum: "the theory of communication should become the metadiscourse of all forms of human communication, so that the structure of this communication becomes evident in order to be able to change it." A "communicologist" is one who has the instruments at hand for the modification of human communication, and theory is what should provide these instruments. This was the programme for my intended chair. . . .
>
> As for classification of the field's scope, I shall mention some of the categories: (a) Nerves (audio, visual, tactile, olfactory communication, etc.). Methods: physiology, behaviourism, etc. (b) Function (mass, elite, closed circuit communication, etc.). Methods: sociology, social psychology, etc. (c) Dynamics (discourse, dialogue, radiation, tree, ellipsis communication, etc.). Methods: cybernetics, game theory, etc. (d) Symbol (denotative, connotative, imaginative, conceptual communication,

> etc.). Methods: literary criticism, aesthetics, etc. (e) Information (original, banal, kitsch communication, etc.). Methods: information theory, etc. (f) Message (imperative, indicative, exclamatory, inquisitive communication, etc.). Methods: logical analysis, etc. (g) Channels (unidimensional, multidimensional, diachronic, synchronic communication, etc.). Methods: *Gestalt* psychology, etc. (h) Social (work, consumer, entertainment communication, etc.). Methods: economy, sociology, etc. . . . and so on and so forth.[9]

As will become evident, the above description is indeed the embryo of what eventually emerged as Flusser's fully fledged *communicology*, a term he coined to differentiate his own theory from the general discipline of media theory at the time.

Flusser is generally referred to as a "media theorist"; however, conventional media theory tends to focus primarily on transmission, on the channels and networks that spread information, hence Marshall McLuhan's "the medium is the message." In contrast, Flusser goes beyond transmission, including in his critique the aspects of production and storage of information. In other words, his "communication theory" focuses on culture, memory, *and* transmission (production, storage, and distribution). In the Synopsis to *Communicology*, he writes:

> This stress on transmission (on what has become the custom to be called *media*) is unfortunate because it tends to cover up the essential aspect of communication, which is that it transforms humans into accumulators of acquired information.

This combined triad of *production*, *storage*, and *distribution* is central to all his work post-*Communicology*, which he explores from several different angles and which is generally referred to as his "media theory" work of the 1980s. After *Communicology*, Flusser wrote *Post-History* (1979),[10] *Vampyroteuthis infernalis* (1981),[11] *Towards a Philosophy of Photography* (1982),[12] *Into the Universe of Technical Images* (1983),[13] and *Does Writing Have a Future?* (1987),[14] all of which expand on his apparatus theory as a whole.

My main reason for establishing these links between Flusser's various works is to dispel a general, erroneous, view that his ideas seem to "pop out of nowhere," often earning him the attribution of being a "visionary," which in my opinion serves to devalue and sometimes undermine his work as a philosopher. Flusser was a wholistic, rigorous, and methodical thinker. The misplaced impression of discontinuity within his philosophical project is largely due to the erratic way in which his work was published both during his lifetime and after his death. If we strictly follow the trajectory of his unpublished writings, what emerges is a completely different image of the philosopher, one of both consistency and continuity in the development of an overall philosophical project. There are in fact no breaks in his work, and all of his monographs and courses show a continuous, gradual development of his ideas, which expand progressively, growing and mutating along the way. For this reason, in talking about Flusser, I tend to point to the year when a piece of writing was produced rather than the year when a particular work was published, although in very few cases both dates coincide.

My point is that Flusser's production was continuous; every winter he produced a manuscript, either specifically as a monograph or as the final result of a series of lectures. After writing *Communicology*, he started planning a series of lectures titled *Post-History*, which became the basis of his subsequent book of the same title, published for the first time in Brazil in 1983. There was never a break in his production, and as one book was rejected by a publisher, another was already in the works, which meant that as he moved on in his work and thought, the rejected manuscript was then simply archived.

This was also the case with, for example, *The Last Judgment: Generations*, which after being dropped by the Brazilian publishers in 1968, was archived, only seeing the light of day again in 2017. This is a peculiarity of Flusser's oeuvre that needs to be appreciated to dispel the image of an erratic writing practice. In fact, if all of his books had been published soon after being written, it is my guess that Flusser would be a far more widely read author today.

Much of my own editing and translation of Flusser's work focuses on an attempt to present the work by placing it on a correct production time line to help readers study his work according to its own inner logic of development. In line with this effort, I have helped edit the bibliographical list of Flusser's work on the online project monoskop.org to reflect his production time line for any reader who wishes to read Flusser chronologically. Readers of *Communicology* may wish to consult this resource as they continue to grapple with Flusser's thought.

And as a final thought, in light of everything that has transpired technologically over the last few decades, the fact that when we read *Communicology* today, expressions such as "network dialogue," "totalitarian apparatus," and "the synchronization of elite discourse and network dialogue" no longer seem alien to us attests to Flusser's forward-thinking critique of human communication systems and their effects on our sociopolitical situation, which ultimately attests to the freshness and contemporary nature of the book you are about to read.

I wish to thank a few people who made the publishing of this work possible: Soraya Guimarães Hoepfner, Márcia Cavalcante, and Michael Marder for their encouragement and for helping establish the bridge with Erica Wetter at Stanford University Press. I am also grateful to Miguel Flusser for continually supporting my work and for the many hours of eccentrically challenging conversations, which indirectly give me valuable insight into his father's mind. I thank my cat, Federico, for the unrelenting support and company during the gruesome COVID-19 period. And of course, I thank Erica Wetter and the team at SUP for all their support and for believing in the potential of Flusser's work.

Notes

1. Mentioned in letters at the time to Milton Vargas, José Bueno de Aguiar, and Dora Ferreira da Silva. He translated the work from English to French later in 1978 (mentioned in a letter from August 1978 to Gabriel Borba) to offer to French publishers but also had no positive results. The French version was published recently as *Mutations dans les relations humains? De la communicologie*, ed. Marc Partouche (Paris: Le Bon Voisin, 2021).

2. "Two Approaches to the Phenomenon, Television," in *The New Television: A Public/Private Art: Essays, Statements, and Videotapes: Based on "Open Circuits: An International Conference on the Future of Television" Organized by Fred Barzyk, Douglas Davis, Gerald O'Grady, and Willard Van Dyke for the Museum of Modern Art, New York City*, ed. Douglas Davis and Allison Simmons (Cambridge, MA: MIT Press,

1977), 234–47. Talk presented at the "Open Circuits: The Future of Television" conference at MoMA, New York, January 23, 1974.

3. *Kommunikologie. Schriften, Bd. 4*, ed. Stefan Bollmann and Edith Flusser (Bensheim: Bollmann, 1996); the German translation was reprinted in 1998 and 2007.

4. Biblioteca Vilém Flusser, ed. Rodrigo Maltez Novaes and Rodrigo Petronio (São Paulo: É Realizações) [an ongoing series].

5. Mentioned in a letter to Dora Ferreira da Silva on March 17, 1974: "Nam Jun Paik: Korean, director of 'The kitchen.' Leader of the New York aesthetic contestation. . . . Thesis: art is like copulation, always the same and always variable and pleasant. He makes videos and films that confuse temporal and spatial orientation, for example: he makes the left hand coincide with the right by the fourth dimension (Moebius space)."

6. This work was written only in Portuguese, intended as a rebuttal to Foucault's *Les mots et les choses* (1966); despite being considered for publication in 1968, it was dropped by the publisher probably as a result of the hardening of the military dictatorship in Brazil and the introduction of censorship. The book was published for the first time in Brazil in 2017, fifty-one years after it was written. *O Último Juízo: Gerações*, ed. Rodrigo Maltez Novaes and Rodrigo Petronio (São Paulo: É Realizações, 2017).

7. Mentioned in a letter to Milton Vargas on March 7, 1977.

8. *The Surprising Phenomenon of Human Communication*, ed. Rodrigo Maltez Novaes (London: Metaflux, 2016).

9. *Groundless*, ed. and trans. Rodrigo Maltez Novaes (London: Metaflux, 2017), 260–64.

10. *Post-History*, trans. Rodrigo Maltez Novaes (Minneapolis, MN: Univocal, 2013).

11. *Vampyroteuthis infernalis*, foreword by Abraham A. Moles, ed. and trans. Rodrigo Maltez Novaes (New York: Atropos, 2011).

12. *Towards a Philosophy of Photography*, trans. Anthony Mathews (London: Reaktion Books, 2000).

13. *Into the Universe of Technical Images*, trans. Nancy Ann Roth (Minneapolis: University of Minnesota Press, 2011).

14. *Does Writing Have a Future?*, trans. Nancy Ann Roth (Minneapolis: University of Minnesota Press, 2011).

COMMUNICOLOGY

SYNOPSIS

• • • Human communication is the art of accumulating acquired information. Since the general tendency of nature is toward loss of information, human communication is therefore an antinatural process (*artificial*). Of course, it does not *infringe* any laws of nature. It may be perfectly explained as a natural process. But if explained thus, it will not show its essence; it will escape understanding. One can see what communication is about only if one takes it to be a symbolic process. This requires the observer to assume an *intersubjective* point of view, one that admits that what is observed has a meaning. If observed thus, it may be seen that communication is a process that stores symbols in individual memories (*minds, spirits, souls*) and in collective memories (*civilizations, cultures*). From such a point of view, it does not matter whether the accent is put on the individual or on the collective information accumulators (whether *culture* is considered to be a product of *minds*, or the *mind* a product of *culture*). *Communication is seen as a tissue composed of individual memories that form a collective memory by exchanging symbols.*

Information is acquired by distribution within the tissue of communication. This method is called *discourse.* It distributes information stored in one memory among other memories. New information is created through the exchange of previously acquired information. This method is called *dialogue*. It exchanges information stored in various memories aiming toward a synthesis, which becomes new information. The two methods imply each other: discourse presupposes dialogue, and dialogue presupposes discourse. Communication is satisfactory (it accumulates acquired information well) only if there is an equilibrium between the two methods. If one prevails over the other, human relations may be said to be in a *crisis*. At present dialogue is dominated by discourse to a degree rarely, if ever, attained in the past. *Human relations are in a crisis because all dialogues are dominated by omnipresent discourse.*

Several structures of discourse and dialogue may be distinguished: (1) theatrical discourse (such as schools), which tries to preserve information by making the receivers responsible for it; (2) pyramidal discourse (such as armies), which tries to preserve information by authoritarian methods; (3) tree discourse (such as the sciences), which tries to preserve information by branching it out in progressive specializations; (4) amphitheatrical discourse (such as broadcasting), which tries to preserve information by stereotypical massification; (5) circular dialogue, which tries to produce information by elitist synthetization; and (6) network dialogue (public opinion), which produces new information by vulgarization of acquired information. At present, mass-media amphitheaters and networked public opinion are being synchronized and tend to reinforce each other. *This synchronization of the radiation of stereotypical information, together with small talk about it, is an aspect of our crisis.*

This domination of radiated discourse over the situation, and the consequent degradation of dialogue, may be seen as the result of a revolution in communication techniques or as the result of a revolution in the type of symbols in which information is coded. Under the first perspective, it must be asked: Why do discursive structures like TV and the press dispose of such advanced technology, while the dialogical structures are generally archaic? Although there are many answers, they will not be satisfactory unless the second perspective is also taken into consideration. It will then be seen that our situation consists of two levels: a level of elitist communication and one of mass communication. The *upper* level programs the *lower* one by radiating information coded in a new type of symbol, technical images. Specialists translate information coming out of the various dialogues of the scientific, technological, and other tree discourses into technical images and then broadcast them to the mass level of communication. *This mass culture, now turned universal, degrades the sophisticated technical images into an archaic small talk, and it is programmed to do so.*

Technical images (such as photographs and films, but also blueprints and road maps) are unlike traditional images, not so much because they are produced in a different way but because they mean something different. Traditional images may be said to mean *scenes*. Technical images mean something much more abstract, although many of them look as if they have the same meaning as traditional images. Their meaning is deceptive. It may be deciphered only if technical images are seen to be a late result not of traditional images but of linear texts. *If we are to understand our crisis, to understand how and why humanity is being programmed for passive reception, we must make an effort to decipher the technical images that program us.*

It will be seen that there are many types of codes in which the information within our memories and within the world around us is stored. But if we concentrate attention on the present crisis, we find that three types of codes are immediately concerned: codes that consist of images, those that consist of symbols ordered in lines, and those that consist of technical images. In the codified world around us, these three types of codes follow one from the other: linear texts come later than traditional images, and technical images later than texts. In our own memories, the three types of codes overlap. There is, at present, a discrepancy between the information stored in our memories and the information stored in the world around us, and this discrepancy is due to the conflict between the various codes within our program (the way we store information). *We are not suitably programmed for the situation we are in, and this is an aspect of our crisis.*

Each code requires a specific method for information manipulation and for deciphering the information coded. The method of codification and decodification of images can be called *imagination*, the one for codification and decodification of linear texts can be called *conception*, and the one for codification and decodification of technical images can be called *technical imagination.* Imagination is the capacity to project supposedly real relations upon a surface (make images) and to reproject supposedly real relations from a surface (decipher images). Conception is the capacity to *explain* images by unrolling them into lines (describe them) and to reconstruct images from texts (read texts). Technical imagination is the capacity to project texts upon a surface (make images of concepts) and to reconstruct the texts from those images (see through the technical images). *We are programmed for imagination and conception, but not for technical imagination.*

Each of the three methods of codification gives a specific meaning to symbols, and therefore to the world and to life within it. To each corresponds a specific level of existence, of consciousness, and of action. The level corresponding to imagination can be called *magical existence.* On that level, the world is experienced as a context of scenes, time as a circle of eternal recurrence, and life as a search of a *just* place in the world. The level corresponding to conception can be called *historical existence.* On that level, the world is experienced as a process of becoming, time as a sequence of unique and irrevocable instances, and life as a search for progressive perfection. The level corresponding to technical imagination has not yet been attained, and although it begins to condense, it is difficult to formulate it. But it will no doubt be a radically new form of existence, and life will have a radically new meaning if it is ever consolidated. *Unless we attain the level of consciousness corresponding to technical images, we shall not decipher the programs of which we are the receivers.*

The obvious way to render technical imagination conscious is to observe how technical images are produced and how they are received (even if they are not being appropriately deciphered during reception). The first thing we see is that technical images are produced by complexes that can be called *apparatus-operator.* Those complexes (for example, photo camera–photographer or TV broadcasting system–television operator) establish a new form of relation between tool and human: no longer the tool serves the human, or the human serves the tool, but both function for each other. Therefore, *classical* categories cannot be applied to this new situation: an apparatus is a new type of tool and requires a new type of political thinking, and an operator is a new type of human and requires a new type of anthropological thinking. *Unless we give up traditional categories, we shall not understand the problems posed by the apparatus-operator complex, which is central in our situation.*

The *apparatus-operator* complex is the place where linear texts are being translated into technical images (for instance, film scripts into moving pictures). It may be said that they are the place where history in the strict sense of that term is being translated into programs to be radiated. Those places suck in history and vomit programs. From the point of view of history, they are the *end of history*, the *plenitude of times*, and it is in their direction that history has tended ever since it started. From the point of view of the receivers of the programs (for instance, the cinema-going public), they are the place where history *repeats itself* and may be contemplated. *The fact that every commitment to history will be sucked in by an apparatus-operator complex, even if it is committed against that complex, is an aspect of our crisis.*

The climate of mass culture is pseudo-magical because the inability to decipher technical image programs is not a technical difficulty (technical images are not *mysterious*) but a refusal to decipher them on the part of the receivers (they are believed with *bad faith*). The explanation is that people fear to *see through* the programs they are fed: they prefer semiconscious reception to the responsibility of full awareness. And this fear is justified: The conscious use of technical imagination would undoubtedly imply the abandonment of experiences, values, and knowledge cherished for countless generations. It implies a leap just as radical as was the one that resulted, four thousand years ago, in historical existence. *People prefer to be programmed for pseudo-magic, to the challenge of questioning the fundamental categories of historical, conceptual reason.*

Technical imagination is a step back from linear thinking. It is thus fundamentally the abandoning of the *objective* point of view, which is the place where linear thinking stands. This implies not only that the traditional distinction between science, politics, and the arts will become meaningless for technical imagination but also that *intersubjectivity* will become a new criterion for the validity of knowledge and action. The abstract and empty concepts of *time* and *space* will be substituted by technical images of *space-time*, which will not be measurable by absolute and deliberate scales but by scales that are relative to existence and given by existence. This implies that *proximity* and *interest*, coupled with *intersubjectivity*, will become the measures of knowledge, value, and action, and this again implies the abandoning of *humanistic* values. *Whatever the new human will be, he will not be Christian or Marxist but something dreadful, as is everything that is new.*

Although we cannot imagine an existence in technical imagination, this overcoming of history and reason by the capacity to give meanings to history and reason, we may be certain that our situation has only two possible issues: it will either stifle technical imagination and lead to an omnipresent *apparatus-operator* complex, in which the whole of humanity will become a mass of operators; or it will explode through the conscious application of technical imagination. *Either totalitarian massification or technical imagination will penetrate the masses and render it aware of the possibilities dormant in our situation.*

Even now, we can vaguely distinguish those possibilities, and they are gigantic. We possess, even now, all the tools and all the methods to transform human society into a *true cosmic democracy*, namely, a dialogue that will result in a quantity and quality of new information, compared to which the whole of human past communication must seem like a hesitant introduction. A mutation of human relations is technically, economically, and even politically possible, which would, if become real, result in human existence of unimaginable and inconceivable wealth of knowledge, experience, and evaluation. But of course, to say this is to speak nonsense. This possibility can become real only if there is sufficient technical imagination to realize it, and if there is such technical imagination, it is not a possibility but only a chimera. We have therefore to be content with the following statement: *Our crisis will result either in a perfectly imaginable totalitarian apparatus or in a totally unimaginable explosion of technical imagination.*

If communication is defined as the art of accumulating acquired information, there is, sotto voce, a second connotation. Commitment to communication becomes a commitment to the *mind* and to *culture*, to memory, to the immemorial, and against death and oblivion. And this again implies that any commitment to communication is one to immortality in the memory of others. *Fundamentally, we are in a crisis because to commit oneself to communication in our situation is to commit oneself either to a totalitarian apparatus or to a dreadful explosion.*

Now, this may not be a *valid reading* of our situation. This book will not submit its reading as if it were so. In fact, it is the belief of this writer that there are countless points of view with regard to any concrete situation, that this is what makes it *concrete*, and that each point of view opens a specific vision. The book intends to present a single point of view with regard to our crisis: the point of view of the codes that program us. From such a point of view, this is what can be seen: *the decadence of linear codes and historical reason, the danger of a fall into second-degree illiteracy and massification, and the possibility of a yet unimaginable new form of human communication.*

If read in such a spirit, as an effort to contribute to a dialogue concerning the mutation of human relations we witness, and as an effort to provoke further dialogue, this book will have attained its purpose. *In this sense, this book is itself a manifestation of the effort to master technical imagination and contribute to the mutation of human relations.*

1

WHAT IS COMMUNICATION?

• • • The human being is not a social animal, like bees or ants, or even cows or wolves: communication with other humans does not come naturally. Therefore, the theory of communication is not a discipline of the natural sciences. Human communication is an artificial process based on artifacts, artifice, and artful inventions. Therefore, the theory of communication is a discipline of the type called *humanities*, which has the unnatural aspects of humans for a subject. Although it is obvious that humans do not communicate naturally with other humans (speaking does not mean to naturally emit sounds, like a bird's singing, nor is writing a natural gesture like *dancing* is for a bee), still we often meet with the opinion that a human is a *zoon politikon*, an animal that lives in groups and cannot live outside them. And, in fact, it may be said that a person who does not know how to speak is an *idiot* (which literally means a "private person"), and this implies that such a person is not fully human. The contradiction here involved—that humans, unlike social animals, do not communicate naturally, but they are not fully human if they do not live socially—is, however, only apparent. In reality, humans are not *natural animals*, and everything about them, including their social life and the way they communicate with others, is artificial.

There are, of course, what can be called *instinctive* forms of communication in humans, for instance, between mother and child, between lovers, and even spontaneous motions that may be considered instinctive signals that communicate something (for instance, danger) to others. But it is difficult to state exactly to what extent these forms of communication are natural (to what extent suckling or making love is not influenced by culture), and although these forms of communication may be the most fundamental ones, they are not characteristic of human communication. The reason is that humans are animals with relatively weak instincts (whatever that term may mean) and must rely on artificial patterns of behavior for their survival.

The artificial character of human communication, the fact that humans transmit information to others and receive information from them by means of tools specially designed to communicate, called *symbols*, and that they must learn the use of those tools if they want to live with others (they must not only learn how to speak but also learn a specific language), is not always sufficiently appreciated. Once we have learned the use of a set of symbols (for instance, the meaning of certain gestures like nodding, or certain drawings like a cross), we tend to forget that they are artifacts designed for communication and are surprised if we meet people who do not *understand* them (who do not know that to nod means *yes* and a cross means a crossroad ahead). The codes of which such symbols are a part (the code of gestures, the traffic code) have become sort of second nature to us. We tend to forget that the codified world that surrounds us, the world composed of meaningful elements, is an artificial tissue designed to permit human communication and that it hides and covers a meaningless context in which each of us is entirely alone, in solitary confinement and *incommunicado*: the world of nature. We tend to forget that, and, indeed, this tendency of ours to forget the artificial character of human communication is the ultimate purpose of communication: we communicate with each other and thus create the arts and sciences, philosophy and religion, in short, society and its products, in order to forget our fundamental solitude, our solitude toward death.

Communication is an artifice designed to make us forget that we are going to die and that therefore to live has no meaning. It is a device against death, the only device we dispose of. By nature, humans are lonely animals because they are the only animals that know they are going to die. In the face of such knowledge, every form of social life becomes useless: nobody can substitute for me in the hour of my death, and, potentially, the hour of my death is every hour. But of course, it is impossible to live with such knowledge. Communication is the device to make us forget such knowledge and thus make it possible for us to live. The meaningful codified world that surrounds us and that hides and conceals the meaningless world of nature in which we are going to die in solitude is the artifice that allows us to survive our knowledge of the brutal meaninglessness of our death and of the death of all others. In short, humans communicate with others, not because they are *political animals* but because they are lonely animals that cannot live in loneliness.

Human communication is artificial, not only in the sense that it is a device against loneliness but also in the sense that it goes against nature. In fact, it may be defined as a tendency that opposes the general tendency of nature. According to the second principle of thermodynamics, nature tends toward an ever-greater equilibrium, away from the improbable and toward increasing probability: it is an *entropic* process. Human communication tends toward ever-increasing information, away from the probable and toward increasing improbability: it is a *negentropic* process. Nature, as a whole, progresses toward uniformity, toward a loss of information, and, in fact, natural time can be measured by an increase of entropy, for instance, by the progressive decadence of radioactive carbon atoms (*carbon test*). Humans communicate in order to create and conserve information, and, in fact, human time (historical progress) can be measured by the accumulation of information. Although this is only approximately true (there are negatively entropic processes in nature, and there is the phenomenon of oblivion in human communication), it is true essentially. If the codified world is abandoned to the action of nature, it will be disinformed and reduced to the probable state of a heap of stones like the ruins of ancient cities. And cities are the result of an effort of human communication to impose highly improbable forms on stones and other relatively uniform elements of nature and to preserve those improbable forms.

But to say that human communication is a device against loneliness, and to say that it is a process opposed to the general tendency of nature, is to say the same thing. The stupid tendency of nature toward the ever more probable, toward the heap of stones, toward what is sometimes called *thermic death*, is nothing but the objective aspect of our subjective experience of loneliness, of the brutally stupid fact that we are destined for death and oblivion. Whether we approach the phenomenon of human communication from an existential point of view (as an effort to overcome loneliness by contact with others) or from a formal point of view (as an effort to create and preserve information), the phenomenon reveals the same essential aspect: human communication is, essentially, an effort to deny nature, both human and extra-human. This is why we are, all of us, committed to it.

The keyword in this commitment of ours to communication is *memory*, both in the formal sense of *store of information* (as it has become familiar through computers) and in the existential sense of *immortality* (as it is used if we say that a dead person lives on in the memory of others). Of course, the two meanings of the word *memory* are one and the same: Mozart is immortal because some of the information he created is stored in our memories, and ever since the Internal Revenue Service has been computerized and now stores some information concerning us, we have all become, to some extent, immortal. We are, all of us, committed to communication because we do not want to die and do not want those we love to die, and the only form of immortality accessible to us is to be stored away in the memory of others. We are committed to communication because we want to be remembered, and by the same token, we become memories for others. Thus it may be said that to communicate is to create information to be stored away in memories so as to become memorable and not to die altogether. In short, communication appears as the artifice that makes memories, stores for acquired information, about us (and thus make us, in a sense, immortal).

It is obvious that if we conceive of communication as the artifice that permits us to lead memorable lives (to become *famous* or *immortal in the memory of others*), we cannot avoid strictly political connotations. Nonetheless, it must be mentioned that politics, within the context of Western civilization, is originally closely linked to two entirely different concepts of *memory*, the Jewish one and the Greek one. (This duplicity in the Western tradition, the fact that it stems basically from both Greek and Jewish roots and that it has never succeeded in really synthesizing them, explains, in part, its inner contradiction and therefore its outer dynamism.) For Jewish tradition, *memory* is the place where history is stored, and to remember is to relive the past. Jewish feasts are feasts of rememoration. As a consequence, politics in the Jewish context is a commitment to history—an acceptance of the past in view of the future. For Greek tradition, *memory* is the place where ideas are stored, and to remember is to see ideas. Greek philosophy is a technique to rediscover ideas concealed by oblivion. As a consequence, politics in the Greek context is a commitment to the realization of ideas. Although both in the Jewish and Greek traditions politics is a commitment to memory (a commitment to immortality), two entirely different concepts of politics are at the root of Western civilization. If we look at the political scene, we can see that both are at work and that they are incompatible.

Thus, it appears that human communication is the antinatural, artificial effort to create new information and to store it away in memories, to preserve and protect it from the entropic action of nature. In short, human communication is the art of accumulating acquired information. This is not the definition of *communication* one would expect to find in textbooks. Usually, neither the creation nor the conservation of information but the transmission of information is stressed in such definitions. This stress on transmission (on what has become the custom to be called *media*) is unfortunate because it tends to cover up the essential aspect of communication, which is that it transforms humans into accumulators of acquired information.

It is easier to say such a statement than to grasp its impact. An accumulator of acquired information, a cumulative memory, is a miracle the marvel of which we do not realize only because we, ourselves, are it. As said before, it goes against the laws of nature. We pay lip service to this miracle if we say that humans are *historical animals* because, unlike all other animals, they transmit acquired information from generation to generation. It may be suspected that the whole bundle of problems and pseudo-problems around concepts like *spirit*, *mind*, and *soul* has to do with this capacity of ours to become memories for acquired information (to become *immortal*). This book is, unfortunately, not the place to discuss how such a miracle is possible, how communication does this. Suffice it to say that, as a matter of course, communication does not cancel out the second principle of thermodynamics. Seen objectively, human communication is, of course, a *natural process* and as such subject, like any other process, to progressive loss of information. There is no *miracle* if we look at communication from the point of view of the sciences of nature.

But this is precisely not the appropriate method to look at human communication if one wants to grasp its essence. It is no good to say that while typing this text information is lost because the energies involved tend to be transformed into heat. The essential aspect of the process of typing this text is that it tends to increase information in the memories of its future readers, and this is an aspect outside the competence of the sciences of nature. It is not an objective but an intersubjective aspect. Intersubjectivity is, basically, an agreement between subjects about what is called *meaning*: it is a consensus. This text is going to inform its readers if and only if they agree with the writer about the meaning of the letters, words, sentences, and so forth of which it is composed. It will inform them only if they have the *key to the code*. Communication makes cumulative memories out of us because it codifies the world, gives it a meaning to which we agree. Such a meaning cannot be verified through objective observation, only through intersubjective participation. A Martian, if observing human communication, would not find anything remarkable about it: It would look like a complex set of gestures, sounds, scribblings, and so forth, and the idea that these phenomena *mean*, that they are symbols, would never occur to the Martian, who would possibly explain these phenomena but, not being a participant in the intersubjective consensus that gives them meaning, would never *interpret* them. Thus it must suffice, for the purpose of this book, to say that communication makes cumulative memories of us on an intersubjective level and that the miracle is not one that can be observed objectively. In other words, in spite of communication, we shall still die in loneliness if we look at ourselves objectively and there is no such thing like *mind* or *spirit*. But if we look at ourselves intersubjectively, we may, thanks to communication, live on in the memories of others and make others live on in the cumulative memories that we, ourselves, are.

At this point, however, one must take up the proposed definition from a different angle. If one defines communication as proposed, it reveals two aspects of the production and conservation of information. Both are, of course, negatively entropic aspects. Production of information is negatively entropic because it substitutes a less probable for a more probable situation, and conservation of information is negatively entropic because it prevents the establishment of a more probable situation. For instance, the typing of this text is a negatively entropic process because it distributes the letters on the sheet of paper in a highly improbable manner (it *produces information*). And if one files this text and keeps it in a drawer (a *memory*), it is a negatively entropic process because it prevents the sheet of paper from being burned and thus transformed into ashes, which is a far more probable situation than a sheet of paper covered with letters. Thus, both the typing of this text and its filing (both the production and the conservation of information) are statistically highly improbable events; they are unexpected from the objective point of view of the sciences of nature. Still, typing texts and filing them away are two different aspects of communication.

If we approach this difference from an objective point of view, we shall not be very successful. How long will it take for the text to be typed by *chance* (for instance, by a gorilla), and how are the *chances* that the typed sheet will be filed away (for instance, by wind) instead of being washed away by rain or burned by a cigarette? This demonstrates that the sciences of nature (including what might be called *objective psychology*) do not offer happy approaches to the phenomenon of communication. The questions to ask, if one faces the difference between the production and the conservation of information, are of a quite different, and not statistical, order—questions that have nothing to do with probability but have to do with decisions. In short, *political* questions, questions concerning freedom. Let us, again, resist the trap of establishing a premature link between politics and the theory of communication, and let us be content with the statement that, if we are to grasp the difference between production and conservation of information, we must ask how people decide to create new information and how they can do so, and how people decide to preserve the information they already possess and how they can do so.

Before trying to answer these sorts of questions, a word of caution is in order. It is the opinion of the author that the theory of communication should concern itself with these sorts of questions only and should abandon questions of the statistical type, questions of the objective order, to what might be called *theory of information* or *informatics.* In other words, the author believes that it is useful to distinguish neatly between the objective and the intersubjective aspects of communication and to reserve the theory of information for the first aspects and the theory of communication proper for the second aspects. This caution is in order because informatics is often confused with the theory of communication.

Thus, communication, if defined as proposed, follows two distinct, although closely related, purposes: to produce and to preserve information. It may be said very schematically that the first purpose is pursued by the following method: Information stored in various memories is exchanged with the hope that it will be synthesized into new information. This can be called the *dialogical method.* (The various memories involved in dialogical exchange need not be various individuals but may be contained in a single individual, such as a person, a library, or a computer. The *inner dialogue* in the Platonic sense may be a source of new information just as much as is a dialogue between various individuals.) In regard to the second purpose of communication—preserving information from the entropic action of nature—it may be said just as schematically that it occurs by the following method: Information stored in one memory is distributed so that it becomes stored in various memories. This can be called the *discursive method.* The hope of this method is that the information thus distributed may again be redistributed and thus constitute a never-ending flux, the *eternal discourse* in the strict sense.

If this distinction between dialogue and discourse is made, two things become immediately apparent: (1) One method of communication cannot exist without the other, and (2) the distinction depends on what can be called the *distance* of the observer. First, for a dialogue to establish itself, there must have been previous discourses that have informed the memories that exchange information. And for a discourse to exist, there must have been previous dialogues that have produced the information that is being discoursed. The question of precedence between dialogue and discourse is, therefore, meaningless. Second, every dialogue may be considered to consist of a series of discourses that each aim at an exchange of information. And every discourse may be considered part of a dialogue into which it merges. For instance, a book on a scientific subject may be considered, if observed in isolation, to be discursive communication. If observed in the context of other publications, it may be considered part of a dialogue: the scientific *debate*. And if observed from an even greater distance, it may be considered part of that scientific discourse that has flowed ever since the Renaissance and characterizes our civilization.

Although it is true that there can be no dialogue without previous discourse, and vice versa, and that the distinction between the two methods is a matter of distance of observation, it is still a very important, and revealing, distinction. To participate in dialogue is quite a different situation from the participation in discourse. In fact, as this book will try to show in the field of politics, it is a radically different situation. The very common complaint one hears everywhere, that people can *no longer communicate*, is a good illustration. What people mean by this complaint is not that they are unable to communicate, since never before in history has communication worked so well in both intensity and extension as it does at present. What people mean is that it is becoming increasingly difficult to establish true dialogical situations in which an exchange of information may result in new information and that this difficulty is due precisely to the excellent performance of communication—to the fact that omnipresent discourses inform everybody with the same type of information, which makes every effort to exchange information useless. The desperate loneliness that characterizes the *mass of humanity* is the result of the incapacity for dialogue under the bombardment of stereotypical discourse.

It may be thought that communication achieves its existential purpose (to overcome loneliness) only if a certain equilibrium between dialogue and discourse is established. If, as it does at present, discourse dominates dialogue, people feel lonely, although they are constantly in communication with what is wrongly called *the sources of information*, with discursive emitters. And if dialogue dominates discourse as it did in rural situations before the revolution in communication, people feel lonely in spite of constant dialogue with a restricted number of partners because they feel expelled from the general discourse of human communication. (Obviously, the loneliness of the crowd is different from the loneliness on the farm: one lacks dialogue, and the other lacks discourse.)

The concept of equilibrium between dialogue and discourse permits, among other things, the establishment of criteria in historical and biographical studies. One may distinguish, for instance, in Western history, periods of prevailing dialogue (such as the ancien régime with its *round tables*, its *constitutional assemblies*, its *common reason*, and so forth) from periods of prevailing discourse (such as the early nineteenth century with its Romantic discourses, its *progressiveness*, its tendency toward *evolutionary biologizing*). And in biography one may distinguish between periods of reception of discourses (such as schooling and training) from periods of participation in dialogues (such as political or cultural commitments) and from periods of emission of discourses (such as teaching or managing a business). No doubt, such criteria have always been applied, more or less deliberately, by biographers and students of history; it is a banality to speak of *formative* and *creative* periods in the course of a life or to speak of the elliptic, dialogical quality of the baroque in comparison to the arrow-like, discursive quality of Romanticism. Still, it can do no harm to render those criteria more precise with the help of the theory of communication. And all this shows that the distinction between discourse and dialogue is a meaningful one, even if one method of communication does imply the other.

But the moment one accepts such a distinction, it becomes too rude and crude for an analysis of the communication situation we are in. It is obvious that a discourse that emanates from the screen of a cinema is not of the same type as the discourse of a grandmother telling fairy tales, nor is a dialogue between two teenagers over the phone of the same type as a dialogue in a philosophical symposium. The critical thing to seize here is that such a difference of types is not only due to a difference in the type of information that is being communicated. It is, at least as much, due to a difference in the structure of the communication. The difference between the reception of a movie by a moviegoer and the reception of a fairy tale by a grandchild is not only a difference between the *messages* received but also between the ways they are being received: in the cinema one sits motionless and receives passively, but one may ask the grandmother questions and thus influence the emission of the message. And the difference between the dialogue over the phone and the dialogue at a symposium is not only a difference between the information exchanged but also between the ways how they are exchanged: over the phone people hear each other, and at the symposium they face each other.

It is, of course, possible to make a catalogue of the type of information that is communicated both in dialogue and discourse. One may, for instance, distinguish between factual information (indicatives), evaluative information (imperatives), and aesthetic information (optatives). Such a *semantic* analysis will establish a difference not only between the cinema and the grandmother but also between various movie programs. But it may be shown that a structural analysis, one that distinguishes between various ways of transmission of information, prepares the field for a posterior semantic analysis and permits an easier mapping of the communication situation. For this reason this book now proposes a short sketch of the communication situation from a structural viewpoint. One cannot deny, of course, that structure and meaning, *semantics* and *syntax*, imply each other (although one need not accept that the *medium is the message*), and constant reference to meaning will therefore accompany the following considerations. Still, the emphasis of what follows will be on structure. But the reader should keep in mind that what is aimed at here is a map, not a photograph, of the situation.

1.1. DISCOURSE AND DIALOGUE

Discourse is the method of distributing available information to preserve it against the entropic action of nature. Most of the problems involved in such a definition lie outside the scope of this book—for instance, the problem of the meaning of the word *distribution*, where information is concerned. It cannot have, obviously, the same meaning as it has where something material is concerned because the distributor of information (the emitter) does not lose it, and each of the receivers gets it in its totality and not as a parcel of distribution. Another example of the problems involved in the definition of *discourse* that cannot be dealt with here is the meaning of the word *available*, which involves the function of memory. Information contained in a book, stored in a library, is *available* in a different sense from the one in which information is *available* in a human memory if one succeeds in recalling it. In short, most of the problems involved in the definition of *discourse* here proposed must be left untouched because their consideration would lead to the development of a whole theory of communication, which is not the purpose here.

However, there are two problems involved in the definition that relate to the present purpose, with the consideration of various structures of discourse. One is that discourse, if it is to be successful, must avoid the information it distributes being perturbed during distribution. It must avoid *noise* entering the information during transmission because its purpose is the conservation of the original information. We may call this the problem of *fidelity* to the information. The other problem is that discourse, if it is to be successful, must permit the receiver of the information to store it in such a way that it may be retransmitted. It must make of the receivers potential future emitters because its purpose is the *eternal* flux of the information. We may call this the problem of *progress*. Since, as it will be seen later, these two problems are in some respects contradictory (*fidelity* seems to contradict *progress*), the question is to find structures of discourse that would conciliate *fidelity* with *progress*. Here this question will be considered not from the point of view of informatics (mathematically) but from that of communication proper (in terms of human participation).

For this purpose, four models of discursive structures were chosen, each of which solves in its own way the two problems and their contradictory aspects. These models are abstractions: they cannot be found, in their purity, in the actual situation. And they were chosen for their political connotations: they are meant to permit establishment of a link between communication and politics later in the argument. Still, the choice of the four models has been imposed by the phenomenon of communication itself and is not a violation.

1.1.1. Theatrical Discourse

Theatrical discourse obeys the following structure:

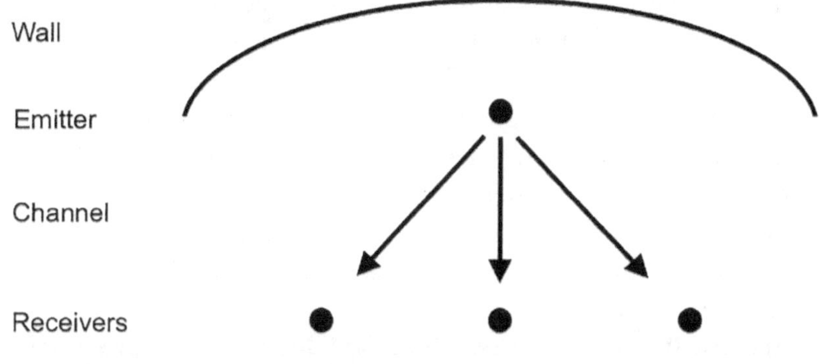

SKETCH 1.1.1

The sketch reduces the structure to a *bare skeleton*, but one can still recognize it. It is the structure not only of a theater proper but also of, for instance, a classroom, concert hall, and, most important, a specific type of family. If thus reduced to a skeleton, it is composed of the following elements: (1) a concave wall, (2) an emitter whose back is to the wall, (3) channels through which information flows from the emitter, and (4) receivers arranged in one or several semicircles facing the wall. These four elements are not always as clearly visible, but they are always present, even if sometimes in a modified form, where a theatrical discourse takes place.

These are the functions of the elements within this structure: (1) The concave wall is a shield against outside noise and an amplifying shell within the discourse's situation; (2) the emitter is the memory in which the information to be distributed is stored; (3) the channels are material media (in most traditional theatrical discourses they are of air), which carry the code in which the information is being emitted; and (4) the receivers are the memories in which the information is to be stored after distribution. The whole structure forms, ideally, a circular shape as in a Greek theater.

The characteristic aspect of this structure is that emitter and receiver face each other during the discourse. *Fidelity* to the original information is maintained by the fact that the *theater* is a closed, shell-like structure that eliminates much of the noise from outside. *Progress* of the original information is made possible because the receivers can leave their places, step toward the wall and turn around, and thus become themselves emitters. But it is precisely this possibility of *revolution*, of a turning around of the receivers, that limits *fidelity* in theatrical discourse. Although it is relatively well shielded against outer noise, it is unprotected against noise from the inside. The receivers can turn around during the discourse, and since they face the emitter, they can also turn the channels around and *answer* the emitter. The theatrical structure places the receivers in a *responsible* situation, that is, a situation in which they can answer and thus introduce noise into the original information. Thus, the original information is changed into new information because the discourse is changed into a dialogue. In short, what characterizes this discursive structure is that it is *open to dialogue*. Thus, theatrical discourse is less suited for fidelity than for progress.

1.1.2. Pyramidal Discourse

Pyramidal discourse obeys the following structure:

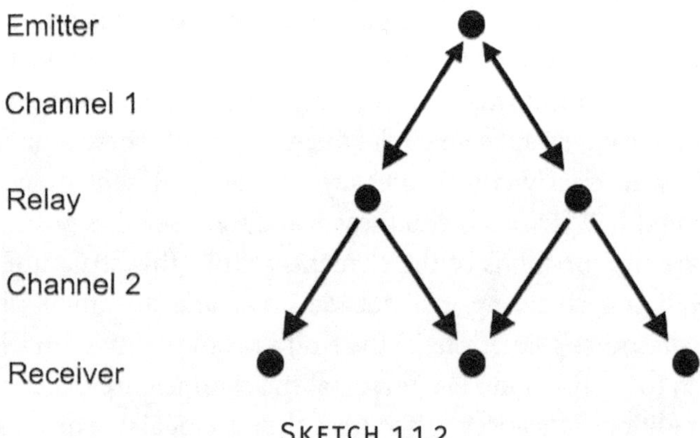

SKETCH 1.1.2

As in the model of theatrical discourse, this sketch is a skeleton of the pyramidal structure of discourse. But unlike the previous model, it does not simplify the actual situation considerably: pyramidal discourse already has a very simple and orderly structure. In fact, this simplicity is its advantage over the sometimes-bewildering complexity of theatrical discourse. Examples of pyramidal discourse occur in the army, church, political parties such as communist and fascist hierarchies, and specific types of administrations. It will be argued later that the prototype for this structure in our civilization is, very probably, the Roman republic. It is composed of the following elements: (1) an emitter, (2) channels through which information flows from the emitter toward relays, (3) channels through which the relays can check the information with the emitter, (4) relays, (5) channels through which information flows from the relays to the receivers, and (6) receivers.

These are the functions of the elements within the structure: (1) The emitter is the memory in which the information to be distributed is stored but is also, at least in theory, the memory in which that information originated, and the emitter is the *author* of the information; (2) and (3) the channels linking emitter to relays (*author* to *authority*) are material media (usually, sheets of paper) that carry the (usually written) codes in which the information is being emitted; (4) the relays are memories that recodify the information to eliminate all noise that might have penetrated it during transmission, so they form usually several layers of decreasing *authority* in the direction of the receivers; (5) the channels through which the finally recodified and purified information flows from the ultimate relay toward the receivers are the material media that carry the information (usually orders); and (6) the receivers are the memories in which the information is to be stored after distribution.

The characteristic aspect of this structure is the hierarchy of relays that guarantees *fidelity* to the original message by eliminating all noise through gradual recodification. Thus, the relays have two complementary functions. They check the information received with the *author* to verify which noise has penetrated. This can be called their *religious* function because it reconnects (*religare*) the relays with the author. And they retransmit the information to further relays after having purified it. This can be called their *traditional* function because it passes on (*tradire*) the information.

Thus, the pyramidal discourse is well suited for the conservation of information but not for its *progress* during the discourse. The receivers are placed in an *irresponsible* position, in one that makes it impossible for them to respond to the information. They not only cannot answer the author directly but also cannot do so even through the intermediary of the relays. And this is why they are condemned, by the pyramidal structure, to passive reception and cannot retransmit the information unless, of course, they advance within the *pyramid* and become relays. In that case, they can *assume authority* and become transmitter relays. In short, pyramidal discourse is *closed to dialogue*, excludes the possibility of *revolution*, and is well suited for the preservation of the information from noise but not for *progressive* transmission.

To overcome this limitation of pyramidal discourse, to open it up for dialogue and thus render it *progressive*, structural changes were introduced that have resulted in a new structure of discourse, tree discourse.

1.1.3. Tree Discourse

Tree discourse obeys the following structure:

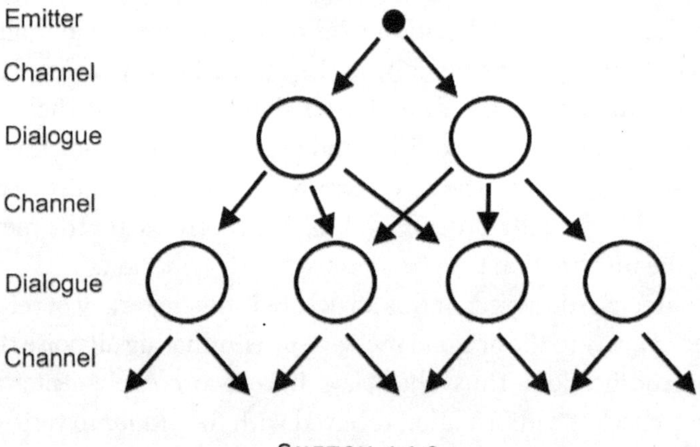

SKETCH 1.1.3

The sketch shows that the substitution of dialogical circles for the pyramidal relays involves two further changes in tree discourse: the channels of transmission cross and recross, thus destroying the simplicity of pyramidal discourse, and there are no ultimate receivers of the information, a fact that radically changes the character of the discourse. The two most important examples for the tree structure are the discourses of science and of technology, but it has also become the model for a number of other discourses that tend to become *progressive*, such as in the arts, some political institutions, and industrial and business organizations.

The tree structure is composed of the following elements: (1) an emitter, (2) channels through which information flows toward dialogical circles, (3) dialogical circles, and (4) channels through which information flows from dialogical circles toward further dialogical circles.

These are the functions of these elements: (1) The emitter is the memory in which the original information to be distributed is stored, but one loses sight of the emitter as the discourse progresses; (2) the channels that link emitter to dialogical circles and (3) those that link dialogical circles with other dialogical circles are the material media (in the case of science and technology, usually books and periodicals) that carry the codes in which the information is being emitted; and (4) the dialogical circles are memories that receive the information to synthesize it with other information available into new information and then transmit it.

The characteristic aspect of this structure is the progressive recodification of the original message by the dialogical circles and the branching out of the original information resulting from this. One may call this aspect the tendency toward progressive *specialization*. It guarantees the *eternal flux* of the information and does so in an explosive fashion. The information explodes into specialized bits, each of which is coded in specialized code, and these *bits* fly away from the original information, sometimes crossing each other in their centrifugal progress. But as far as *fidelity* to the original information is concerned, the tree structure may be said to be ambivalent. On the one hand, it produces ever-new information, and in this sense, it abandons the original information; it *overcomes* the information. On the other hand, all new information produced during tree discourse is methodically linked with the original information, and in this sense, tree discourse preserves the original information.

But it is not only the explosive progressiveness that characterizes this discourse. Also, there are and can be no ultimate receivers of the information. The reason is that during the progressive recodification of the information, during the process of specialization, the original information becomes subdivided into a number of difficult codes that are inaccessible even to the emitters of the information in other branches of the discourse, let alone to some *nonspecialized* receiver. In other words, tree discourse has no receiver because it becomes less and less decodifiable as it progresses. This hermetic aspect of tree discourse, in spite of its openness to *noise*, especially of tree discourses—*science* and *technology*—must be appreciated together with its explosive progressiveness if one is to judge the efficiency of its structure: it does overcome the rigid limitations of pyramidal discourse and does become progressive, but at the price of becoming progressively less *meaningful*.

To oppose this tendency toward hermetic specialization, and therefore toward the loss of the very purpose of discourse, which is to distribute available information to preserve it, another discursive structure has become ever more important, amphitheatrical discourse, which is a development of theatrical discourse.

1.1.4. Amphitheatrical Discourse

Amphitheatrical discourse obeys the following structure:

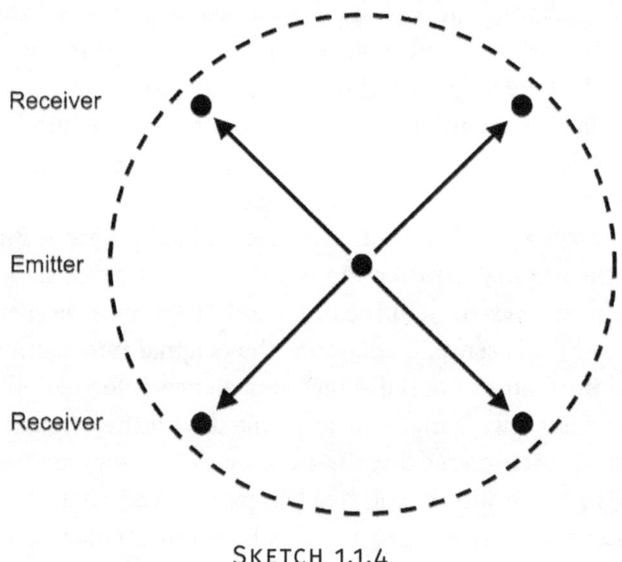

SKETCH 1.1.4

The sketch shows the fluidity of the horizon of the amphitheatrical discourse situation, once the concave wall of the theatrical structure is abandoned. Examples for this type of structure are what is called *mass media*, such as the press, TV, and posters, but it should not be forgotten that its prototype is the circus, such as the Roman Colosseum.

The amphitheatrical structure is composed of the following elements: (1) an emitter who stands in *empty space*, (2) channels that radiate from the emitter and through which the information flows toward an ill-defined horizon, and (3) receivers who happen to stand in the field of transmission. These are the functions of these elements within the structure: (1) The emitter is the memory in which the information to be distributed was stored in a code suitable for amphitheatrical discourse, that is, *programmed*; (2) the channels are the material media (for instance, newsprint or Hertz waves) that carry the code in which the information is being emitted; and (3) the receivers are the memories in which the information is to be stored after distribution. The whole structure has, ideally, cosmic dimensions: there is no limit to it.

So much has been written about mass media lately, and most of it in such a polemical spirit, that we tend to lose sight of the characteristic aspect of amphitheatrical discourse: there is no existential rapport between emitter and receivers or between the receivers. In a sense, it is the most *human* because the most unnatural form of communication: it is utterly artificial. In another sense it is the most inhuman form of communication: the participants do not recognize themselves or their partners as *humans* within it. This is what is called *the masses*: the transformation of human memories into ideal information conserves, like a tin of sardines, in other words, tins of programmed information. This ideal is (almost) achieved by the following factors: The receivers are placed into entirely irresponsible positions because there is no method for them to answer the emitter or even to discover the emitter behind the information. There is no possibility of a dialogue about the information received because the receivers dispose of the same information, all of them, and they do not meet each other. And there is no possibility of a *revolution* because the receivers have nowhere to *turn*: they float within the field of radiated information without any center of gravity, therefore without orientation. Thus, amphitheatrical discourse is a near-perfect method for the preservation of information: the receivers cannot but preserve it.

The uniformity of the information thus radiated, and therefore the uniformity of the few codes in which it is radiated, is an effective countermeasure against the hermetic specialization of tree discourse. (However, as will be shown later, amphitheatrical discourse cannot exist without tree discourse since it is itself the results of a branch of tree discourse.) But as far as *progress of information* is concerned, amphitheatrical discourse is utterly ineffective. Not only is it quite impossible for the receivers of its information to ever become emitters, but also the type of memory that is the emitter (a complex of cybernetic memories such as computers, video libraries, record collections, and film libraries) renders any retransmission on the side of the receivers unnecessary: the emitter is *immortal* and can emit the same information ever and ever again (*forever*). This consideration, and the consideration of the types of codes that prevail in amphitheatrical discourse (discussed later), has led some observers to expect *the end of history* (meaning the end of politics) if amphitheatrical discourse should prevail over all other discourse structures. This is the communicological equivalent of what is called, in the field of politology, the establishment of totalitarianism. In short, amphitheatrical discourse excludes dialogue, excludes revolution, and excludes *progress* and is thus an ideal method for the preservation of information.

Thus, if one does not shun extreme simplification, there are at present four basic discursive structures: (1) the theatrical structure, characterized by *responsibility*; (2) the pyramidal structure, characterized by *authority*; (3) the tree structure, characterized by *progressive specialization*; and (4) the amphitheatrical structure, characterized by *massification*. It is, however, impossible to apply this radically simplified scheme to the situation of communication we are in without also considering the other method of human communication, the dialogical method.

Dialogue is the method by which information stored in various memories is exchanged with a view to synthesizing it into new information. As was the case with the proposed definition of *discourse*, there are many problems involved in this definition that cannot be dealt with here without extending dangerously the scope of these considerations. It becomes, for instance, necessary to define the terms *information* and *new*, if the definition of *dialogue* is to be meaningful, and both these terms involve difficulties of various orders. Also, one must consider the problems of production, creation, and so forth, which are involved in the definition and pose both very ancient and very modern questions. Finally, the very term *dialogue* involves, both logically and historically, the whole problematic of dialectics. All these and similar considerations will be left in abeyance, although they will be present sotto voce in discussion of the dialogical method of communication.

The problematic aspects of dialogue to be considered here concern the methods applied with a view to synthesizing various types of information. Although there are many methods being tried out at present (in experiments such as brainstorming and group dynamics), it is curious to observe that only two methods are actually in use and are, therefore, the subject of political, philosophical, and theological speculation. (Let it be said, at this point, that Western tradition seems to have occupied itself far more with dialogue than with discourse as a subject of analysis, which is surprising.) The two dialogical structures that will be considered briefly are not, as was the case with the discursive structures, deliberately chosen from a multitude of observable discourse structures but are the only two that have any importance in the actual scene of communication.

1.1.5. Circular Dialogue

Circular dialogue obeys the following structure:

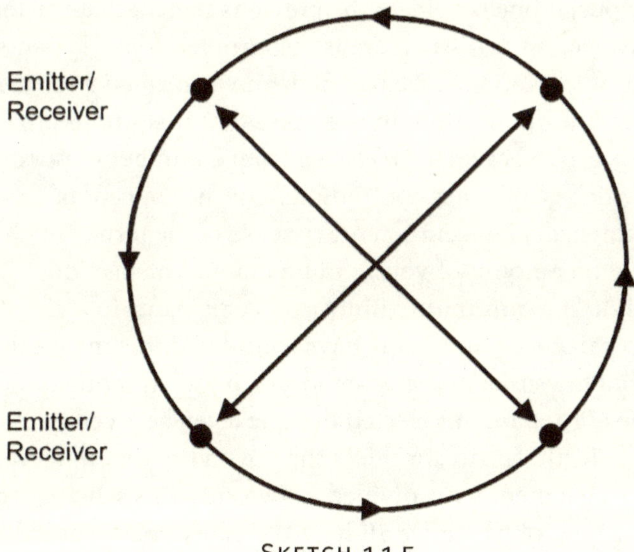

SKETCH 1.1.5

This is, of course, the structure of the *round table*, such as parliaments, committees, laboratories, and symposia. The principle of this method is very simple: Find the common denominator of all the memories participating in the dialogue (what Rousseau called *common reason* and was called the *State reason* in the eighteenth century) and establish it as the *valid information.* But behind this geometrical simplicity hides a complex situation. The memories involved in the dialogue differ among themselves not only with respect to information about a problem to be dialogued about (to be *decided*), but they also differ with respect to other information, with respect to their various *competencies* (amounts of available information), and with respect to the codes in which the various information is stored. And this complex difference occurs on many levels, from the level of *conscious information* to the deep levels in which it is difficult to distinguish between acquired and inherited information. Thus, it is very difficult to find a *common denominator* where a dialogue between very different memories is involved (why *liberal democracy* works so badly), but this is also why the information resulting from a successful circular dialogue is not at all a *common reason* (as enlightened philosophers expected) but a partial synthesis of conflicting information and, in this sense, *new* information. The very *failure* of this method is thus its true justification.

It is obvious, if one considers the previous sketch, that the foremost problem involved in this structure is the number of participants in the exchange of information: Circular dialogue is a *closed circuit.* It is an *elite* form of communication, in the sense that it is limited to a group and that this group is somehow *elected* from a number of possible participants (which is an inner contradiction of the concept of *democracy* in the enlightened, eighteenth-century sense of the term, which can be overcome by no amount of voting in no amount of elections). There is a clear limit to the minimum number of participants in a circular dialogue—two partners—and many have considered this the ideal dialogical situation: the situation between lovers, between mother and child, between the master and his elected disciple (even between humans and God), and so forth. (Plato considers the possibility that *inner dialogue*, in which a single memory is divided in two, and this schizophrenic dialogue, *reflection*, of which we all have the experience, would limit the circular dialogue to one partner only, although this is *dialogue* in an extraordinary sense of the term.) There is, however, no clear upper limit to the number of participants in a circular dialogue, which poses a practical, political problem. Some may hold that this is indeed the basic political problem. It should, however, be stressed that there is probably an optimal number of participants and that such an optimal number is a function of the intended *new information*. That number is different in the case of, for instance, scientific information and that of normative (*legal*) information. Those who make a claim for *participation* should specify both in what sort of dialogue concerning what sort of information they want to participate and their *competence* for it.

It is obvious from these considerations of circular dialogue that the number of participants involved is a function of the difference between the partners. The smaller the difference, the greater the number of possible partners, and vice versa. However, it should be stressed that the greater the difference between the partners involved in a dialogue, the greater the chance for meaningful new information, if the dialogue is successful (which is a way of restating the well-known principle that communication and information are inversely proportional: the more one informs, the less one communicates; and the more one communicates, the less one informs). Since dialogue, as opposed to discourse, is a form of communication that seeks information, not communication (which seeks the production, not the preservation, of information), it should be clear that circular dialogues between a restricted number of widely different memories are more interesting than those between great numbers of similar memories. For instance, although communication between an American industrialist and a Chinese Red Guard may be very difficult, dialogue between those two is far more interesting, because potentially far more productive of new information, than is a congress of thousands of American industrialists or millions of Red Guards. This shows that the manipulation of circular dialogue poses strategic problems because it is structurally a closed circuit and functionally a search for new information. If it is successful, it is probably the highest form of human communication. But as may be seen from the above considerations, it is rarely successful.

1.1.6. Network Dialogue

Network dialogue obeys the following structure:

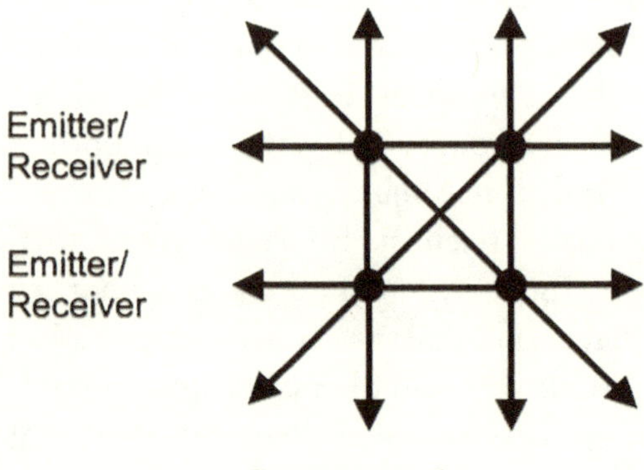

SKETCH 1.1.6

This form of highly diffused dialogical communication, which propagates information by constantly changing it, is the fundamental net (*reseau fondamental*) that absorbs and sustains all other forms of communication. Examples are rumors, mouth-to-ear communication, small talk, and, in a better-structured form, the post office and the telephone network. (It is important to stress that radio and TV do not form networks; they might claim to do so but are broadcasting systems. They *cast information broadly*, they radiate amphitheatrically, and they are discursive and not dialogical structures.) Network dialogue does not deliberately aim at the production of new information, as does circular dialogue, but it does spontaneously result in new information in what can be called *ever-changing general consensus*. It is this changing, ever-*new* information, that public opinion institutions try to measure.

Contrary to circular dialogue, network dialogue is an *open circuit*, and in this sense it is *truly democratic*. And contrary to circular dialogue (rarely successful), it always succeeds because it is structurally successful; it always results in new information because, being open to noise from all sides, it always deforms the original information. Our elitist tendency to despise this form of dialogue is not a good approach. Trotsky used to say (if I am not mistaken) that although one may not know who is right, one does know that the majority is never right, and it is obvious that *common sense* (as opposed to *common reason*) is not the most enlightened method to grasp the problems that defy us. Although contempt for network dialogue is not a good approach, neither is adulation: the *vox populi vox Dei* idea or the *silent majority* adoration. The phenomenon of network dialogue must be approached for what it is: the ultimate reservoir of all information, the constant elaboration of information through vulgarization, and the background noise of every effort at production and conservation of more elaborate information. In short, it is the lowest common denominator of humanity's effort to oppose the natural tendency toward entropy and therefore is itself somehow entropic.

The fact that network dialogue is the foundation of communication is, of course, more or less consciously known to every political commitment, past or present. People committed to politics aim, on a low level, *to be talked about* and, on a high level, to inform the network dialogue so as to change it, which implies to *change humanity*. This can be called a low- and high-level attempt to *manipulate public opinion*. And mass media are, of course, totally conscious and highly disciplined methods to do so. But it is curious to note that very rarely has there been made an attempt to materialize some of the unused virtual ties dormant in network structure. No noticeable technical improvement has been introduced to it since Neolithic times (save, of course, the post office and the telephone system), and people gossip more or less as they did in pre-historical surroundings. If we compare this archaic state of network dialogue with the sophistication of amphitheatrical discourse (and such a comparison imposes itself by the fact that those are the two *totally open* forms of communication), we feel that we are approaching one of the roots of the present situation in communication.

The argument submitted in this section can be summarized as follows: If one attempts to organize the forms of communication according to structural criteria, one finds, broadly speaking, the following communication structures: (1.1.1.) theatrical discourse, which tries to preserve information by making the receivers responsible for it; (1.1.2.) pyramidal discourse, which tries to preserve information by authoritarian methods; (1.1.3.) tree discourse, which tries to preserve information by branching it out in progressive specialization; (1.1.4.) amphitheatrical discourse, which tries to preserve information by stereotypical massification; (1.1.5.) circular dialogue, which tries to produce new information by elite synthesis; and (1.1.6.) network dialogue, which produces new information by degrading available information through vulgarization. Structures 1.1.4. and 1.1.6. are highly successful and, in fact, are synchronized at present in what tends to amount to total depoliticization (totalitarianism) through apparent total politicization (universal participation). Structures 1.1.1. and 1.1.5. are in a very specific crisis, and structures 1.1.2. and 1.1.3. need reevaluation. The following section proposes an analysis.

1.2. HOW THESE STRUCTURES WORK

The preceding section contains the following apparent contradiction: It affirms that the amphitheatrical structure of discourse is a form of communication that excludes dialogue and is therefore held by some to announce the end of history and the establishment of totalitarianism. But it claims that the network structure of dialogue is synchronized with amphitheatrical discourse, that amphitheatrical discourse aims deliberately at informing network dialogue, and that it is precisely this synchronization that may be taken as a symptom of depoliticization and the establishment of totalitarianism. It is obvious that the contradiction is only apparent, because *network dialogue* is not a true dialogue in the sense of a method of production of new information. The resulting information is a degradation of the information it has received from discourse. Still, the fact that network dialogue appears to be an exchange of information to those who participate in it (and this means all of us) and that therefore the so-called *power of the press, the broadcasting systems, and other mass media* is felt to be a sort of link between discourse and dialogue (as if *public opinion* were a partner, not only a passive receiver of mass media information) is to be considered within every consideration of the situation we are in. Thus, the apparent contradiction between the statement that mass-media information cannot be dialogued and the statement that dialogue is at present synchronized with mass-media information is key for understanding our situation in communication (and possibly also our political situation) and is the key for the curious feeling we have that, at present, we are being depoliticized precisely because politics pervade almost entirely the world we live in.

But that key cannot be used to open the door to our scene if one would restrict the problem only to the central relationship between amphitheatrical discourse and network dialogue. It is true that total depoliticization, the true totalitarian state, would be a situation in which all communication was reduced to synchronization of, for instance, TV programs and gossip. But this is not (yet) the situation we are in. Therefore, it is necessary to consider all the other communication structures mentioned in the preceding section before approaching the central problem.

1.2.1. Theater and Circle

No doubt, theatrical discourse and circular dialogue seem somehow to be the basic structures of communication. They seem to be *tribal* forms, well suited for small groups of people and entirely unsuited for the compact, moving mass of billions of persons now covering the surface of the earth and slowly pressing northwest. Indeed, if we consider the theatrical structure, we see the Paleolithic cave wall, with the sage of the tribe sitting with his back to the wall and facing the young warriors, and we *hear* the myths he is telling. And if we consider the circular dialogue, we *see* the Paleolithic hunters gathering around the campfire, and we *hear* how they make decisions concerning the hunt of the approaching herd of ponies. But such a projection of theater and circle into the ancient past, and the implicit admission that they are archaic forms of communication unsuited for the present, would be desperately pessimistic because theatrical discourse is the only discursive structure that permits responsible participation in the transmission of information from generation to generation (in history), because circular dialogue is the only dialogical structure that permits participation in deliberate decision-making, and because the synchronization of these two forms of communication is the only method to live in freedom that one can imagine. To deny the possibility of such synchronization in the present situation would amount to a denial of the possibility of maintaining a form of life worth living.

Some think that it would be dishonest not to admit such an impossibility. They believe that the sheer quantity of people living at present, and their tendency to increase in number in the immediate future, imposes mass communication and therefore excludes freedom (in the sense of participation in history and in decision-making). In fact, the quantitative impact of recent demographic explosions has an influence on communication structures, and therefore on everybody's form of life, which is not always fully appreciated. Still, this is not the first demographic explosion to have occurred. There was one resulting from the first Industrial Revolution. Another resulted from the canalization of rivers at the beginning of the Age of Metals. And still another (and probably the most violent) must have resulted from the invention of agriculture. And each time both theatrical discourse and circular dialogue adapted themselves to the changing situation. Let us not be impressed by sheer and mere number; that there are billions of people today, and probably will be tens of billions of people tomorrow, is not more terrible than during Mesolithic times when the number of people living together in one place increased, more or less suddenly, from tens to thousands. Hope is, therefore, justified that theater and circle (and thus a decent form of living) may survive the present demographic explosion.

We can follow, although very sketchily, the various metamorphoses of the theater and circle, and possibly such a sketch will be attempted in a future chapter. But what is important at this point is the consideration of some recent changes in these structures and of the present *crisis* they are in. The most important form of theatrical discourse in recent times is (in spite of appearances to the contrary) the Victorian family and the Victorian educational system. And the most important form of circular dialogue in recent times is not the parliamentary systems or even the famous dialogues between warring ideologies but the circular dialogue going on within the tree discourses of technology and science. It is, therefore, necessary to consider these recent forms and their present-day *crisis* if we are to grasp our situation.

From the point of view of the theory of communication, the Victorian family consists of a drawing room containing a mother or her equivalent (a maid or some other employee) and two to four children. This forms a theater as it did not exist before the Industrial Revolution, because the family was then composed of three generations and because the fathers were not as yet permanently absent. The fact that this form of theatrical discourse was statistically rare (the proletarian mother worked and thus informed little, and the rural family was still centered around the grandparents even during the nineteenth century) does not diminish its importance. It was the model of postindustrial *paideia* (transmission of basic patterns of behavior, knowledge, and experience from generation to generation). Even if the Victorian family was actually rare, it modeled, until quite recently, what can be called *basic education*, meaning the method by which fundamental information was transmitted.

If we try to free this communication structure from its ideological cover, we find the following situation (see sketch 1.1.1.): The concave wall has become a wall in a room, probably partially covered with pictures. The emitter (the mother or her equivalent) has become a memory that stores information elaborated and codified during Romanticism (for instance, specific patterns of behavior suitable for production and preservation of industrial wealth or specific patterns of experience having to do with *nature* and *culture*). The receivers are children of preschool age. But the important aspects are the channels. The mother reads to the children or tells stories she herself has read. Victorian family discourse is a linearly coded discourse based directly or indirectly on the alphabet and (if we include the piano present in the drawing room) on linearly coded sheet music. This, even more than the semantic contents of the discourse, is what is decisive about it. The importance of code on communication will be discussed elsewhere in this book, but two of its aspects must be discussed at this point.

The receivers (the children) are being programmed to become memories fed predominantly by alphabetically coded information, which implies a specific way to *decode the world*, namely, a historical consciousness. To them, the world will be predominantly a process. For instance, the fairy tales that the mother tells them are not coded within the oral, mythical tradition from which they stem but were recodified by Romantic poets and ethnologists of the Brothers Grimm type, which means they are no longer myths but stories. Thus, Victorian family discourse translates Western *paideia* into linear, processual information. (It destroys its folklore structure.) However, the alphabet, which dominates the codes of Victorian family discourse, is the attempt to transcribe phonetically some spoken language. Since the invention of printing the language thus transcribed is neither a universal one (such as Latin) nor the living language of daily communication (such as a dialect) but a more or less artificial print language (such as literate English, French, Italian, or German). The reason is that the printing press produces tens of thousands of books, for which readership in Latin would be too reduced, and even more reduced if it were to transcribe dialects. The print languages function as the spoken language appropriate for printing. In the Victorian family discourse, these print languages finally overcome the living dialects, and the receivers are being programmed by and for them. Thus structurally, by their codes, Victorian family discourses program their receivers for nationalism.

Obviously, this is not an exhaustive analysis of the Victorian family, even if it is considered only on the aspect of being a theatrical discourse and a model for a specific *paideia*. But it suffices for the present purpose, which is to show how theatrical discourse, this ageless method to transmit information from generation to generation by rendering the receivers responsible for it, had transformed itself in the recent past by programming its receivers for historical consciousness and for nationalism.

It may be said that this form of theater no longer functions, although its remnants are still with us (not to mention its ideology, which still floats about and prevents us from seeing that it no longer functions). The place of the mother in the discursive situation has been taken over by television, and this implies two radical changes: the structure is no longer theatrical, and it is no longer alphabetically coded. The introduction of TV to the family has cracked its closed theatrical shell and transformed it into one among the countless places of reception on the horizon of the amphitheater of broadcasting. And the substitution of the alphabet by the technical image (the TV screen) implies, in the near future, the change of program from historical consciousness and nationalism to some other, as-yet-not-articulated form of consciousness. The decadence of the Victorian family structure implies a revolution in our *paideia*. This will be discussed later in the argument. But at this point, one may conclude that the decadence of the Victorian family implies the end of historical consciousness and of the national state because both these phenomena are based on the alphabet, and the Victorian family is being substituted by a discourse based on image codes.

The Victorian school system, as it resulted from the Industrial Revolution, is structured in three levels: *lower*, *middle*, and *higher* education. The purpose of the *lower* level is to program the proletarian mass for a sort of rudimentary historical consciousness and nationalism and thus absorb it into the process of industrial production (to avoid class consciousness and revolution). The purpose of the *middle* level is to program the new generation of the bourgeoisie with the knowledge, values, and patterns of experience suitable for the management of the industrial establishment (and of the *embellishments* it requires). But the purpose of the *higher* level is to program a bourgeois elite with the knowledge of the codes and methods suitable for participation in the circular dialogues that compose the various tree discourses, especially the discourses of technology and science. The *lower* and *middle* levels of our school system are now in *crisis* because both proletarian and bourgeois youth are programmed in a way unsuitable for our school system when they enter it. But the *higher* level of our educational system is in an even more revealing *crisis*: Our universities have structures that have become unsuitable for the present structure of science and technical progress. The consideration of the university crisis must therefore be postponed until the tree discourse is under discussion.

One of the ideologies that serves to conceal our school system is the alleged *penetrability* of all its levels: ideologically *everybody*, regardless of class, race, or creed, has an opportunity to penetrate even into the highest levels of education. (This is part of the general ideology with which all of us are being programmed on the *lower* level of education and of which some of us are freed on the *higher* level.) The purpose of this ideological cover is to create the illusion in the proletarian mass that it may, if only it makes an individual effort, participate in decision-making and thus avoid a collective effort. But the recent development of tree structure discourse, its violent specialization, is demonstrating very clearly that to participate in scientific or technological dialogues is not to participate in decision-making. Put more simply, it has become obvious that if one attends a university, one may become a specialist, but not necessarily a decision-maker. This new knowledge has two distinct effects: it means that it is becoming less attractive for the proletarian to try for university admittance, and thus the ideological cover is being put out of action; it means that the university student feels politically castrated in spite of his or her admittance to the elite level. In short, the crisis of our education system manifests itself, among other ways, as the new generation's loss of interest in it.

The above argument, as far as theatrical discourse is concerned, can be summed up as follows: The two most important forms of that discourse, as they emerged from the upheaval of the Industrial Revolution—the Victorian family and the Victorian educational system—have not so far succeeded in adapting themselves to the present revolution in communication and are in a *crisis* (which does not imply that both the family and the educational system may be restructured in the future to become suitable for the new situation). There are other theatrical discourses that program us, for instance, concerts and the theater proper. Though important in their own way, their consideration can be postponed for another future context.

In regard to circular dialogue, a superficial consideration of our scene may give the impression that the Industrial Revolution has resulted in a victory of that communication structure, which is now being threatened by the revolution in communication. It may look as if parliamentary systems; open dialogue through book publication; political, artistic, philosophical, and other types of polemics; and even the numerous wars of the nineteenth century and the first half of the twentieth century were manifestations of circular dialogue dominance and as if the present irruption of the mass media onto the scene was an attack on this dominance.

However, a closer examination finds that circular dialogue, which indeed dominated during the eighteenth century and resulted in the revolutions of the last third of that century (the Industrial, American, and French Revolutions), did not truly survive the revolution it had, itself, set into motion. Parliaments, polemics, and wars, in short, what is called *liberal democracy* by its supporters and *capitalist imperialism* by its opponents, are nothing but specters of true dialogical circles as they prevailed during the ancien régime and among the American Founding Fathers. Why those communication forms cannot be considered true dialogues but crossed discourses (why, for instance, the Second World War was not a true dialogue, although the Seventy Years' War was) cannot be discussed at present and is left, provisionally, to the reader's intuitive comprehension.

However, one type of circular dialogue, which composes tree structure discourse, not only survived the upheaval of the late eighteenth-century revolutions but also became one of the dominant communication forms. Circular dialogues, as they occur in laboratories, in seminars and scientific symposia, in specialized scientific and technical publications, and so forth, not only produced most of the information during the industrial period, but they also resulted in the present revolution in communication. And, as far as we can judge, they continue their violent progress. However, circular dialogue inserted in a tree discourse is not quite like a *sovereign* dialogue (for instance, the dialogue of hunters gathered around a campfire); it is *subject* to the structure of the discourse it is part of (see sketches 1.1.3. and 1.1.5.). The new, resulting information is not a synthesis of available information but of a branch of available information, *specialized* information. Thus, there was no true dialogical discourse outside the sciences, techniques, and similar tree discourses, even before the present revolution, and the present communication revolution did not change anything in this regard. (But the impact of this statement cannot be appreciated without a consideration of tree structure discourse, as discussed in the following argument.)

In sum, if we consider theatrical discourse and circular dialogue to be the basic forms of communication, and their synchronization to be a condition for a life worth living, the present scene does not look very hopeful. The most important forms of theatrical discourse, the family and educational system, are in a *crisis*, and we have not had any truly meaningful circular dialogues outside science and technology for several generations. The question of how to synchronize theater and circle seems thus to be a moot question. But this is only part of the map of our communicological situation as we are attempting to draw it in this chapter.

1.2.2. Pyramid and Tree

Pyramidal and tree discourses are, quite obviously, not basic structures of communication. Although pyramidal discourse is a very ancient structure, it cannot be basic since the function of relays is a composite function (see sketch 1.1.2.). And tree discourse is of such recent origin, and its function has been submitted to so many epistemological analyses, that one does not need to look at sketch 1.1.3. to know that it is the most sophisticated and refined form of communication. The surprising thing is that, if one compares the two sketches, the obvious fact that tree discourse is a modification of pyramidal discourse has not always been appreciated. One often hears, for instance, that modern science (the most typical tree discourse) has resulted from opposition to the authority of the church (the most typical pyramidal discourse of the Middle Ages), but one hears less often that modern science is structurally the modern heir to the medieval church. This is surprising, because the structural similarity between the two is so striking but mainly because the hidden pyramid nature, and therefore authoritativeness, of science and similar discourses is one of the reasons for their present *crisis* (if indeed they are in a crisis).

The origin of pyramidal discourse is obscured by the millennia that separate us from it. No doubt, the introduction of relays into the channel that links emitter and receiver (*author* and *obeyer*, or *message bearer* and *faithful*) must have happened long before the establishment of elaborate hierarchies since they characterize even the earliest civilizations. No doubt also, the pyramid of early Sumerian *administration* does not have the same structure as that of modern pyramids, such as the administration of a multinational enterprise or the Soviet system. Still, the striking thing about pyramids is how simple and effective they are for the conservation of original information and how deeply they influence our program, even centuries after their apparent *overcoming* by tree-structured discourse.

The Roman republic is a model for pyramidal discourses as they continue to function in the present situation. Here we consider two of its aspects: the problem of *authorship* and the double function of the relays. As a rule, the *author* of the information is not present in the pyramid, which preserves the information (the author *transcends* communication), and this information is a *supreme authority*, a sort of relay connected with the *transcendent*, that occupies the top. (The *authors* of the information preserved in ancient civilizations were gods, of the Roman republic it was Romulus, of the church it is Christ, of the various armies it is *the sovereign people* or some other sovereign, of the Communist Party it is dialectic materialism, of multinational enterprises it is the shareholder, and so forth). This mythical character of information is quite different from the *myths* of amphitheatrical discourse, which are considered later.

The double function of relays—their constant recodification of the original message to keep it pure from external noise and the way they distribute the information to subaltern relays—posed theoretical and practical problems very early. The recodification of the information demands that the relay be reconnected with the *author* (this is the *religious* function of the relays), but since the author is transcendent, the supreme authority (king, pope, four-star general, general secretary, and so forth) must often substitute for it. (In Rome, because this religious function of the relays was considered to be the most important one, it was called the *magisterial* function.) The distribution of information demanded that there be an executive power, which conditions the subaltern relays, and the final receivers to accept the information. (In Rome, because this function was considered to be the less important one, it was called the *ministerial* function.) Each pyramid has solved the religious and what might be called the *traditional* problem involved in its structure its own way: the religion and tradition of the Acadian Empire are not quite the same as they are within the Exxon administration. Still, no pyramid can work without some form of religion (*faith*, *esprit de corps*, and so forth) and without some form of tradition.

It is precisely to eliminate the problem of a *transcendent author* and the problem of religion and tradition that the structure of the tree, the discourse of science (and other discourses that take science for their model), has been elaborated. Although for about three centuries (from the sixteenth to the nineteenth) this attempt seemed to be successful, it now appears to be a failure. Although the authorship of the information discoursed by science is clouded by the fact that there is constantly new information that originates in the circular dialogues that recodify it, the ultimate *author* is *scientific truth*, which may be defined in various ways but is always mythically transcendent. And although the various dialogues, which have substituted the pyramidal relays in tree discourse, may not want to assume *authority* (because they consider themselves to be free of *religion and of tradition*), they constitute the most characteristic authority in the present situation. (Even more so than generals or party secretaries, dictators or managers, the scientists and technicians are considered to be authorities at present.) This implies that tree discourse is just as religious as pyramidal discourse (so-called *scientism* or *technologism*) and just as traditional (scientific *method* and so forth). Thus, it may be said that the invention of science and similar communication forms is now shown to have been a failure if the aim was to substitute myth for some other kind of source of information (for instance, *doubt*) and authority for some other kind of preservation of information (for instance, *method*). This does not imply, of course, that science is a failure.

But that one discovers its mythical quality and its authoritative aspects is not the only reason that science may be said to be in a crisis. There are two other basic reasons, which have already been alluded to: the progressive hermeticism of its codes and its progressive explosive specialization. It may be said that there is no human memory capable of storing the information discoursed by science because no human memory can have all the scientific codes in its program, let alone synthesize the various bits of specialized information. There may be artificial memories that can do so (computers and so forth), and these cybernetic machines may, in the future, substitute for the *philosophers* (in the sense of being information synthesizers). But it is doubtful whether those hypothetical machines will ever allow human memories to *analyze their system*.

Thus, scientific discourse, having no human memories for receivers of its information, has become inhuman and in this basic sense useless: It does not preserve information (nor yet produce information) that gives the world and life in it meaning. That this is a fact should be obvious to everybody, but the fact is obscured by the dense ideological clouds that cover science. And what is true for science is also true for technology, philosophy, and so-called *avant-garde* art, in short, for every tree discourse to become a victim of hermeticism and specialization.

This is also the reason why our *higher* educational system is in a crisis, and the very word *university* shows it. The pedagogic ideal of universities is the Renaissance *uomo universale*, the memory that stores all available information. Not only has this ideal become nonsense, but the very idea of storing information coming out of tree discourse in human memories (to *teach students*) has become nonsense for two reasons: There is too much information, and it becomes too quickly invalidated by the progress of dialogical reformulation. Students are not capable of learning and/or forgetting all the information coming out of their specialized branch of tree discourse quickly enough to be on the same level of progress within the branch, even if a student should constantly *recycle*. *Higher* education should form system analysts who handle cybernetic memories that store information instead of forming specialists (including specialists for generalization) who can never hope to compete with computers, and thus become frustrated computers.

There is yet another reason for the university crisis. As the bits of information explode and cross during the discursive process, a new type of dialogical circle has been forming lately. These circles do not dialogue information itself but the structure of information (as if the tree of discourse would turn its branches against itself). Two types of this dialogue are old, logic and mathematics. But there are many new ones, such as cybernetics, informatics, decisions theory, games theory, and, why not confess it, the theory of communication. These *formal* branches of scientific (and artistic, philosophical, and politological) discourse do not fit into the current university structure. Universities are structured according to the type of information to be discoursed, but these new *formal* branches are dialogues concerning structure: Mathematics, informatics, or games theory must be taught at the school of natural sciences just as much as in courses on literature; in architectural schools just as much as in law schools. No amount of *cross-education* can adapt the present structure of universities to the present structure of the tree discourse.

To resume the preceding argument (which does not pretend, of course, to be a critique of authority or a philosophy of science but nothing other than a short sketch of present communicological events), the following can be stated: There are at present very important pyramidal discourses at work, just as in ancient times, although some of them have assumed a new form. But there is an archaic flavor about them. They have survived the *liberating* attempt of their transformation into tree discourses (the attack on them made by *doubt*), but they have suffered from it: faith in the church, in the goodness of armies, in the party, or in the company is not as it used to be before methodical doubt coming from science and philosophy, from technical and artistic progress, attacked it.

And there is, at present, the obvious dominating action, mainly of technology and science, of tree discourse. But it is becoming more and more obvious that tree discourse is essentially the same as pyramidal discourse, that scientific truth is a myth, that the goodness of technical progress is an article of faith, and that the religion of progress is just another form of authoritative religion. This, and the tendency of science and technology toward hermeticism and specialization (toward the formation of priests and ministers), permits the conclusion that the heyday of science and technology is over and that tree discourses will suffer the fate of all pyramidal discourses: They will be dissolved in the massifying action of amphitheatrical discourse. This does not mean that science and technology will not continue to produce ever-new information at an ever-more-breathtaking pace. It only means that the *general public* will be less and less interested in this sort of, by now, almost meaningless progress.

There is, however, one result of scientific and technological progress that tends to continue to dominate the scene: the revolution of communication through the development of the amphitheatrical discourse structure and its appropriate new codes. Through this scientific and technical progress science and technology may well have ended not only their own careers but the career of general progress as well.

1.2.3. Amphitheater and Network

If we now turn our attention to what has been recognized to be the central problem in our present communicological situation—amphitheatrical discourse, network dialogue, and their synchronization—we find that it is in no way a new problem. Not only do we know from antiquity that amphitheaters (Olympic games, arenas, circuses) had a massifying and *alienating* function just as the present ones do (for instance, the

Roman cry *panem et circenses*, meaning "if they have bread to eat and games to watch, they will behave like sheep"), but we also know from even more ancient sources that the network dialogue always worked in the direction of degradation of information (for instance, the *murmuring* of the children of Israel and other manifestations of the silent majority and of public opinion in the Bible). If we, therefore, realize that amphitheatrical discourse and network dialogue are at present the dominating communication forms and that they are tending to eliminate all other forms of communication, we are compelled to conclude that there is nothing exceptional in such a situation. This must have been the case in Pharaonic Egypt, in the Greek tyrannies, and under the Roman emperors, in short, wherever a *totalitarian system* prevailed.

However, there is indeed something entirely new to our present problem, something for which there is and can be no parallel in history or prehistory: the fact that our amphitheatrical discourse is the product of scientific and technical discourse. This cannot be minimized by saying that TV is a scientific and technical circus just as the motorcar is a scientific and technical oxcart. Even in the case of the motorcar, it is not only a question of improved performance: a new form of tool, and therefore of human existence, that came into being when motorcars were invented. But in the case of scientific and technical amphitheaters, it can be stated, without exaggeration, that a radically new form of communication, and therefore of the meaning humanity gives to the world and to itself, has been set into motion and that the similarities with previous amphitheaters are more misleading than revealing.

What is meant here is not the banal statement that the invention of the telegraph has made it possible for the press and similar paper amphitheaters to make all events in the world simultaneous and thus, in a sense, overcome geography, or the similar banal statement that the invention of the radio (and to a lesser extent the later invention of TV) has made it possible for broadcasting systems to make this simultaneity accessible to those who do not participate in alphabetic conventions. (However, these statements are banalities, not because they are not revolutionary statements but because they are statements too often repeated to be really grasped in their revolutionary impact.) What is meant here is the less banal, because less overemphasized, although equally revolutionary, fact that the codes that were developed—some of them independently from scientific amphitheaters, others as a result of those amphitheaters, but all of them characteristic of those amphitheaters: The codes of photography, film, TV, and video, in short, what may be termed *technical image codes*—are about to radically change our program and thus not only the structure of society but, even more significantly, the structure of the world we live in. Not only has geography been overcome by synchronization of events, but also history is being overcome by the transformation of events into pictures (be they still or moving).

This is, according to the basic thesis being defended in this book, what is so new in our situation: A new consciousness is coming about, and it can be grasped if one considers the way by which our memories are being programmed. The dominance of scientifically produced amphitheaters, and their synchronization of largely archaic network dialogue, and the pitiless marginalization of all other forms of human communication threaten not only to destroy all social structures and transform humanity into an amorphous, homologized mass, but even more significantly, it threatens to destroy human consciousness of existence—total *alienation*. In other words, it threatens to definitely depoliticize us and thus bring about a totalitarian situation, which is a caricature of the millennium, of Paradise on Earth, of the Kingdom of Heaven. However, it holds the promise for a new and as yet entirely unimaginable form of post-historical existence, of an overcoming of historical categories by entirely new concepts and images, of a new level of existence in the world. This is entirely unimaginable, even though manifestations of it can already be observed all around us.

Before considering this revolution in codes (which will be dealt with in Chapter 2), let us try to draw the map of our situation from the point of view of communication: Our theaters are in a crisis because (with the sole exception of the cinema, which may be no true theater and which therefore merits special considerations) they are structures become dependent, since the Industrial Revolution, on alphabetic codification. Our circular dialogues are in a crisis since that revolution, except for those dialogues that go on in tree discourses and that have become victims of hermetic specialization. Our pyramidal and tree discourses (including all authoritative political discourse and technology and science), although they continue to function, appear like archaic blocks within the mounting sea of amphitheatrical discourse, like melting icebergs in the tropical waters of broadcast technical images. And these amphitheaters, which are transforming humanity into a cosmic circus, are synchronized with a network dialogue of pre-historical character. It is worthwhile to take a closer look at this map.

1.3. SOME CHARACTERISTIC SITUATIONS

One can say (if one is to continue the method of radical simplification, which has been followed so far) that, previous to the revolution in communication provoked by scientific amphitheaters and the codes that characterize it, the situation of communication in Western society had approximately the following structure:

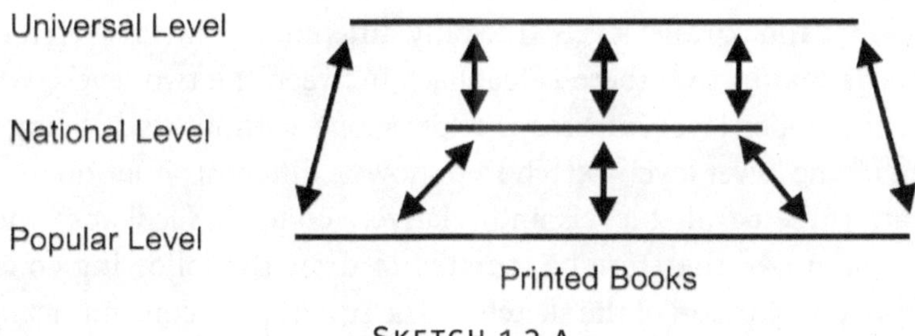

SKETCH 1.3.A

One can hold, if one wants to push the attempt to map the present situation a little bit further, that the previous sketch may be considered to be a development of a communication structure as it prevailed before the invention and general use of book printing.

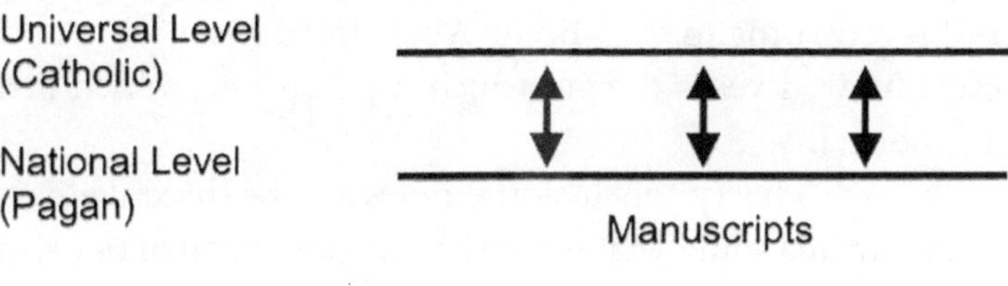

SKETCH 1.3.B

And one can say that recent developments, which are implicit in technological inventions of the nineteenth century (especially the photograph) and became explicit shortly after the Second World War, point to the establishment, in the immediate future, of the following communication structure:

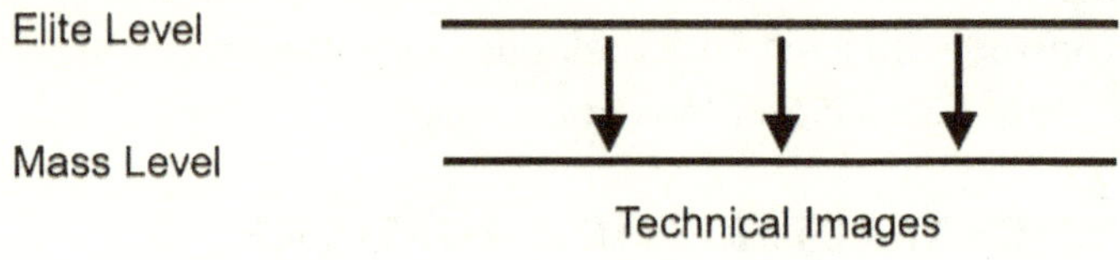

Sketch 1.3.c

If one compares the three sketches from a purely visual point of view (that is, if one does not read the written texts that *explain* the drawings), the similarity between sketches 1.3.b and 1.3.c is striking. Both drawings show that communication in Western society was conducted on two distinct and parallel levels. The only difference between sketch 1.3.b and 1.3.c is that in 1.3.b there is feedback between the two levels, while in 1.3.c the upper level informs the lower one without itself being informed by the lower level. Sketch 1.3.a shows a different situation in that there are three parallel levels and relatively complex feedback among them. One might therefore be tempted to draw the following conclusion from comparison of the sketches: The situation in communication, as it is emerging from the present revolution in communication, is similar to the one existing before the invention of printing, and what is commonly called the *Modern Age* (the period corresponding roughly to the situation in sketch 1.3.a) is an abnormal interruption of what may be considered to be the *normal* communication structure. In fact, one does find people who defend the thesis that Western society (or society in general) is returning to the Middle Ages after a short interruption of about four hundred years during which it *progressed*, which means it behaved abnormally.

However, such a hasty conclusion is not what the three sketches here intend: they aim at a somewhat more sophisticated map of our situation in communication.

1.3.1. Printed Books

Any attempt to locate the printed-book situation in time without reference to geographic space will result in gross falsification. It began to function in the second half of the sixteenth century in western Europe but does not yet function in some parts of what has come to be known as the *Third World*. Thus, it may be said to be a rough communicological equivalent to the concept of the *Modern Age* for historians. And as in the historical concept, there is in the concept of the *printed-book* situation a more or less neat climax: What is for historians the Industrial Revolution is for communicologists the introduction of the public school system. Any question of precedence is, of course, nonsense. It is of no consequence whether *modern humanity invented printing* or *printed books made modern humanity possible*; or whether *the Industrial Revolution introduced the public educational system* or *that system opened the field for the Industrial Revolution*. The difference of formulation is a question of points of view on the same phenomenon and of a subsequent different use of terms.

Still, if one assumes the point of view of communication, the period called the *Modern Age* in history does show some aspects that are not sufficiently emphasized under the historians' point of view. And the most important is not (as it might seem) that modern nations are seen to be consequences of book printing but that the popular level of communication is no longer *pagan* in the Modern Age as it was in the Middle Ages. Both these aspects will be now put into their historical perspective.

As alphabetic writing becomes the dominant code in Western communication, the spoken languages become problems for communication because the alphabet is a more or less successful transcription of spoken language. Before that dominance, when the alphabet was a convention of the clergy, the linguistic problem was of a different order. There was a universal language, Latin, and to learn how to read and write implied learning Latin (as to learn how to write and read numbers implied learning mathematics). There were, of course, other written languages, such as Greek, Arabic, and Hebrew, but each had a different alphabet, and learning a new language implied having to learn a new type of writing. The unlettered, vulgar dialects, as they were spoken in village and castle, were only used for communication on a low level. They were beneath the interest of a clerk, although, as a matter of course, he himself used them in his daily communication.

This problem changed as printed books became common. They were to be bought by a bourgeoisie that had only a very rudimentary knowledge of Latin and could not be bothered to learn it before buying the books. However, books could not be printed in *vulgar* languages because every dialect had only relatively few speakers and because, even within this relatively small number, there was a great variety of subclasses. (Relatively few people spoke Tuscan or Hessian, and there were many varieties of Tuscan and Hessian.) Therefore, some artificial languages had to be elaborated from the vulgar tongues, sufficiently close to them to be easily learned and sufficiently widespread to permit the sale of thousands of books. These artificial languages, such as Italian, French, English, and German, are at the roots of modern nations. (An aside: Since the Jews had had a relatively large literate class during the Middle Ages, and since they wrote an alphabet appropriate to only one language, Hebrew, they escaped somehow from the printed-book revolution. They may thus be said to have been a *nation* even during the Middle Ages or not to be, even now, a nation in the modern sense of the term.)

The problem of whether the modern languages were codified before printed books (such as the Italian of the *Dolce stil nuovo*) or immediately after them (such as Luther's German) is not important. It is the same if I say that printed books presuppose a modern language or that they produce it. What matters is that printed books introduce a level of communication into the situation that is codified in modern languages, first as they are written and slowly, later, as they start to be spoken. In short, the important thing to grasp is that modern national languages were first written and only later spoken; they are made for printing and for linear notation, which gives them a totally different character from that of medieval Latin (which is not really meant to be spoken) and of dialects (which are not really meant to be written).

As noted previously, the fact that modern nations are based on print languages (although they are important for the understanding of Modern Age communication) is not what is so very characteristic of the printed-book situation. Even more characteristic is that people, ordinary people in the villages and small towns, had to learn, at a certain age, to speak a print language. Before the advent of public schools, they had to learn that artificial language to be able to communicate with the *authorities*, to understand the information coming from the pyramidal discourse to which they were subjected. And after the advent of public schooling, they had to learn how to speak and write that artificial language if they were to participate in general communication. And this had a profound effect on their program, their *being-in-the-world*, because it was the end of mythical, magic, ritual existence. The true revolutionary effect of printed books is not that they have produced nations and nationalism (although nobody can deny how important that is) but that they have destroyed, slowly but definitely, a pre-historical form of living. It was the books (and not the various saints) that truly *Christianized* Western society by imposing upon it Christianity's linear, historical consciousness. Each printed book is, in this sense, a Bible.

This imposes two different *readings* of sketch 1.3.a, one concerning the *printed-book* situation before, and the other concerning the same situation after, the introduction of the public education systems. Before that event, this is how the sketch might be interpreted: There was a popular level of communication whose chief codes were spoken dialects, popular music, and dance; a figurative two- and three-dimensional code, now called *folkloric art*; specific codes of gestures; and so forth. The communication structures on this level were circular dialogue (on the village greens and in the marketplace) and network dialogue (gossip and rumors propagated by traveling groups such as gypsies and apprentices). There was a national level of communication whose chief codes were the printed national language, baroque and classical *arts and techniques* (including political-institutional codes), and a spoken language, which was a mixture of dialect and written language. The communication structures on this level were theatrical discourse (in the family and in schools), circular dialogue (in politics, in the workshop, and after dinner), and network dialogue (gossip, common sense, and the forming of public opinion). And there was a universal (for Western civilization) level of communication whose chief codes were written Latin, Italian, and French; the codes of the sciences (including formal logic and mathematics); and the codes of the arts of the sixteenth to eighteenth centuries. The communication structure on this level was the tree discourse of science, technology, philosophy, and the arts and the circular dialogues of political, social, economic, and *ideological* decisions. The popular level communicated with the universal level, receiving information through pyramidal discourse and emitting information through various circular dialogues. The national level was connected with the popular level by pyramidal discourse through which it emitted information and by circular dialogues, but also through theatrical discourse (in church and marketplace), which permitted revolutions. And the national level was also connected with the universal level through theatrical discourse, of which the universal level was the emitter but in which national-level revolutions (such as the Reformation, the various bourgeois revolutions, and finally the Industrial Revolution) took place. These interlevel communications were mostly coded in the various national languages.

The second reading of sketch 1.3.a, concerning the situation after the introduction of public schooling, allows the following interpretation: There was a popular level of communication whose chief codes were the printed languages of the school book and the press; music and dance as they were being coded by the national level for popular consumption; and other pseudo-artistic *kitsch* codes produced by the same method. The communication structures on this level were remnants of circular dialogues (in cells of syndicates and political parties), theatrical discourse in schools and political rallies, and intense network dialogue. The national and universal levels of communication were more or less as they were before the introduction of public schooling, although, of course, the codes of Romanticism (which then prevailed) showed a different structure from the baroque and classical codes prevailing before the Industrial Revolution. But what had changed radically was interlevel communication. The popular level (now better called the *proletariat*) was subject to intense amphitheatrical discourse on the part of the national level (through media such as the press and later the radio), and its codes were almost entirely elaborated by that national level. It had lost autonomy. And the universal level had begun the process of branching out into different specializations, which characterize it at present, and was neatly divided into at least two different *cultures* with entirely different codes: the *culture of science* and the *culture of the humanities.*

Thus, one can see that, although the *printed-book* situation has been more or less structured the same way since the Renaissance up to the Second World War (it is the *bourgeois* structure), the existential climate is entirely different before and after introduction of the public school system. Before it, the popular level was autonomous, lived in a mythical, pre-historical world, and could thus sustain the whole structure of communication. After public schooling, the popular level became dependent on national codes (it *absorbed bourgeois ideology* and became *alienated from its reality*), and it no longer sustained the situation. And in consequence of this *conversion* of the popular level, the function of the national level within the whole structure changed profoundly. Before introduction of the public school system, the national level had been the level of *revolutions*, in the sense of the transformation of discourse into dialogue and thus the production of new information. After the public school system was established, the national level became the emitter of discourses, which aimed at preventing revolutions. In fact, the very concept of *nation* has a different meaning before and after establishment of the public school system. Before, it meant the establishment of dialogical circles. After, it meant theatrical and amphitheatrical discourse (*imperialism*). One is not always aware of the fact that the book as a medium changed completely with the Industrial Revolution. Before, it was the starting point for dialogue (for the production of new information), and after, it became an information conserve, like a tin, which means that before the Industrial Revolution the national bourgeoisie was *progressive*, and it *became reactionary* later.

The present revolution in communication, provoked by science and technology, which means the universal level, exploded into the *printed-book* situation, as it did after the introduction of the public school system. In fact, it exploded precisely at the point where so-called *Western* society had absorbed and *alienated* entirely its popular level (had *eliminated illiteracy*) but where the so-called *Third World* had just begun to introduce public schooling. In other words, it exploded, in the *West*, against an already literate proletarian mass, while it exploded in the rest of the world against a widely illiterate, pre-historical popular communication situation. As one of the characteristics of the present revolution is the cosmic dimension of its amphitheaters, which despise the difference between the West and the rest of the world (and in this curious sense represents the victory of the West over the world), one cannot consider the present communication structure before first touching, however slightly, on the pre-book situation.

1.3.2. Manuscripts

Sketch 1.3.b is meant to map the manuscript situation, or the communication situation of medieval Europe, and to some extent even the situation of the late Roman Empire, of which the Middle Ages are, from a communicological viewpoint, a rather smooth continuation. But the sketch may be applied, in a way, to the communication situation as it prevailed in a great part of the so-called *underdeveloped countries* before the irruption of the present revolution in communication. Applied to Western society, the following is a possible *reading*.

There are two parallel communication levels. The popular, *pagan* level is, in reality, a complex of small communication islands (valleys, villages, and regions), each with its own set of codes and communication structures. It is here called *pagan* (in spite of its official Christianity), not only because *pagan* means "rural" but for the more fundamental reason that Christianity did not really touch it. Christianity is the ideology of linear texts (of the *Bible*), which means that it is a *historical* ideology, while the popular level of communication had practically no written texts and thus no historical consciousness. However, the universal, *catholic* level is indeed extremely uniform and permits communication without great difficulty between all its participants, wherever they may live in Europe. In fact, never before or since has such a universality been achieved in Western civilization. This is why it is here being called *catholic*, not only because its chief communication structure was the Catholic Church but also because *catholic* means "for everybody." Its codes were written Latin, the codes of scholastic philosophy and theology, the codes of alchemy and astrology, the codes now called Romanesque and Gothic. And communication was structured by the pyramidal discourse of the church and by circular dialogues in monasteries and so forth. There were also the theatrical discourses of the schools, but they may be considered to have been preparations for pyramidal discourse (the formation of *clerks*, authoritative relays).

There was constant and intense feedback between the upper, historical level and the lower, pre-historical one, although theoretically the lower level formed the passive receiver of the pyramidal church discourse. The information, as it was emitted from the upper to the lower level, was coded in a way accessible for the lower level, and that means in images: church windows, tapestry, icons. It was recodified from a linear into an image code and thus suffered a transformation in the character of the information: it became *mythical*. (It became *pagan*, in the sense that Christ was no longer a historical actor but became a god in a pantheon.) But the codes of the lower level, as they manifested themselves in the tools, gadgets, and gestures of daily life, were taken over by the higher level for the work of recodification of its information. Thus, although the pyramidal discourse of the church did slowly inject some historical consciousness upon the popular level, it suffered, through this kind of feedback, a constant remythification (of which Mariology is but one example). It may be said that in spite of the neat division of the communication situation, and in spite of the irreversible character of pyramidal discourse, which then prevailed, there was a unity, a *style*, in Middle Age Europe (and possibly also in late Roman Empire Europe) that will not be found later. This may explain why *life was meaningful*: everybody participated somehow in the same codes and in the same communication structures, although of course, there was a great difference between the participation of a priest and the participation of a maidservant.

It may be held that if the printed book had not supplanted the manuscript, this situation, which had prevailed for at least a thousand years, might have continued indefinitely and thus, by its mere duration, might have overcome linear discourse. In other words, it may be held that the *historicity* of Christendom (and of Islam) was restricted to an ever-smaller elite and that mythical ritual became increasingly the climate of the greater part of society (and the Greek part of Christendom is an illustration of this increasing ritualization). The printed book gave historicity a new impulse and made it explosive. The dialogue between iconoclasts and iconolatry in the orthodox part of Christianity is an example of how the importance of image and alphabetic codes was appreciated: before the printed book there was no way to decide which of the two codes was to prevail.

Thus, in the West, the invention of printing made the communication situation incline to the side of the alphabet by creating a literate middle level of communication and as a consequence brought about all the scientific and technological progress we know, because it was this revolutionary middle class that changed the pyramidal into tree discourse. But outside the West, the process was entirely different. It is entirely impossible to make general statements concerning the *Third World*. Places as different from each other as Brazil, Upper Volta, or China cannot be brought down to a common denominator. Still, the irruption of the Latin alphabet is comparable in all those places. It created a level of communication in which the participants knew how to read and write some European language (mostly English, French, or Spanish) and were therefore being programmed by the whole set of codes that characterizes the middle level of the late printed-books situation. In Latin America, where Spanish and Portuguese are spoken by most of the people, the impact was different from that in Africa and Asia, where no European language was spoken. Still, all these places have in common that the new level of communication based on printed books did not establish a *printed-books* but a *manuscript* situation. There were now two levels of communication: the lower level encompassed all the levels previous to the book penetration, and the upper level communicated far more with Europe than with its own lower level. (This is why alphabetization is an ambivalent effort in all those places.)

To put it simply, the historical consciousness of the literate level in the Third World is a European consciousness based on the alphabet, and as it penetrates the lower level, it not only destroys its structures but also introduces a foreign element into it. (In these few, apparently quite neutral words, the whole tragic dilemma of the commitment of Third World intellectuals is contained.) Thus, sketch 1.3.b, if meant to be a map of the Third World just previous to the present revolution in communication, may be read as follows: There is an alienated upper level of communication, based on the alphabet, on imported books, and on other imported codes, that functions, whether it intends to or not, for the place of the origin of the codes, which means the United States and Europe. And there is a lower level that communicates more or less as it did before the invasion of printed books but that has become subject to the higher level. The upper level is *committed* to the lower one: the upper level informs the lower one and thus alienates it from its original form of existence. And as it becomes aware of this, the higher level tries to absorb some of the codes and structures of the lower one to preserve *authenticity* (black culture, Latin American and Arabic *nationalism*, and so forth). The feedback thus established between the two levels is quite unlike the feedback between the catholic and the pagan level of medieval Europe, although sketch 1.3.b may map the two situations. By injecting European codes into the lower level, and by absorbing *traditional* codes that have no possible function within the European structure that now dominates it, the upper level finds itself in a vicious circle of pseudo-historicity trying to deny itself. In sum, the present revolution of communication explodes in its place of origin against sketch 1.3.a, second reading, and abroad against sketch 1.3.b, Third World reading.

1.3.3. Technical Images

If we now turn to sketch 1.3.c, and thus, at last, to the consideration of the situation of communication as it is crystallizing around us after the recent revolution, we find, unsurprisingly, that it is in no way a return to medieval structures, in spite of the similarities between sketches 1.3.b and 1.3.c. On the contrary, in some respects, it is the very reversal of the medieval structure. The mass level of communication is of cosmic uniformity with respect to the codes it utilizes (mostly technical images) and to its communication structures (mostly network dialogue), and this cosmic uniformity reminds one of the uniformity of the medieval *catholic* level. And the elite level of communication is subdivided into countless hermetic dialogical circles, each of which has its own specialized code (of the various branches of science, technology, the arts, even of sports, and so forth), and these islands of communication are just as separated from each other as were the valleys and villages of the medieval *pagan* level. But this reversal of upper and lower level of communication in our situation (as compared to that in the Middle Ages) is not what distinguishes us most from our medieval elders. The decisive difference is that there is no feedback between the mass and the elite levels: The so-called *mass culture* is irresponsible in the sense that it cannot answer to the information it receives from the elite level. But, and very curiously, the distinction between the mass and elite level is one of communication, not one of individual participation. There is no elite in our situation, only elitist communication. In other words, we all belong to the masses when we eat hot dogs or watch television. It is only when we are engaged in our specialization that we have recurrence to the elite communication level.

This is a very curious situation: On the one hand, we are, individually, all of us, part of the mass communication level, and on the other hand, there is no feedback from this level to the elite level, in which some of us participate sometimes. This implies that there is no feedback between one part of the individual memory of a specialist and the other: A technician in metallurgy or a bacteriologist cannot link their experience while watching a TV commercial with their experience while *working*. The reason is that the two codes involved in the two receptions of information are too different to permit translation. But this explanation does not do away with the fact that we are facing here a violent alienation, bordering on schizophrenia. And we have to face this. As we do so, we are finally facing what is understood, in this book, to be the central problem of our situation: the synchronization between technical amphitheatrical discourse and archaic network dialogue, which implies totalitarian massification.

Sketch 1.3.c, which aims at mapping the situation as it begins to form around us, intends to show that our situation is literally held together by the amphitheatrical discourse that is radiated from the upper toward the lower level. If by a miracle, the press, TV, radio, and the other broadcasting systems should shut down for a relatively short period (say, a month), the structure that sustains our communication (and thus our society) would fall to pieces. It is true that science and technique could, in that case, go through the motions of continuing on the upper level, and the gossip of network dialogue would probably grow more intense for a while, but very soon the upper level would disintegrate into its dialogical circles and the lower level into small islands of small talk with nothing to talk about. The amphitheatrical discourse provides us, even now, with almost all the information we dispose of in daily life, and it will do so more fully in the near future. It beats the rhythm to our movements; from the morning paper and morning news to the late show on TV, it inundates us with music, and it surrounds us with images in the streets and subway. And it does so all over the world, from Greenland to Mauritania, from Kyrgyzstan to Andalucía. It transforms the lonely farmhouse in the midwestern United States and the one in Southeast Asia into a receiver of cosmic communication, and it transforms a member of the teeming masses of Calcutta and Cairo into a lonely receiver of one of the loose ends of amphitheatrical discourse. This is a new situation, and all the historical categories (sociological, political, psychological, or even religious ones) fail to seize it in its desperate perfection.

It is important to note that the impact of amphitheatrical discourse is not on a well-articulated popular communication structure but on an uprooted proletariat in the so-called *developed* countries and on a population estranged from its true communication forms by the invasion of a European alphabet in the *Third World*. The *mass culture* created by *mass media* does not have to destroy any *popular culture* created by some *authentic means*, either in the Western countries or in the rest of the world: It destroys only the pitiful remnants of *folklore*. It is a mistake to blame *mass media* for the disappearance of phenomena such as Slovak peasant dress or the Sioux war dance, which were destroyed by the public education system and by the increasing cheapness of printed books. *Mass culture* with its hot dogs and football games is not heir to truly popular culture with fondue bourguignon and rain magic, but it is heir to an uprooted popular culture with portable lunch in tin pots and May Day parades. In short, the process of massification provoked by amphitheatrical discourse should not be examined against the colorful background of medieval communication or against the even more colorful background of Asian or African popular communication but against the gray background of communication through cheaply printed books communication.

Even if one admits that the TV commercial does not substitute for an epic story within an oral tradition but for a cheap printed novel of *love* or a detective story, even if one admits that *mass culture* substitutes for a culture that is in no way admirable, one cannot help feeling awe while contemplating its manifestations. It is not that the phenomena of mass culture are *worse* or *uglier* than the phenomena of the previous culture. On the contrary, they are *better* and *less ugly*: a plastic pen is better than a wooden pen, and a bottle of Coca-Cola is less ugly than an early twentieth-century soda bottle. What is so awful about the manifestations of mass culture is that they do not have any relationship to the concrete situation of their receivers (consumers). A shampoo has no relation to the hair of its Nigerian, Indonesian, or Tartar consumer, let alone to the existential situation of those consumers, and Ray-Ban glasses have no relation to the light prevailing in the rain forest, the shantytown, or the tundra where it is consumed, let alone to the economic, social, or historical situation of its consumer.

This awful contempt that mass-culture phenomena have for mass-culture participants reflects the fact that mass culture is not made for the masses, but the masses are made to behave according to mass culture. Ice cream is not manufactured for ice-cream eaters, but participants of the masses are manufactured into ice-cream eaters. In other words, amphitheatrical discourse *informs* the masses, imposes specific forms of behavior (and of experience) on them, and this information is elaborated on the upper level of communication with no regard to the communication going on at the lower level and with no feedback from it. And what is so awful about it is that it should not work but does work so perfectly.

It should not work because one should expect the receiver to have enough consciousness to refuse information, which has no relationship to the individual's situation. One should not expect a Brazilian peasant to eat pizzas as a Neapolitan sailor would, or a Parisian salesman to use hats as a Texas cowboy would. But the fact is that the consciousness of one's situation is the consequence of one's program. One knows who one is and where one is as a result of the information one receives. And that information depends on the codes in which its symbols are ordered. Popular communication prior to the explosion of technical amphitheatrical discourse (whatever one may say about the deliberate alienation it intended to produce in the proletariat) was coded alphabetically and therefore required a specific effort, called *reading*, from the receiver of its information. It is true that popular communication prior to the Second World War did program its receivers for alienated behavior such as going to war or buying things nobody needed, but it could not entirely eliminate some consciousness and self-consciousness in the receivers, because spoken and written language (the codes of popular communication) demand that one follow their lines to get at the information, and this process is one of synchronization (of *thought* and *reflection*). A demagogic leaflet cannot inform someone without the person at least having to rudimentarily think about it, because one has to read it. But technical amphitheatrical discourse is coded in technical images: The Brazilian peasant sees the pizza on a color photograph in a magazine, and the Parisian salesman sees the cowboy hat on a poster in front of a movie theater, and they *consume* those cultural goods without thinking because they are being informed about them (programmed for them) in a code that needs no *reflection* to be decoded. Consciousness as we understand it—stepping back from oneself and seeing oneself in one's situation—is an attitude rendered superfluous by the codes of technical-imaginary amphitheatrical discourse. The Brazilian peasant and the Parisian salesman do not need to step back from themselves to see themselves; they see themselves as the emitters of amphitheatrical discourse see them—as Parisian salesmen today and as Texas cowboys tomorrow. This is why mass culture works so well and why it is so awful.

Chapter 2 is dedicated to the problem of codes, and there is no need here to go into it further. It is sufficient to say that mass culture works perfectly well because it renders the masses almost entirely unconscious, almost perfect objects for manipulation, and that it succeeds in doing so thanks to the technical image codes through which the information programming it is being radiated. This is, of course, an exaggeration as far as our actual situation is concerned. We, as participants in the masses, are not being entirely informed and programmed by images. We are still receiving alphabetic information. And there is information that comes in through image codes (such as paintings), which are not technically manipulated. In sum, we have not yet become mere objects of manipulation, and we do have, sometimes, some sort of consciousness about our concrete situation. In other words, we still know how to read and write (although the younger generation knows it less well than the older one), and therefore mass culture is not yet perfect. (This is, by the way, why this book can still be written.) However, even the most optimistic observer cannot deny the tendency toward a situation as shown in sketch 1.3.c.

If we continue this projection into the immediate future, we find how the program elaborated on the upper level of communication, coded in technical image codes and radiated through amphitheatrical discourse, is preserved and changed within *mass culture* (the level of reception). Earlier, we called the method of how this is done dialogue through network. It is an archaic method, but it is quite satisfactory from the point of view of the elite emitters of the program. In network dialogue, the information received through broadcasting by mass media is being *exchanged* between the receivers by word of mouth, through gestures, and through alphabetic texts thanks to the post office. The telephone network is the only truly technical innovation in the word-of-mouth dialogue since pre-history. Of course, it cannot be said to be a true *exchange of information* since all information available, except for immediate experience (which is itself becoming stereotyped), is the same for all receivers. Still, the consensus that is thus being formed, and that is the reduction of all available information to a common lowest denominator, is in fact *new* information in at least two senses of that term. It is *new* in the sense that it is a translation from technical image codes to more archaic codes, and it is *new* in the sense that it fluctuates under the impact of ever-new information being broadcast. (The collective memory of the masses is a *bad* one, in the sense that consensus changes not through the accumulation of information but under the impact of new information.)

It has been said that there was no feedback between the mass and the elite level of communication. This statement requires clarification. There is a process elaborated in specific branches of tree discourse of science and of technology through which mass consensus can be measured and made available for elite communication (for instance, public opinion polls, market research, and sociological research). These methods of the social sciences and of social engineering are being presented within the prevailing ideology as if they were methods to *consult* the *public: The people demand war; they demand a new type of soap; they demand a new type of entertainment.* But in reality, those methods are the proof of almost total reification of the masses by the elite level: They are by now truly an *inert mass*, which is being measured as if it were inanimate. Public opinion polls and market research are not meant to find out what *people want* but to find out their state of *mind* to manipulate them in the most appropriate manner. They are not a form of feedback between the lower and the upper level of communication. They are a method by which the upper level synchronizes the lower level with the information to be radiated. In sum, the relationship between the elite and the mass level of communication is not, as it was in almost every previous period, one of dialogue (during which the higher partner felt menaced by the lower one), but it is the relationship between subject and object of communication and manipulation. This relationship did not exist in previous situations (or at least, it did not exist in its present, pure form) because it is the result of modern scientific technique.

If we return to sketch 1.3.c to visualize this synchronization between amphitheatrical discourse and network dialogue, we find to what extent traditional categories of *explanation* fail us: We are tempted, of course, to say that the elite level manipulates the mass level to satisfy its own *designs*, *wishes*, *necessities*, and so forth; that we are facing *class oppression*—warmongers manipulate the masses to sell arms; soap manufacturers, to sell soap; entertainers, to make money. This is a valid analysis of the situation, but it fails to grasp its fundamental aspects. The designs, wishes, necessities, and so forth of the elite decision-makers and programmers are themselves products of mass-media programs. The soap manufacturers have a TV program made to sell soap but wish to sell soap because they were programmed for that wish by television. (And this is true for almost all decision-making on whatever political, economic, social, or artistic level.) In other words, the participants of the elite level are themselves participants in the masses.

This discovery of the inherent automaticity in our communication situation, of the vicious circle it tends to turn into, is so shocking that many want to deny it, even if they see it. They accuse those who point to it of *selling out* to the system by mythologization. They say that if one denies a human interest behind the system, if one makes of the system a sort of God-like machine, in sum, if one does not admit that the amphitheatrical discourses are the tools of some human interests (hidden or not), one submits to those interests by arguing against the possibility of doing away with such interests (of revolution). But though the motives of these people (usually called the *left*) are noble, they are, unfortunately, mistaken. It is not that the *hidden interests* are being denied by the analysis of the automaticity inherent in our situation. For those interests are there, and they are not very well hidden; it is easy to point them out if one watches American or Soviet television. But if one removed those interests, nothing would change in the situation because they are not the cause but the effect of such a situation. A proof of this is that even though the interests in America and the Soviet Union are not of the same type, the communication situation in both territories is indeed of the same type. (This is what can be called depoliticization.)

The explanation of this vicious automaticity lies in the fact that the decisions made concerning the programs to be radiated (that is, the decisions concerning the future behavior, knowledge, and experience of humankind) are not being made in true dialogical, elite circles, as was the case in every previous communication situation. There are, at present, no such true dialogical circles (no *hidden centers of decision* in this sense). All the circles that look dialogical (cabinet meetings, meetings of chiefs of staff, of party or business administrations, and so forth) are in reality circular dialogues within a specific branch of a specific technical discourse. The ministers, generals, and bosses that meet are not, as in previous situations, men who exchange information to synthesize it into new information (a *decision*). They are specialists, functionaries, technicians who exchange a specialized sort of information in a hermetic code to arrive at even more specialized new information and pass it on to some further dialogical circle. This is the fundamental difference between aristocracy and technocracy (or between capitalist and manager, or between leader and *apparatchik*): In the first case decisions are made on the basis of available information; and in the second case, on the basis of specialized information. In other words, in the first case, there is a true elite, and in the second case, there is elitist communication between participants of the masses.

It is difficult to admit, although it is an obvious fact, that there is no elite at present. The difficulty is ambivalent. On the one hand, it is difficult to admit that the abolition of the elite (an age-old ideal) has resulted in vicious automaticity instead of freedom. On the other hand, it is difficult to admit that the abolition of the elite was not the result of some revolution but an event brought about, and going on almost unnoticed, by total massification. In short, it is difficult to admit that a *classless society* is not a society where humans are no longer wolves to other humans but a society where exploitation of humans by humans goes on without there being any class to profit from it. The *vulgarity* of our so-called *great leaders* is thus not an aesthetic problem; it is how we have to face the difficulty of having to admit that the age-old ideal of the abolition of the elite has been accomplished.

Let us now try to *read* our situation (not as it is now but as it tends to be in the near future), on the basis of sketch 1.3.c, as follows: There is a mass level of communication, which has become universal for the whole earth, and it is being informed by technical amphitheatrical discourse through technical image codes. This information is preserved and changed within *mass culture* through archaic network dialogue. The program of the broadcast through amphitheatrical discourse is decided by circular dialogue of specialists in hermetic codes, which form, when doing it, part of an elite communication, subdivided into branches distributed all over the world but which, when not doing it, are themselves part of *mass culture.* This gives the whole situation the automatic character of a vicious circle.

It may well be asked whether such a situation still fulfills the purpose of human communication, whether it creates and conserves information to overcome loneliness and death by giving life a meaning. Before answering negatively to such a question, some further aspects must be considered.

2

WHAT ARE CODES?

• • • This chapter considers some aspects of the problem of codes. And this requires a brief return to the initial considerations, where human communication was questioned. It was, somewhat apodictically, stated that human communication is an artificial process, in the sense of it being opposed to *nature*, both to *human nature* and to *the world of nature*. This is not the place to go into philosophical speculations about the meaning of the term *nature* or about the justification of a distinction between *nature*, on the one hand, and *art* or *culture* or *spirit*, on the other. Still, the distinction between the natural sciences and the humanities does pose a methodological problem that cannot be ignored by those who want to study human communication. Is it *better* approached by the methods of natural science, or are the humanities competent for it? It has been decided, from the start, to follow the methods of the humanities, which decision must be justified.

Since the late nineteenth century, it has generally been held that natural sciences try to *explain* phenomena by pointing out their causes, while humanities try to *interpret* phenomena by pointing out their meanings. (A cloud is explained if one knows what caused it, and a book is interpreted if one knows what it means.) It would be naïve to believe that it is the phenomenon itself that imposes the choice of methods (that the cloud demands explanation, and the book, interpretation).

One can interpret clouds (magicians and some psychologists do so), and one can explain books (physicists, chemists, and some psychologists do so). Thus, it would seem that anything may be approached by the explanatory method and then becomes *nature*, or by the interpretative method and then becomes *art* or *spirit*. One may hold that, for a believing Christian, the whole world is *art* (God's creation), which implies that one should approach it in order to discover its meaning, and that, for a nineteenth-century scientist, the whole world is *nature*, which implies that it may be explained, at least in theory. In other words, it would seem as if one were free to apply either the method of natural science or the method of the humanities to any given phenomenon and that the decision to apply the interpretative method to human communication in this book is a *subjective* decision.

But the matter is not as simple as that. One *feels* that clouds should not be read and that, if one does so, one imposes something human on them. Or one *feels* that books should be read and that if one explains them instead of reading them, one somehow betrays their essence, renders them inhuman. In other words, although all phenomena may be *humanized*, some are being violated in that process, and although all phenomena may be *naturalized*, some hide their essential aspects in that process. Thus, the decision to apply interpretative methods to human communication, although not imposed by the phenomena, is not a *subjective* decision. It was made because there is the hope that it is the method best suited for the essential aspects of human communication; however, not everybody shares such hope.

There is, at present, a tendency to *explain* humans as animals, and everything human (including communication) as the result of biological evolution. This blurring of the distinction between humans and the so-called *higher* animals is, curiously enough, not only the result of the tendency to *explain* everything, and thus make of humanity a natural phenomenon, but also the result of the opposite tendency to *humanize* higher animals and *interpret* them as if they were idiotic humans. One explains speech as the result of the evolution of the vocal cords (or of sounds made by other primates) and also interprets some gestures of chimpanzees (or dogs or, on another level, ants) as meaningful communication. The preceding argument intends to show that both these tendencies are perfectly justified: One can explain human communication from natural causes (as a development of mammalian communication, of human anatomy, and so forth), and one can interpret animal behavior to have a meaning (one can say that a specific posture of a goose means *danger!*, and even that a specific motion of a dog's tail means *good morning*). But the preceding argument intends to show also that such explanations and interpretations lose somehow the essential aspects. If I explain speech from vocal cords, I have lost what is essential to human speech, although I have pointed out some of its important aspects. And if I interpret the posture of a goose as meaning something, I have unduly anthropomorphized that poor goose (made it into something not fully human), although I have made the gesture more *understandable* for humans. (In the case of the dog's tail, the matter is different: dogs have indeed become humanized in the process of domestication.)

Thus, having decided to apply the methods of the humanities to human communication, this book does not deny that the border between human and some animal communication is fluid but has decided that this fluidity is not essential for the understanding of human communication. And this is the sense in which it insists on the *artificiality* of human communication. But this implies another, quite different although related, consideration. This book states that the *artificiality* of human communication manifests itself in its antinatural tendency toward the accumulation of acquired information. But if one explains it from biological evolution, this evolution itself may appear to be precisely such accumulation. Thus, to accumulate acquired information would appear to be a natural process, and there would be nothing unnatural for the tendency of human communication to do so. The decision to apply humanistic methods to the phenomenon of human communication implies, precisely, an interpretation of *accumulation of information*. Nobody can deny that biological evolution is a negatively entropic process, in the sense that it evolves ever-more-complex and less probable organisms. But there are two reservations to this affirmation. One is that all organisms will die and thus lose their information, so it may be said that biological evolution is a negatively entropic epicycle on the general entropic tendency of nature, both as far as individual organisms and the whole stream of life are concerned. (Although a hen is more *informed* than an egg, it will become dust, and although humans are more *informed* than an amoeba, the whole stream of life will be burned to ashes once the sun explodes or draws closer.) The other is that biological evolution is the product of chance and necessity, therefore a statistical process toward less probable forms and statistically *condemned* to return to more probable forms. It is, *essentially*, not negatively entropic, although it is actually productive of new information and accumulative of information.

However, obvious entropic aspects mark human communication. The phenomenon of oblivion exists in every individual memory, a phenomenon that is not *accidental*: no memory can function without it. Thus, information is continuously lost in the process of communication. But there is also oblivion on a far larger scale: Cities and whole civilizations are destroyed and *forgotten*, and it may be said that the enormous majority of information created by humans during their presence on earth has been lost forever. Although this is true, human communication, as opposed to biological evolution, is *essentially* negatively entropic. First, because contrary to biological evolution, it does not preserve information on an *objective* level, which is subject to the second principle of thermodynamics and must *return to ashes*, but on the intersubjective level of symbolic codification. (It can be forgotten, but it need not be forgotten.) Second, because contrary to biological evolution, it is not the product of chance and necessity but of a deliberate search for meaning. Thus, the decision to apply the interpretative methods to human communication, and thus distinguish it deliberately from animal communication, implies a *qualitative leap* between the highest animal and the lowest of humans, thanks to which the *essence* of the animal changes, and it becomes antinatural, negatively entropic, a *memory accumulating acquired information*. *Nature* ends with such a leap, and the *spirit* is born.

But before considering this leap (which is, let it be repeated, not an *objectively observable phenomenon* but the result of an intersubjective interpretation of human communication), it must be stressed, again and again, that the terms *symbol* and *code*, which will be important for the following considerations, will be used in a very specific sense, which flows from the original decision in favor of the interpretative method. *Symbol* will mean any phenomenon that has been agreed upon to substitute for another phenomenon, whether that convention is fully conscious or not on the part of the participants. And a *code* will be any system that orders symbols, whether the rules of that order are consciously elaborated or not. Thus, every biological phenomenon lies outside the definition of *symbol*; no animal behavior is *symbolic* in the sense of the definition because the definition implies that every symbol is the product of human convention, a tool for human communication. And the use of the term *code* outside the domain of human communication (as in *genetic code*) lies outside the definition of *code* here submitted because the definition implies that every code is a system ordered by humans in their search for meaning. And all this may be summed up as follows: The decision to consider human communication to be a phenomenon best approached by the interpretative method implies the decision that there are meaning and value in human communication, and the decision to distinguish human communication methodically from all other forms of communication implies the decision that one should not look for meaning and value outside the domain of the human presence in the world. It is, in summary, a *humanistic* decision.

Undoubtedly, the *qualitative leap* mentioned previously, by which a primate turned around and against its surroundings to become human, is one of those phenomena of human presence in the world that have been forgotten. Not quite, though: Numerous myths (such as the one of the expulsion from Paradise) tell about it. But although this event (which is, in the sense of the German word *Ursprung* an *original leap*) is forgotten, it is not inaccessible to our interpretation, in various senses of that term. Anthropologists find skeletons of human-like apes surrounded by circles of stone and bare bones, dated approximately two million years ago, which may be interpreted as the *first humans*. We can observe in children patterns of behavior at a very early age, which we can interpret as the *first truly human manifestations*. And if we apply the method of *reflection*, of observing ourselves, we may discover a motion of somehow turning against the world that surrounds us and taking a distance from it, which we may interpret as a manifestation of our fundamentally *human existence*. This book need not go into the philosophical aspects of this *original event* (or its religious aspects). It has no need to discuss the meaning of *existence* in the sense of a *standing outside* (*ek-sistere*) or the meaning of *original sin* in the sense of alienation (expulsion) from nature. It can take for granted the fact that humans *exist* (that they stand outside nature somehow) and the fact that they *sin* (that they have an evaluative dimension). In short, this book can take for granted that humans are *insane* animals (in the sense of not being healthy or normal as an animal), and it can do so because it is going to analyze, although very sketchily, the product of humans' existence, of their insanity and alienation, that is, the codified world with which they surround themselves.

In fact, this is the criterion for the discovery of the presence of true humans in the world: that they are surrounded by ordered symbols. The two-million-year-old ape-like animal in Southeast Africa is truly a human being, not because the skeleton is human (it is not) or because it made tools by working on natural objects to change them (it did not) but because it assembled stones and bones to form improbable structures (circles). The circles are unlike the structures made by beavers or ants, not because they are less probable but because they mean something. We no longer know what they mean (we have lost the key to that code), and we may never decipher their meaning. Still, we do know that they mean something because we do such things ourselves; we recognize ourselves in the animals that made those circles. This two-million-year-old ape was a true human because it felt the urge to give meaning to something, just as a baby does after a certain age and just as we do. And we can also interpret why it felt that codifying urge: because it could not stand life without meaning. That ape was insane, and its insanity manifested itself in codes composed of symbols, in what we must call *culture*. This is what we mean when we say that beaver dams are natural and the circles made of stones and bones by that ape are artificial.

Codes composed of symbols are methods by which humans try to bridge the abyss that separates them from the world after they have made their leap into existence. Some of the aspects of this bridging were discussed in the first part of this book. What must be retained at this point are two aspects of the codifying activity: that anything may serve for symbolization and that symbols may be ordered in many structures. Not only stones and bones, sounds and gestures, knots in strings, coins, letters, numbers, paintings, tools: every natural or artificial phenomenon can be agreed upon to represent something. And the symbols thus agreed upon can be arranged in point-like patterns like a mosaic, in straight or curved lines, on plane or curved surfaces, as three-dimensional structures of any form, synchronically (the whole set of symbols at once) or diachronically (one at a time). Thus, there is no limit to the number of possible code structures. Humans surround themselves with a complex shell made of many types of codes that are composed of many types of symbols, with the hope that the shell will give meaning to their lives and free them from solitary confinement at an individual level.

The difference between various cultures, and between various stages of the same culture, is the difference between various complexes of codes. This is why it is so difficult to decipher a culture (to decipher the meaning a specific society gave the world and life within it). It is not sufficient to decode the most important codes of that culture in order to interpret it, nor is it sufficient even to decipher all the codes that compose such a culture. To understand a culture, it would be necessary to weigh the importance of each code with relation to all the other codes within its codified world. (To *decipher* the Kra culture, it is not enough to have deciphered the code of masks, dance, family order, the Kra language, and so forth; one must also know how masks are related to language, dance to family order, and so on). Thus, it would seem that the only culture one may ever hope to decipher is the one into which one was born, because one might suppose that one has learned how to *read* the codes that compose it.

But even such an apparently modest endeavor is condemned to failure where a codified world as complex as ours is concerned. Not only are we unable to relate all the codes that compose it (the code of fashion to the code of civil law, the code of serial music to the traffic code, the Morse code to the code of cooking), but we are also unable to learn how to read even the most important codes of our own codified world (the code of nuclear physics, of symbolic logic, of concrete poetry, of multinational economics). In other words, we are lost within the coded world that surrounds us. In this sense, we are at least as much determined and oppressed by the codified world as we are by the world of nature from which the codes are supposed to liberate us. The meaning that our codified world impresses upon the world of nature from which we have alienated ourselves cannot be the meaning of our lives, because we do not *understand* it. Possibly simpler codified worlds (such as Kra culture) do succeed in their task to permit those participating in their communication to lead meaningful lives (although we can never know whether, in fact, they do so). But we have become alienated from the codified world that was supposed to overcome our alienation from the world of nature.

The purpose of this chapter cannot be, of course, to try to do something about this, but it will try to shed some light on the problem.

2.1. HOW SOME CODES EMERGED

If one assumes a bird's-eye view on the tissue of human communication, it looks as if spoken languages were a sort of preferential code. In fact, there are observers who believe that to talk and to think are closely related processes, that one cannot take place without the other, and that humans are programmed, to a large extent, for the language they were born into. Many consider the symbols of which spoken languages consist (specific sound patterns, called loosely *words*) to be a special sort of symbols: for instance, *in the beginning was the Word*, or *logic is the science of the order of words*. There are, indeed, attempts to define humans as *talking animals*. This book does not try to deny the importance of spoken language for human communication. But it does pose the following question: Is an analysis of spoken languages a good method for an understanding of our present crisis, or are there other codes better suited for that very specific purpose?

To answer this question, let us consider very briefly what sorts of codes spoken languages are. They consist, all of them, of the same type of symbols; sound patterns produced by organs of speech such as the tongue, lips, teeth, and vocal cords (although the method of production may vary from code to code). But as far as the rules that order these symbols are concerned, they vary considerably from language to language, although one may distinguish, very vaguely, between three types of rules. The first type, *fusional languages*, orders the symbols into series (*words* into *sentences*) and manipulates the symbols to fit them into order (it *conjugates* and *declines* words). Examples are Arabic, Sanskrit, and English. The second type, *isolating languages*, organizes the symbols (mostly in pairs) into a mosaic pattern and intones each sound pattern in three to five intonations, thus isolating one sound from all others (separating *syllables*). Examples are Cantonese and Mandarin. The third type, *agglutinating languages*, puts the symbols together by means of special sound pieces (*prefixes*, *infixes*, and *suffixes*), and only thus do they acquire meaning. Examples are Inuit and Tupi-Guarani.

Such a catalogue is a brutal simplification of the true situation; therefore, most linguists consider it no longer valid. But this is precisely why it serves the present purpose. It shows how the codes of spoken languages are *open* with regard to each other. For instance, the participants of what is called *Western civilization* are programmed, by *fusional languages*, to an extent far beyond their awareness of such. Thus, the order of the words in the sentences (which distinguishes between a subject and a predicate) is projected into the universe of meaning so radically that it is being accepted as a *world order*; we accept that the world is structured by *subject-object* relations without being aware of the fact that this is a linguistic category that does not prevail in types of languages different from ours. Still, even in our organization of spoken symbols (*fusional*) there are *isolating* and *agglutinating* elements, which are difficult to call *words* in the sense of *meaningful sounds*. For instance, in English, *put* becomes meaningful only if paired in a mosaic pattern such as *put off*, *put in*, or *put on* and is thus *isolating*; and *becoming* consists of a *root*, *come*, and of a prefix *be-* and a suffix *-ing*, and the whole is meaningful only if put together in an *agglutinating* fashion. Thus English, which may be considered to be typically fusional, shows how deeply isolating and agglutinating structures infect it. It is therefore difficult to try to understand a codified world (a *culture*) by an analysis of the structure of the language that programs it.

Another difficulty is the ephemeral character of the medium of spoken language. Before the invention of the gramophone, the sound patterns that compose those languages could be stored only very indirectly (for instance, through writing). Although the words we utter and hear, and whisper in our innermost self, are among the most ancient symbols, although their roots probably point to the very origin of humankind, etymology cannot reconstruct them beyond a very limited time span. This is what makes spoken languages such *mysterious* codes: their *original meaning* is lost forever. But this is also why it does not seem to be a good method to try to analyze them to understand our present crisis.

And there is this consideration: If we look about, we see how profoundly all of the codes that program us are being remodeled by the present turmoil. But the spoken languages seem to be least affected. Of course, even they change under the impact of the communication revolution, and they change profoundly. But it seems as if they formed, nonetheless, a sort of solid bedrock of human communication, affected by the present earthquake but still somehow *beyond* it. Thus, they are not well suited to serve as starting points for an analysis of the present transformations, and other codes must be chosen. But a word of caution: The analysis that follows cannot pretend to be an investigation into human communication since it will not consider one of its most characteristic codes, spoken language. At best it will be an analysis of the present communication crisis. And this is its purpose.

The very brief consideration of the function of spoken languages within our program may serve as a reminder of the function of the codified world in general; it is just as important *how* it stores information as what *sort* of information it stores. The rules that order the symbols within a code form dragnets by which the world is fished and transformed into information. Thus, the world acquires the structure of the code that *fished* it. The rule of specific languages such as English, which distinguishes between a *subject* and a *predicate*, becomes, for people programmed by that language, a *category of the world*, and when they discover this, they tend to believe that the linguistic rule is somehow a *copy* of a *true* subject-object relation. The proof that such a belief is mistaken is, of course, the fact that in agglutinating languages such as Inuit there is no distinction between subject and object. This confusion about the relation between the codified world and the universe it means is characteristic of situations like ours.

If we accept the fact that we experience, understand, and evaluate the world we live in under the shape of the nets, which the codes weave around us, we begin to see an avenue of access to an analysis of our crisis. The following hypothesis is then in order: Within Western civilization the code of alphabetic writing is the *official* bearer of what might be called the typically Western sort of information—science, politics, philosophy, literature, and religion. This means that insofar as we are Western, we experience, understand, and evaluate the world we live in under the shape of the rules of alphabetic writing. This is a code that is, at present, in a crisis. And this implies that our way of experiencing, understanding, and evaluating the world is in crisis, at least as far as we are Western. Thus, it seems to be a good idea to try to analyze this code if we want to understand our situation, and thus now we attempt to do so.

The first part considers the process during which linear writings were developed near the eastern shore of the Mediterranean Sea between 4000 and 1500 BC, which is the period called *pre-history* in our schoolbooks. The second part deals with the origin of the alphabet, its struggle with other codes, and its victories and defeats and covers the period between 1500 BC and AD 1900, called *history* in our schoolbooks. (The thesis that *history* and *alphabetic writing* are closely related is implicit in such a division.) The third part deals with the rise of revolutionary new codes that have menaced the alphabet since the second half of the nineteenth century; although there are no schoolbooks covering that period, it might be called *post-history.*

One consequence of such a structure is that critical points will appear that are not quite apparent in more usual accounts of the history of western civilization: approximately 1500 BC (the Minoan texts); approximately 800 BC (Homeric and Prophetic texts); approximately AD 1500 (printed texts); and AD 1850 (photographs). The first and last critical points will appear to be axes: the beginning and the end of history proper. The two middle points will appear to be high points: the origin of the West and conquest of the world by the West. In short, this is the sketch we will follow:

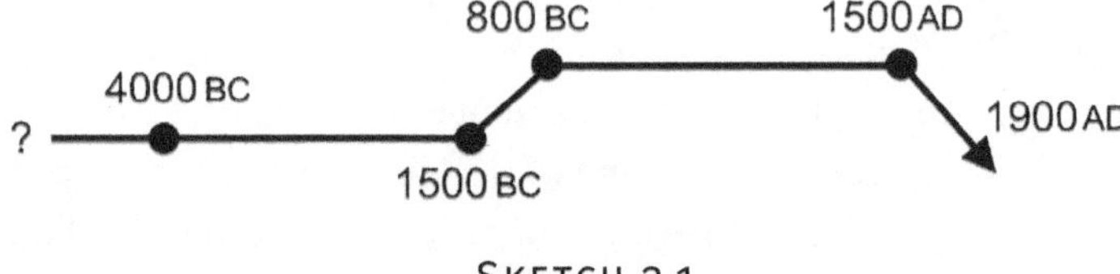

SKETCH 2.1

Let us not exaggerate the importance of this sketch and its implicit pessimism: The history of western civilization, which it illustrates, is one that means an analysis of the present code crisis, not a critique of our civilization, past, present, and future. It can do no harm to stop and contemplate it: it may be an exercise in technical imagination (the effort to make images of concepts).

2.1.1. Pre-alphabet

The alphabet is a code consisting of twenty to thirty simple geometric designs called *letters*. They are symbols said to mean specific sounds of spoken languages and are ordered to form lines according to rules called *orthography*. It is, however, obvious that the meaning of letters cannot be sounds. The number of spoken sounds (however we might define that term) is far in excess of the number of letters—the letter **A** means a different sound in *apple* and in *father*. Surprisingly, and in spite of this, the same sound may be meant by various different letters—**K** in *keep* and **C** in *cope* mean the same sound. Thus, the alphabet is, from the point of view of its *repertoire* (the symbols it is composed of), a very unsatisfactory code: it is ambiguous.

It does not fare better from the point of view of its *structure* (the rules that order the symbols). The basic rules are simple: They order the letters in lines that usually run from the upper left corner toward the lower right corner of a surface in a series of horizontal parallels and thus form a sort of net of threads upon which the letters follow each other like beads on an abacus. The letters thus lose their original character of geometric designs and become point-like. But there are further orthographic rules that have to do with the sequence of specific letters, with blank spaces between them, and with similar problems, and these rules are incomplete and inconsistent. The result is that the link between the text that thus comes about and the pronunciation of the spoken language it means is problematic. (English orthography is a good illustration.)

This is, however, not the main defect of the code: it contains symbols that are alien to it but cannot work correctly without them. Symbols such as **?** (meaning an intonation of the voice, but not a sound, and which is therefore not a letter) and **2** (an ideogram) pervade it. And there are even symbols such as – (minus), the meaning of which is left deliberately unclear. In sum, for such and similar reasons the alphabet must be considered an ambiguous, inconsistent, and hybrid code, one not very suitable for communication.

But of course, we know that the contrary is true. It is so extraordinarily well suited that it has changed very little since it was invented. Even such superficial aspects such as the order of enumeration of the letters it is composed of (A, B, C, etc.) has remained practically unchanged for three thousand years. It has changed much less than almost all the other codes, including the spoken languages it means. (We have lost the key to the Etruscan language, but the alphabet, which registers that language, poses no problem.) There must, therefore, be hidden aspects of the alphabet that render it so extremely successful.

It is true that every child can learn to handle it (which is not necessarily true of all the linear codes, such as Chinese writing). It is true that although the letters are so very ancient (one can see their pre-historic character, if one looks closely at the shape of the **X**s and **P**s), they are not in the least archaic: they are perfectly suitable for modern machinery like the typewriter. And there are other and similar arguments in favor of the alphabet. But this has nothing whatever to do with what was meant by its *hidden aspects*, which the following considerations try to discover.

The origin of our letters is relatively well known. Still, the invention of the alphabet is *mysterious* in a curious sense of the term. In the first half of the second millennium BC people on the eastern shores of the Mediterranean and on the islands opposite began to write our letters. We know the names they gave those letters. For instance, they called the first one *alpha* (which means *bull* in Aramaic), the second one they called *beta* (which means *house* in Aramaic), and the third one they called *gamal* (which means *camel* in Aramaic). This suggests that the letters had been originally pictograms of the objects their names mean. In fact, archaeological research supports such a supposition. For instance, the following very sketchy account of the origin of the letter **A** is suggested:

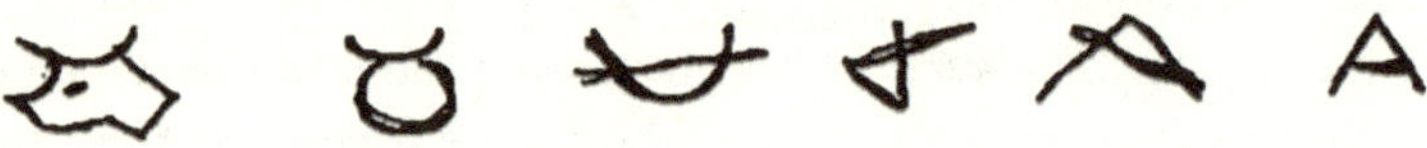

SKETCH 2.1.1.A

The first symbol in the series is an Egyptian hieroglyph meaning *bull*; the others are symbols of the Sinai script, the Moabite script, two early Greek alphabets, and the Latin alphabet. The repeated rotation of the design upon its axis cannot hide the fact that it is a pictogram showing a bull (especially its horns).

But we feel that this cannot be the whole story. And when we try to put ourselves in the situation of those who invented the letters, we are seized by a kind of dizziness, as if we had lost our grounding. To help us, researchers suggest that the following stages bridge the abyss between pictogram and letter: pictograms, ideograms, hieroglyphs, and then letters. These would be the various stages of linear writing. And they suggest the following definitions: A pictogram is an image that means an object according to some convention. An ideogram may be the same image, but it now no longer means the object but a general situation suggested by that object (an *idea*). A hieroglyph may be the same image, but it no longer means an *idea* but a word that means that idea in a specific language. And a letter may be the same image, but it no longer means a word but the sound with which the word begins. At first glance this seems to be a reasonable account of the story, but there are two objections: it is not supported by the facts, and it does not grasp what is essential to the various codes it aligns.

A pictogram is a conventional image and therefore an *abstraction* from what can be called a *naturalistic* image. This suggests the following process: There is an individual who steps back from a scene and paints the picture of a bull on a cave wall. And there is another individual who steps back from the wall painting and draws a pictogram of a bull by simplifying the painting. Thus, the pictogram seems to stand on a more abstract level than the painting with regard to its meaning: two steps *back* from it. But facts do not support this. Pictograms seem to be as ancient as paintings: they appear on the walls of Lascaux and Altamira. *Naturalistic* paintings may be shown, under analysis, to be just as conventional as are pictograms. In most codified worlds pictograms precede naturalistic paintings (the *geometric* period is more archaic than the *realistic* one). Naturalistic painting may be shown, in many instances, to be a step toward *nature* away from abstraction, and not away from *nature* toward abstraction (it is a *decadent*, *Romantic* code, like present-day *hyperrealism*). In sum, the ontological level on which pictograms are produced is mysterious and problematic.

It looks as if an ideogram is an abstraction of a pictogram in the sense that it means a *class of objects* (an *idea*), whereas a pictogram means a member of that class of objects. But this is an incorrect interpretation. A pictogram means a *class*: for instance, it means *all the eyes* and is a generalization of the meaning of a portrait, which means *that eye there*. If we were to define *theory* as *discourse containing names of classes*, pictographic codes would be seen to codify theoretical discourse. Ideograms are no further step in the theoretical direction. In fact, they are steps in a quite different direction, one that has not been fully exploited by Western civilization. If we look at highly developed ideographic scripts (for instance, Chinese and Japanese characters), we can intuit the fundamental difference between what is loosely called the Western and the Eastern *mentality*: one is inclined toward *theory* and the other toward what might be called, for the lack of a better expression, a *Gestaltic* mode of understanding. Still, ideographic scripts do play a very important role within our Western program, for instance, codes such as numbers (1, 2, 3, etc.), chemistry (H, He, etc.), logic (A, E, etc.), and so forth. In order to fix their ontological standing, we would have to agree to what we mean by *idea*.

The problem posed by hieroglyphs is completely different, in the sense that we have lost the key to this type of writing. Of course, we still have *rebus*, and we know that the principle of this codification is a play with words: the picture of an eye may mean *I*, and the picture of an ink bottle coupled with the picture of a fishing line may mean *incline*. Thus, we know that the writer of hieroglyphs steps back, not so much from pictograms but from spoken language. But what we can no longer intuit, because this type of code has been abandoned, is for us the curious, even bizarre, way of thinking of the Egyptian or Toltec *literati*. We know what it means to *think pictographically*: it is a method to grasp objects without recourse to language. We know vaguely what it means to *think ideographically*: if I think $\mathbf{H_2O}$, I grasp an aspect of the idea *water* without recourse to a specific language. (This is why Chinese ideograms may be used as an intralinguistic code.) We know what it means to think *alphabetically*: we do it all the time without being fully aware of what we are doing. But we have no way to intuit what is going on in the mind of a person who thinks in rebuses while writing. The level of consciousness corresponding to hieroglyphic codes (the Egyptian, Mexican, and Bantu levels) has been lost for Western civilization.

Thus, there is little sense in saying that the three codes just discussed are steps toward alphabetic writing. Each is a step in a different direction away from the image, and each opens up a different level of consciousness. To each code corresponds a different *universe of meaning*, and to say that the three codes *prepare the way for the alphabet* is to be victim of *imperialistic* prejudice in favor of Western codification. But there is one aspect common to pictographic, ideographic, hieroglyphic, and alphabetic writing: they are codes that order their symbols into lines; they are *linear writings*. (However, the alphabetic code does this more radically than the others and in this sense is indeed the most explicit of the four forms of writing.) And it is this aspect that is decisive for the deciphering of the codes under discussion.

Sometime during the late fifth millennium BC, people began to align pictograms (impressed upon soft bricks with styluses, thus giving a *cuneiform* impression) alongside images impressed upon the bricks with seals. Even now, after six thousand years, it is breathtaking to look at these bricks and see what happened: a leap from the surface into a line, from an image into a text, from a scene into a story. We see what has happened, we know that we are, ourselves, results of such happening, and still we cannot believe we are seeing this:

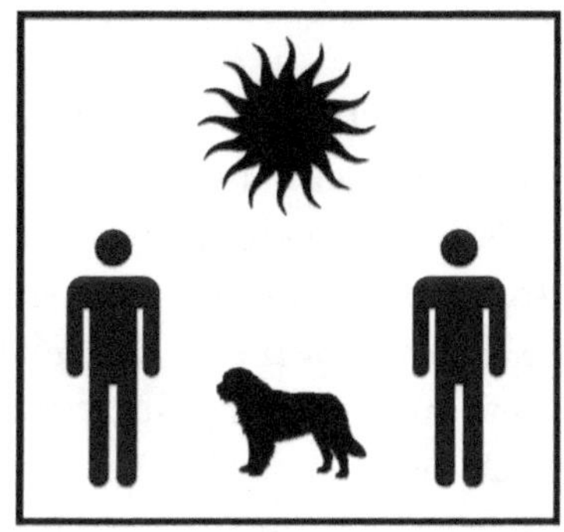
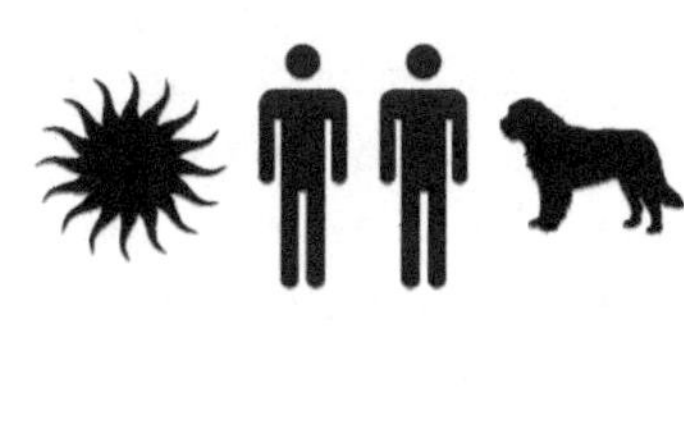

SKETCH 2.1.1.B

Both sketches contain the *same information*, but the image on the left means a scene (two men and a dog under the sun), and the text on the right means a process (the sun and a man and a man and a dog). In the image on the left the symbols are related to each other in the same way their meanings are supposed to be related within the actual scene the image refers to. Those are *imagined* relations. In the text on the right the symbols are related to each other according to a specific rule: like pearls are related to each other on a string. Those are *conceived* relations. In fact, what happened is this: The text on the right is a *development out* of the image on the left, an *explanation of* that image; it was *implied within* the image and has now become *explicit*. In sum, the line of the text has been drawn out of the surface of the image, and it means the image. It *tells* the image, it *recounts it*, it *calculates* it, by aligning its symbols on a string like beads on an abacus or little stones (calculi) in a line. It is a *tale*, a story, and a history, which means an image that in turn means a scene. And by thus meaning an image, it translates the scene meant by the image into a process. The origin of history is in the abyss between the left and the right side of the illustration, and this is why we are in awe when we look at Mesopotamian tablets.

The following section looks into such an abyss. Suffice it to say that on the left side of sketch 2.1.1.b are meant to stand the countless millennia that separate the origin of humans from the origin of history, while on the right side are meant to stand the six millennia of history, which began somewhere in Mesopotamia and are about to end here with us.

2.1.2. Alphabet

The mistaken attempt to *explain* the origin of the alphabet from the other linear codes has led to the opinion that letters are symbols that mean the first sound of the word meant by the hieroglyphs they *originally* were. Thus, **A** means the first sound of the word *alpha*, which is the Aramaic word for *bull* and which was meant by the hieroglyph from which the letter **A** stems. The important thing is not that such an opinion is factually mistaken: the original **A** means a sound that does not exist in English, a consonant typical of Semitic languages; and original alphabets do not contain letters meaning vocals. But this is not what is important.

The important aspect of the mistaken explanation is that the question, What is the meaning of letters? is not one that has to do directly with their shape. The question, What does **C** mean? has almost nothing to do with the fact that its shape suggests the back of a camel. **C** means various different sounds in English, in German, in Spanish, in Italian, and in Portuguese, and these various meanings are fixed by more or less arbitrary rules of orthography that vary from language to language. And those orthographic rules are somehow based on phonetic rules that are just as arbitrary: the meaning of letters is based on a convention of a convention. The meaning of the letter **C** is the result of a convention concerning a previous convention concerning spoken sounds. This is a sort of extreme abstraction that has nothing to do with generalization: If I write alphabetically, the world of objects has disappeared beyond my horizon, not because I have generalized it but because I have put a series of conventions between myself and that world. When I write **C**, the camel has disappeared, not because I have stepped back from the hieroglyph meaning *camel* in Aramaic but because I have severed the link between the hieroglyph and its meaning. Therefore, the hieroglyph does in no way *explain* the letter.

The extreme refinement and abstraction of alphabetic writing (its structural and functional simplicity due to a series of conventions) shows that it is an extraordinary, indeed unique, invention. In fact, it was invented only once (on the shores of the eastern Mediterranean about 1500 BC) in an extraordinary situation. We now know much more about that situation than did previous generations. Thousands of tablets have been found in Syria and Crete that were produced about the middle of the second millennium BC. They are covered with texts coded in the same alphabet but meaning two languages: proto-Hebrew (called *linear A*) and proto-Greek (called *linear B*). Some of those texts deal with themes developed several centuries later by the Homeric epics and by the Bible. They show that Ulysses and Abraham were originally the same figure, that the Trojan army was organized on the same principles as the Hebrew army, that there is a common origin to Homeric and biblical *literary style*, and many more such common roots to Greek and Jewish culture. Although this is not surprising, given the geographic and historical vicinity of both cultures, the fact that Western civilization has only one root (Minoan Semites who learned how to speak Greek and Philistine or similar Greeks who learned how to speak Hebrew) must be digested. The consequences of the knowledge of the profound unity of prophecy and philosophy on the ground of alphabetic codification are as yet uncertain.

The extraordinary, prevailing circumstances when the alphabet was invented could be called *extreme linguistic confusion*. For instance, in the Sinai town of Ugarit the following languages were spoken, among others: the northern Semitic Syriac, Canaanite, Aramaic, and proto-Hebrew; the eastern Semitic Babylonian, Acadian, and Assyrian; Coptic Egyptian; Indo-European Arian, Hittite, and proto-Greek; and languages of dubious origin such as Lydian and Minoan. This confusion (of which the Bible tells us concerning *construction of the Babylonian Empire State Tower*) is quite different from later language confusions (such as the present ones in India or Africa) in that it did not concern the rural population but the elite. No living language could be used as a lingua franca (such as English in present-day India), and no dead language (such as Latin in medieval Europe) because each spoken language claimed to be elitist (universal). We can observe failures in the direction of a living *koine* in Ugarit (Acadian and Aramaic) and in the direction of a dead one (Sumerian). The question of finding a code common to the elite was one of survival, and this is how it was solved.

We have tablets covered with texts in one alphabet but meaning six different languages. The information of the six texts is the same. Thus, if a person is a member of the elite (knows how to read), he needs to know only one of the six languages to communicate with others. He may point to the text written in the language spoken by his partner. Those tablets are dictionaries and a sort of guide (like the Michelin): the alphabet is meant to serve as a bridge between different languages. But this does not yet explain its origin: to know that it is an elitist code. We must ask what sort of information it was intended to carry, and this implies the question: What sort of information was the elite who invented the alphabetic convention interested in?

We now have the answer to this decisive question. Merchants invented the alphabet, and the information it was meant to carry is of the type *stock list* and *bill of lading*. The importance of this discovery for the understanding of Western civilization cannot be exaggerated. The alphabet, which is the code of history, of science, of philosophy, of religion, in sum, which codifies our experience, knowledge, and evaluation of the world, is one that has been invented to permit the counting, measuring, and weighing of exchangeable goods. The alphabet was not created by priests for priests, or by priests for kings and warriors, but by merchants for artisans and merchants. The struggle between the alphabet and other codes (and especially images), which characterizes the whole of history, is one between a mercantile and other types of thinking. When alphabetic texts become *sacred* (as in Homer and the Bible), it is the sacralization of accounting. And if the prophets fight against *idolatry* (the making of images) and Plato despises the *figurative artist* (the image maker), they do so in the name of calculation (*reason*). Finally, if the alphabet is menaced at present by technical image codes, it is *reason* (in the sense of rationing, dividing, and multiplying) that is menaced.

It took many centuries (from the invention of the alphabet around 1500 BC to the elaboration of the *sacred* Homeric and biblical texts around 800 BC) before this demythologizing and rationalizing function of the alphabetic code became apparent. Therefore, it may be said that only then what might be called *Western history* became a program. And not until the invention of the printing press about AD 1500 was this function understood in all its implications. Therefore, it may be said that only then did *Western history* become fully conscious. Therefore, one may conclude that it took fully three thousand years before people learned how to write and read correctly. We know very little about the first stage of learning. But about the second stage (from the Bible to Luther, from Homer to Gutenberg) we know quite a lot, although it is difficult to grasp what we know: we possibly know too much about it.

We are not accustomed to seeing this long stretch of time in one piece. There seem to be interruptions (the rise of Christianity and the fall of Rome, for instance), and there does not seem to be much in common between a citizen of Periclean Athens, a baron of Carolingian Gaul, and a scientist of the Granada of the Reconquista. Still, from the point of view of communication, the period is of one piece. It is the time of the struggle between linear codes (chiefly the alphabet) as the elite use them and other codes (chiefly images) as *the people* use them: the struggle between a calculating, rational, historical, and conceptual form of existence and a magical, mythical, ritual, and imaginative form of existence. Letter against image: this is the nucleus of Western history from the manuscript to the printed Bible.

At the beginning of that period, it had not yet become quite clear for the *writers* (the clerks, the scribes, the literati) that the alphabetic code was essentially different from ideographic ones, such as the number code, in that it was able to count not only merchandise but also events and that it could make up not only catalogues but also stories. The *clearness and distinction* of the letters in the line, and the linear progressivity of the line itself, had not yet fully penetrated the minds of those who had invented it. The literate elite grasped what *to tell* means only in about the fifth century BC. And it is important to note that the elite were Greek and Jewish, cultures programmed from their very beginning by alphabetic writing. Both these cultures are *bookish* from the start—they are *born tellers*.

But there are two different methods of telling, and two different tales result from those methods. The Talmud tells a different story from the Aristotelian one, the happy end of Platonic utopia is different from the ending of the history of salvation, and the Greek system of telling (*logics*) is different from the Jewish one (*pilpul*). Never did Western civilization succeed in synthesizing fully those two different ways of counting and recounting (these two different forms of alphabetically programmed consciousness). This is what makes Western civilization such an extraordinary structure: it is divided into a Jewish and a Greek half by a sort of inner dialogue, which results in constant tension and renders the civilization explosively dynamic.

Nevertheless, one should not forget that this dialogue is one between texts (Aristotle and the Bible, for instance) and, therefore, restricted to a very small elite before the invention of printing. The fundamental dialogue was the one between the literate elite and the illiterate population. Apparently, what is called *history* was the affair of that elite, while the enormous majority of the Western population continued to lead a pre-historic life, untouched by the events on the upper level from 1500 BC to AD 1500. In reality, of course, this was not so. The pre-historic, pagan, population of Western society did not merely serve as a mute background to the development of philosophy and religion, literature and politics, science and esoteric speculation. The people sustained and nourished that development both materially and with its own imaginary codes; it provided such development with meaning and questioned it constantly by the mere fact that the people denied it as a way of living. Up to the invention of printing, historical consciousness (*reason*, conceptual thinking) was constantly menaced and did not stand on solid ground because the illiterate mass that sustained it did not participate in it. History (the alphabet) was in the strict sense *superficial*.

This changed radically when printing was invented. The alphabet, and thus historicity and conceptual thinking, began to penetrate the whole of Western society, which permitted it to explode and spread throughout the earth in a matter of fewer than four hundred years. This explosion may be seen from a variety of points of view, but in the present context it is seen as follows: As the bourgeoisie was being alphabetized by printed books and thus penetrating the level of historical consciousness, the essential aspect of the alphabetic code became finally apparent; it permitted, together with the codes characteristic of mathematical thinking (ideographic codes), the establishment of the discourse of the exact sciences. This discourse resulted in a second one: technological discourse. And those two discourses permitted the alphabetically programmed mind to impress itself upon the world. The rest of humanity watched in awe: it could not decipher what was happening; it lacked the key to the codified world, which was thus exploding. This is why humanity became such easy prey to Western domination: it did not understand the meaning of what the West was doing. We have an example of how this happened: the conquest of Mexico by a handful of Spaniards. It was not the technical superiority of the fifty or so Spanish guns over the hundreds of thousands of Aztec bows that explains the Spanish victory: it was the incapacity of the *magical* mind of the Aztecs to decipher the meaning of the Spanish action (which was a historical action).

The period between the invention of printing and the invention of the photograph (called the *Modern Age*) may be seen as the one that translates the virtualities dormant in the alphabetic code into action. In every field, not only in science and technology but just as much in politics and what is now called the *arts*, the rational, progressive mentality changed the surfaces of the earth in such a way that the life of an eighteenth-century peasant resembled more the life of a peasant in Ugarit than it did the life of a nineteenth-century industrial worker. Thus, it looks as if the Modern Age is the victory of *reason* over *magic*, of concept over image, in short, the triumph of Western civilization. But there is a different reading of this period, as suggested by sketch 2.1. It could be said that the period between the Bible and Gutenberg is one during which the universe of reason, of conceptual thinking, of linear existence, slowly unfolds by constantly absorbing the universe of magic, of imaginative thinking, of mythical existence. This constant absorption of images and their translation into texts is what makes this period so incredibly fertile: prophecy, philosophy, science, and the idea of Christianity, of humanism, of freedom, of personal responsibility result from it. But with the invention of printing the sources of *inspiration* of rational thinking begin to dry up, to be filled as it were, with printed paper. Of course, the motives elaborated during the previous period are only now put into practice. Still, there is now, in the absence of *magical contestation*, something hollow about them. The alphabetically coded world, once it triumphed during the Modern Age, no longer seemed to provide its participants with a true sense of participation; it no longer seemed to give life true meaning.

This is not meant to be a critique of modernity but is a way to look at modern humanity from the other end of the story. The second half of the twentieth century shows humans to have been curious creatures—sort of bona fide writers and readers of letters. As the Modern Age advanced, they tended to believe more and more in the rules of the alphabetic code: in *explanations*, *theories*, *calculations*, *measurements*, *ideologies*, *programs*, *planning*, *discoveries*, *inventions*, *conquests*, in short, in *progress*. And they tended to forget more and more that all of these things are methods to provide human life with meaning. Our generation, which stands outside the Modern Age without being able to free itself from its heritage, looks with astonishment at those people (our own grandparents), who had such good faith in science and technology and who were (to put the matter briefly) so desperately optimistic. Of course, this is a caricature of the bourgeoisie, and we know that under the surface things did not look as smoothly one-dimensional. Sigmund Freud, among others, has shown it. However, there is some truth in the caricature, and we know it because what distinguishes us from modern humanity is that we no longer even pretend to believe in *theories*, *ideologies*, *discoveries*, and *progress*, if we are honest. We are no longer as literate as they were. In our program, *reason* is again challenged by a different code, such as the one before printing was invented. But the challenge is a new one: no longer must we translate from image to letter but from letter to a new type of image.

2.1.3. Post-alphabet

While considering the origin of linear codes, as we can observe it on some Mesopotamian tiles, one is impressed by the leap from level to level. One can almost see how the writer of texts leaps out of the image into a line in order to describe the image, how the writer dared to abandon the world of images and penetrate the world of concepts. If one considers such an *ontological* revolution, it looks like an impossible endeavor. How can one leap from an image into a text without having first invented the rules of the text? And where does one stand while inventing those rules? Whoever invented linear writing could no longer be within the image they wanted to describe, but could they be within the text they were inventing?

We know unfortunately, and from experience, that such is not an impossible situation. We find ourselves in it. And if it were an impossible situation, then we find ourselves in an impossible situation. Because, like the inventor of linear writing, we must, all the time, leap from an already-established code into one that is not yet really invented. We must invent while leaping. We must, all the time, dare to abandon the level of the conceptual world, of the world of texts, and penetrate the world of technical imagination, which offers us no foothold. We must, like the inventor of linear scripts, invent a new form of existence without being able to foresee what sort of existence that will be. We must, all the time, translate from line into technical image and invent this code while translating. In short, we know from experience the sort of situation that prevailed when history was invented.

The first historical generations, those who invented linear writing, must have been menaced by a sense of loss of meaning. They must have lost faith in the meaning of the codes by which they were surrounded: in the images around them, in magic and in rites, in the power of imagination. Those meanings must have lost their validity for them. But they knew no other sort of meaning. In their desperation, they must have decided to invent some new sort of meaning. It must have been easy for them to leap out of the image: it was no longer really valid. But to leap out of the image meant to leap into nothingness: there was nothing except the image to stand between them and death. The motive of the leap was to make the image credible again: to *describe* it, *explain* it. They dared to leap over the abyss, and they invented linear codes, because they knew that there was nothing else for them to do: images had to be explained somehow, or else life was no longer worth living.

We know that they did much more than explain images by inventing linear writing. *They* invented theoretical reason, and historical consciousness, and political commitment, and personal responsibility, and technological progress. But they did not know it and did not pretend to do so. All those concepts were completely meaningless for them. Of course, the decision to explain images by linear codes implied all those concepts. But the tragedy of the first generations of history is that they created a level of consciousness that they themselves were entirely unable to inhabit.

The previous description is, of course, mutatis mutandis, valid for our own situation. We are losing faith in the codes that surround us, and our lives are menaced by a sense of loss of meaning. We no longer trust *progress*. It is easy for us to leap out of the world of linear texts because they are no longer really valid. But when we penetrate the world of films and TV programs, of traffic lights and posters, we have a feeling that we are losing consciousness while doing it (meaning *historical consciousness*). There is no other level of consciousness accessible for us. We can no longer exist in history because we do not believe in it, but we cannot exist outside history because we are not programmed for a post-historical existence.

The loss of faith in the conventions of linear codes becomes apparent in the mid-nineteenth century. Unfortunately, it is not possible to discuss the reasons within the limits imposed on this book. They have to do, in part, with a critique of the structure of science (for instance, of the relation between *observational* and *theoretical* discourses), which has led to a corrosion of the pillars of the scientific edifice (for instance, by logical analysis). In part, they have to do with a critique of the ontological premises of linearity (the ontology of *becoming*), which has led to the corrosion of the pillars of the ideological edifice (of Christianity, of humanism, of Marxism). And there are many more such reasons why faith in *progress* began to falter.

There is, however, a quite different type of reason. The invention of printing had resulted by then in a veritable avalanche of printed matter in the form of the daily press, cheap books, pamphlets, and leaflets, which inundated the codified the world. Such an inflation of texts had, as an inevitable result, the devaluation of textual message. People could no longer believe in what they were reading, and the amount of texts available prevented them from choosing the texts they believed trustworthy. Thus, the value of tales and explanations, of long and short stories, in sum, of the linear code as a means of giving life a meaning, diminished.

And there is yet a third factor. Around the mid-nineteenth century, the texts of science began to supply explanations of the world that were entirely unimaginable and that, when imagined, became *wrong*. The world that science tells us about cannot and must not be imagined. And the better one knows how to read such explanations of the world, the less one is tempted to try to imagine their meaning. This also pertains to physical and biological, psychological and economic discourses, but it pertains, to a lesser degree, to every *disciplined* discourse. This is a catastrophic development for linear writing. The alphabet is a code that was invented to describe images, explain them. It has now become autonomous of this purpose; it has abandoned images and tends to become unimaginable, which implies that it now serves a different purpose. It no longer works to give life a meaning. It no longer provides a *vision* of the world.

All those factors are self-enforcing. The less one believes in texts, the more one criticizes them, and the more one criticizes them, the less one believes in them. The less one imagines what they mean, the less they mean, and the less they mean, the less one imagines their meaning. And this self-reinforcing circle must result in an involution of reason. Texts become more and more opaque, they become impenetrable for meanings, and reason becomes a sort of paranoia: it serves texts. Texts are no longer used for explaining the world, but explaining is done for the sake of texts. The world of texts tends to become fantastic.

Something similar must have happened when the linear codes were invented. The world of images must have become fantastic. Imagination must have mutated into hallucination. Images must have become opaque, and people could no longer *see through them*. This is why they must have tried to *explain them*. They must have tried to conceive their meaning to again be able to imagine their meaning. To avoid the transformation of imagination into hallucination, people must have attempted conceptual thinking as a therapy against the transformation of imagination into insanity.

The invention of the photograph must be seen in a similar context. As texts become opaque, as conceptual thinking tends toward paranoia, as science and technology begin to weave a fantastic world around us, a world that defies understanding, the only possible therapy is to try to imagine the meaning of all this. A new type of imagination is needed if we are to avoid the transformation of linear reason into insanity. The photograph is the first of a series of codes (here to be called *technical images*) that aim at imagining what is going on around us, at imagining the concepts that make up our codified world. Of course, this whole book is dedicated to the discussion of *technical imagination*, or better, to serve as an introduction to the analysis of *technical imagination*. Thus, no useful purpose would be served to attempt a discussion of it at this stage, but the important aspect of the new codes must at least be mentioned here.

Images of the type *photograph*, *video*, and *hologram* but also of the type *blueprint* or *analogical model* have in common (and are in this quite different from traditional images) that they are the result of texts and that, if analyzed, reveal the texts from which they resulted. They thus occupy an entirely different ontological place from the one occupied by traditional images. Behind a painting stands a painter who tries to imagine a scene. Behind a photograph stands a text of optics, of chemistry, and so forth, a *theory* that tries to conceive a process. Traditional images are mediations between humanity and the world. Technical images are mediations between humanity and texts. Traditional images imagine scenes, and technical images imagine texts. Technical image codes mean texts; they are post-alphabetic both in the sense that they no longer function like texts and in the sense that they could not have been invented without alphabetic writing.

The invention of the photograph was a revolutionary event of the first order of importance. It signaled an earthquake on the level of historical existence. But it was not recognized as such when it happened. At first, it looked like a sort of innocuous game. Then people thought of it as a competition with traditional images such as paintings. Later some of its inherent virtualities became apparent, and people tried to compare the invention of the photograph with the invention of printing. And even now it is difficult to admit that the only comparison that grasps its impact is the invention of writing. Not even now, when the progeny of photography program every motion of the masses, are we capable of fully appreciating its impact.

The explanation of this slowness of understanding technical images (and not only the photograph) has to do with the curious difficulty they offer for those who handle them. Although we have been surrounded by technical images for more than a century and have been exposed to them from early childhood, we have not yet even begun to learn how to use that language for meaningful communication: how to say what is meaningful, let alone find out what new meaning they permit to articulate. Thus, it is not their omnipresence in our surroundings (the fact that we see posters, neon lights, traffic lights, and colored bottles all around us) that suggests the radicality of the present communication revolution but the feeling that it has not yet really exploded.

The difficulty in learning to use technical images is not a technical one: they are easy to handle and are projected to be easily handled. The difficulty is one of leaping out of the world of linear writing. In order to be able to film *correctly*, one need not learn very painfully how to handle a camera or a filmstrip, but one must learn that it is a code that must not be handled like letters or numbers. It took thousands of years for people to learn that linear writing has quite different characteristics from those of image making and that it should not be used to describe only images but also for other information (for instance, scientific information). No wonder we still tend to use technical images for retelling stories told by linear texts instead of trying to find out what else may be done with them. And when we do try to find out, we believe we are *doing research, or experimental art*, instead of being aware of the fact that we are spelling.

This is an extremely dangerous situation. The danger is not so much related to the fact that we do not *understand* the messages that program us through the new codes or that the generation gap increases, as one generation is still predominantly programmed by the alphabet it does not believe in and the other by technical images it does not see through. The real danger is that by leaping from texts to technical images, by abandoning historical consciousness without achieving a new one, we might lose consciousness altogether and fall into the abyss of unconscious programming: that communication ceases being a bridge between humans, and between humanity and the world, and becomes a prison. This is the essence of our crisis.

2.2. HOW THESE CODES WORK

The attempt to understand our crisis by proposing a *genetic* explanation of the new codes that surround us is, of course, quite insufficient. It will now be complemented by what can be called a *functional* explanation. No longer will it be asked, how did the code of technical images come about? but rather, how does it work in the context of our codified world? This implies a shift in the point of view with regard to the crisis. It is no longer seen as an external, political event but as a rupture in our inner program, a crisis of consciousness, or, as one now says, an *identity crisis*. Because if one considers what is going on from a *historical* point of view (as did Chapter 1), the three codes (image, line, technical image) seem to follow diachronically one from the other. But if one considers what is going on from a *functional* point of view, the three codes are seen to be simultaneous within our program, and the problem is how to synchronize them.

The following sketch illustrates this shift of focus:

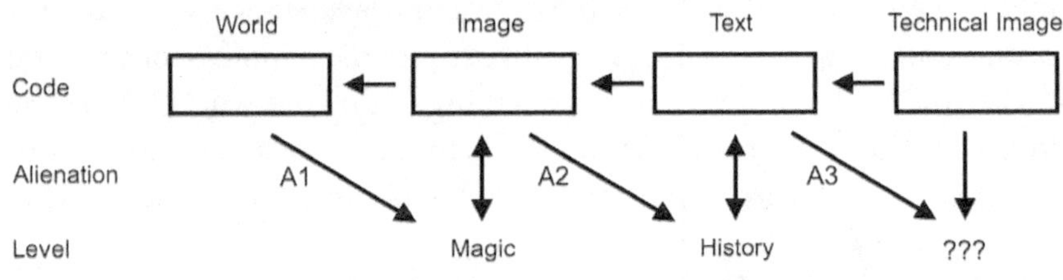

SKETCH 2.2

From the point of view of *historical* explanations, this is how the sketch may be read: Humans are animals who several hundreds of thousands of years ago were expelled and became disintegrated from the *world* (alienation 1, A1). They try to reintegrate themselves through symbols (image). Feedback between them and their codified world (shown by the two-sided arrow) permits them to establish an existential level (magic). As that feedback goes on, images become opaque for the *world*, and humans abandon the world of images (alienation 2, A2). They try to reintegrate themselves through new symbols (text). This establishes again feedback between them and their codified world (shown by the second two-sided arrow), and this results in a new existential level (the historical one). Again, as that feedback goes on, texts become opaque for the images, and humans abandon the world of texts (alienation 3, A3). They try to reintegrate themselves through new symbols (technical images). But so far, they have not yet established a corresponding level of existence and possibly never will (shown by ???), and technical images program them without them being able to adequately manipulate the images (shown by the one-sided arrow). Read thus, the sketch becomes an illustration of the *history of culture* (along the line titled "Code") and of the *history of consciousness* (along the line titled "Level").

If read as a *history of consciousness*, the sketch may be less brutally naïve than it looks at first glance. It shows the dialectics of mediation. As soon as humans lose *immediacy* by becoming conscious and stepping back from the *world* (A1), they must mediate or become insane. This mediation is shown to be a negation of a negation (images negate the negation that is human existence). This double negation becomes a position (images become opaque and cease to be mediations). Humans become a mirror of images (a negation), and they must mediate or become insane. This new mediation (texts) is again a negation of a negation (of humans being a mirror of images) and thus tends again to establish itself as a position. As texts become opaque and no longer mediate with images, humans become a mirror of texts, the negation of texts. Again, they must mediate or become insane. Technical images are their present attempt to escape insanity. They now find themselves within the prison walls of a library against which they project technical images in order to negate them and thus affirm their existence.

This type of reading of sketch 2.2. (which is more or less in agreement with Hegel's *Phenomenology of the Spirit*, Schopenhauer's *Will and Representation*, Marxist *historical materialism*, and even the Heideggerian concept of the *step back*) is not the one that this chapter has in mind (although, of course, the sketch was proposed to permit just such a reading). Instead, the chapter proposes to look at the sketch from the point of view of the three question marks in its lower right corner. In sum, it proposes not to read the sketch as if it were a linear text (from left to right) but to look at it as if it were an image. And this is what one may see from such a focus.

Where we now stand (if to *stand* is the correct verb to describe our lack of position), we are surrounded by technical images, by texts, and to some extent even by images of the traditional type. Those are the codes that program us, that permit us to behave within the world. But each does so in its own way. They must be deciphered, each in its own way. To understand what texts mean, we have to learn how to read them. This requires a specific level of consciousness, which we may call *conceptual thinking*. To understand what traditional images mean, we use a capacity called *imagination*, but we are not quite sure how we acquired it. And we seem to be able to decipher the technical images without understanding their meaning. In sum, where we now stand, texts are the only codes of the three codes shown in the sketch that we really master.

We master them because we learned at school how to read and write, while nobody taught us how to look at images or technical images. We are programmed for a level of consciousness corresponding to linear writing, a level called in the sketch "History." But we no longer *believe* in our program, in what we learned. Texts no longer mean for us what they intend to mean: images that mean the *world*. They have become opaque and mirror us. We no longer see images through them but now see ourselves in them. (Instead of seeing an image of the world through a text of classical physics, we see Newton. Instead of seeing an image of society in Marxist texts, we see the authors. Instead of seeing the image of the soul in the *Brothers Karamazov*, we see Dostoyevsky.) We possibly learned *too well* how to read and write; we know too well that texts are human artifacts and therefore do not believe them.

It seems that we have somehow *forgotten* how to decipher traditional images directly; texts stand between them and us. Of course, there are moments when we can *imagine* without also having to *conceive*; this moment is called in the sketch the level of "Magic." And such a moment may compose the greater part of our existence. Still, the imaginary world is for us a challenge and needs an explanation. It does not satisfy us. We are not integrated into it (like children or the so-called *primitives* are). The world codified by images (paintings, tapestry, stained-glass windows) does inform us, is meaningful, but we cannot take refuge in it if we want to escape from the menace of texts become meaningless. Imagination is no salvation from insane conceptual reason. On the contrary, it accentuates alienation. Relatively innocuous phenomena such as drug addiction and magic rites but also phenomena such as Nazism are there to prove it; we cannot undo the fact that we have learned how to read and write (how to explain images). If we assume the *magical level of consciousness*, we are bound to do it in bad faith. Naïveté, like virginity, cannot be willed. Imagination as a retreat from conceptual reason is barbarism.

The technical images that now surround us so intensely are shown in sketch 2.2. to be the true challenge in our situation. If we could master them, as we master linear codes, we might be saved from the insanity of empty, because meaningless, concepts. Thus, the challenge is precisely the opposite from a retreat into imagination. We should not abandon the attempt to conceive the world by trying to take recourse to an antirational imagination. On the contrary, we should learn a new type of imagination, one that imagines concepts (a transrational imagination, here to be called *technical imagination*). But so far, this is not what is happening; technical images program us without our having learned how to manipulate them.

This is the result of what might be called a *synchronic* reading of sketch 2.2.; it then becomes an illustration of our present program. This chapter attempts to analyze it from such a focus.

2.2.1. Images

Let this be a definition of *image*: a surface with symbols. This is not a common definition. It includes surfaces such as maps and blueprints, not usually called *images*, and it excludes all three-dimensional objects, some of which, such as statues, are sometimes called images. If one accepts the definition proposed, it becomes obvious that what characterizes an image is that the symbols covering its surface are related to each other within that surface in a way that somehow copies the relationship supposedly existing between the objects meant by the symbols within the *real world*. Thus, images are projections upon surfaces of supposedly *real* relations.

There are objections to such a definition. Many images do not attempt to project *real* relations but *ideal* relations. They do not show how things are but how they could or should be, that there are not only road maps within the world of images but also blueprints. This argument stresses that *imagination* is precisely not the capacity to project an image of an existing situation but to project one of a possible, or a desirable, situation. That imagination is *prospective*.

This objection is, of course, a good one. But let us consider it closer. The wall paintings at Lascaux may be considered *projective images*: They do not aim to show a *real situation* (to serve as lessons on the anatomy of ponies) but to show a *possible and desired situation* (to serve as magic for hunting ponies). They do not show how ponies are but how they should be hunted. However, there is nothing magical about Michelin road maps: They do not show how roads should be but how they are. But of course, Michelin maps serve a purpose. They are meant to show what one should do if one wants to drive from one town to another. They are *good images* if they serve that purpose, just as much as the Lascaux paintings are *good images* if they serve for hunting.

Thus, it is true that imagination is a capacity to see how things ought to be and what can be done about it—that imagination is *deontological* (motivated by values). But it is just as true that one cannot see how things ought to be and what can be done about it if one does not see how things are. The Lascaux paintings are *good hunting magic* because the anatomy of ponies shown there is a good one, and Michelin maps are *good images* because they show the existing roads correctly. Therefore, imagination is *epistemological* (shows the *real situation*). In fact, the deontological and epistemological aspects of imagination can never be separated; it is impossible to see how things are without being motivated by the wish to change them, and it is impossible to wish to change things without knowing how they are. All images are both road maps and hunting magic, which eliminates the objection.

There is another, and even more violent, objection to the proposed definition of *image*. Most images are neither road maps nor blueprints but surfaces meant to please. And it is precisely those pleasant surfaces, not a Michelin map or hunt magic, one means when talking of an image. A painter is neither a geometer nor a designer but a producer of interesting surfaces that interest for their own sake. This can be called the *aesthetic* objection. It states that imagination is the capacity to produce *beauty*.

There is something questionable about such an objection. What does one mean by a surface interesting for its own sake? By *beauty*? A Byzantine icon is beautiful because it serves for prayer, just as much as the Lascaux painting is beautiful because it serves for hunting, and a Michelin map is beautiful because it serves for driving. Or a Byzantine icon is beautiful because it shows how saints are, just as much as the Lascaux painting is beautiful because it shows how ponies are to be hunted, and a Michelin map, how roads are. Thus, *beauty* cannot be separated from *truth* and from *desire for action*. But this is not what the *aesthetic objection* has in mind; it means that imagination *seeks beauty* above truth and action, that *art* (pleasant surfaces) is different from science (road maps) and technology (blueprints). This is what makes it questionable.

Fortunately, it does not withstand examination. If we compare a painting by Goya with a painting by Matisse, we see that the difference is one of perception and evaluation of the world. We see the world differently if we look at a painting by Goya than if we look at one by Matisse, and we want to do something different about it. The Goya and Matisse paintings are models for experiencing the world and in this sense are both road maps and blueprints. This is what makes them *art*. And it is only when surfaces insist on being *nothing but beautiful*, *pure delight*, *pure sensation* that they are no longer useful for truth or action. Then they are kitsch, not *pure art*. The *aesthetic* argument is questionable because it argues in favor of kitsch, decadent imagination.

The two arguments against the proposed definition of *image* help, therefore, to clarify it instead of doing away with it. Let us repeat the proposed definition: images are surfaces covered with symbols that project supposedly *real* relations upon surfaces. It now becomes clearer what such a definition implies: Images are surfaces meant to mediate between humans and the *real* world. They *inform* about the world, and the more they inform, the more *beautiful* they are (beauty = information). They show how the world *really* is, and the more they do so, the *truer* they are. And they do so because humans want to do something about the world, and the more images serve that purpose, the *better* they are. Images are surfaces that are more beautiful the truer and better they are—the truer, the more beautiful, and the better they are, the better, the more beautiful, and the truer they are. The aesthetic, epistemological, and deontological aspects of images cannot be separated because they are implicit in image making (in the human effort to give a meaning to their existence).

This definition of *image* implies one of *imagination*: It is the capacity to project supposedly *real* relations upon a surface (to make images) and to decipher such images (to see the supposedly *real* relations through them). Or it is the capacity to project the supposedly four-dimensional relations upon two dimensions and to reproject the four dimensions from the two dimensions of the image surface. In sum, imagination is the capacity to codify and decode the imaginary world. It is important to note that, according to the proposed definition, imagination has nothing to do with the form of the symbols on the surface but only with the relations between those symbols. This is illustrated in the following sketch:

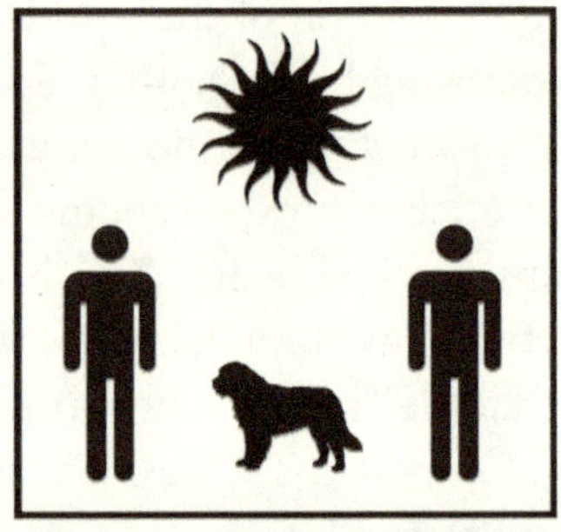

SKETCH 2.2.1.A

This is an image containing four symbols, one meaning *sun*, two meaning *human*, and one meaning *dog*. They are related to each other as their meanings are supposed to be related in time-space—*above*, *to the right of*, and so forth. The symbols are pictograms, but this is not what makes an image out of the illustration. To show this, let us compare it with the following example:

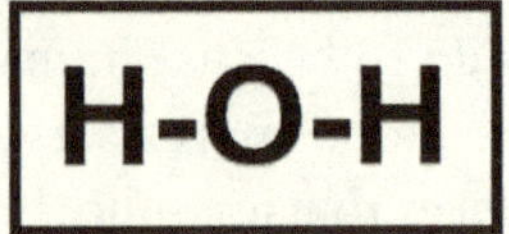

SKETCH 2.2.1.B

This is an image containing three symbols, one meaning *oxygen* and two meaning *hydrogen*. They are related as their meanings are supposed to be related in time-space: *center, horizon*, and so forth. The symbols are ideograms, but this does not prevent the illustration from being an image. It is an image because it is a projection of supposedly real relations upon a surface. Imagination, as here defined, has nothing to do with trying to imitate the appearance of objects (to make *pictures*). It is the capacity of projecting relations, of codifying four dimensions into two dimensions.

Since this is an important point, it should be emphasized. Suppose one were to translate the two illustrations above into linear texts thus:

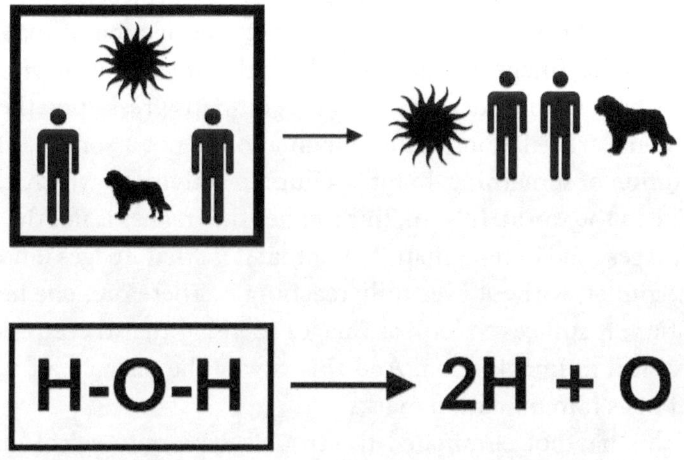

SKETCH 2.2.1.C

Such a translation would leave the symbols untouched, but it would change the relations between them. They would no longer be of the type *above, to the right*, or *in the center* but of the type *after* and +. And those are not *imaginary* relations but *conceptual* ones. They no longer try to reduce a four-dimensional situation upon a surface, but they order the symbols in lines. This is why the translations are texts, not images. Thus imagination, as here defined, is the capacity to abstract from four into two dimensions.

But if one defines *imagination* as here proposed, one poses the problem of mediation within an ontological context. One asks, in effect, what is the connection between the imaginary and the *real* world? This is, of course, not the kind of question this book wants to answer. Therefore, it will try to reformulate the context. Images are made because humans have lost immediate contact with their surroundings. If they had immediate contact, they would need no mediation: an *integrated* being needs no road maps to know where it is, no blueprints to know what to do, and also no *information*. In fact, it not only does not need any knowledge, but it is also incapable of knowledge. Imagination is proof of alienation, and images are the results of an effort to overcome alienation.

This implies that images cannot be copies of known situations. On the contrary, they are made precisely to render unknown situations imaginable. And it implies that imagination is a projection toward the lost *reality* over the abyss of alienation, not a projection of that *reality* upon humanity. Images are not something that mysteriously *press upon humans* (*impressions*) but something that humans press upon the world (expressions, articulations). And imagination is not a sort of inarticulate intuition of something, but it is a human activity by which humans try to live in the world. In sum, this implies that *reality* is not the source of the images (and of imagination) but that it is what images (and imagination) aim at, without ever fully reaching it. Therefore, one need not be Kantian; it suffices to look at images to grasp that there is nothing metaphysical to imagination. And this is why the term "real" must be thought of as if in quotation marks.

But this has not eliminated the troublesome ontological question about the connection between the imaginary and the *real* world. How can imagination abstract from the *real*, and project this abstraction upon a surface, if it cannot contact the *real*? The answer to this question may be extremely complex within philosophical contexts, but within the context of code analysis it is surprisingly simple: *Reality* is a convention made for the purpose of image making. Or imagination is a projection of conventional dimensions upon a surface, of conventionalized situations upon two dimensions. In other words, images presuppose that the *real* be thus so that it permits elimination of *depth* and *time* from it and then is *frozen* on a surface.

This is, of course, no answer to the troublesome ontological question because it poses the question, How can conventions concerning the *real* be established? Or what is the *ontological ground* of human communication? Fortunately, this book has no need to go into this question. It can leave it, but not without a sensation of awe concerning the bottomless mystery of human existence. It is sufficient, for the purpose here pursued, to stress that imagination and image making are based on some very specific conventions that allow surfaces to mean something. In short, it is sufficient to state that imagination is the technique to make conventional surfaces (images) and to decipher the meaning of such surfaces. Imagination is not some *gift*, but like all techniques in general, and codifying techniques in particular, it must be learned.

The curious thing about imagination is that we have forgotten that it must be learned. The code of images is so very ancient (probably as old as humankind itself) that we have forgotten the convention that sustains it. We believe that if we look at pictures or films, at photographs or drawings, we know what they mean without having to learn anything. We believe that we are born with the capacity to understand images (which is a pernicious mistake when technical images such as TV are concerned). Of course, there are images for which *imagination fails us*: X-ray photographs, geographic maps, and drawings from unusual angles. They are shocking because they suddenly reveal the conventional character of images. But we tend to suppress this experience because we are programmed to *believe in images*. In fact, this is probably one of our most basic programs.

There are codes whose conventional origin is completely conscious. Nobody would believe if one said that within Morse code the symbol • • •, meaning the letter **S**, is somehow contained within the letter **S** itself because everybody knows that the Morse code was conventionalized in a way to mean letters because it is a recent addition to our program. Specialists learn how to manipulate it. But with imagination it is different; there are no specialists in imagination. Everybody is programmed for images since earliest childhood. And thus the curious feeling arises that the meaning of a symbol within an image is somehow contained in what is meant by the image. In short, we are programmed, from early childhood, to believe that images are not conventional, that imagination need not be learned. Although we may observe how children learn to decipher images (and how chimpanzees learn it with enormous difficulty), we still believe that *reality* is somehow like the image that means it. This profound *metaphysical* faith is what can be called the *magical level of consciousness*: reality is like the images that mean it.

If one believes this, the question of a distinction between the imaginary and the real world becomes a practical question. The imaginary world then becomes a sort of skin, or frozen surface, of the real world, a reduction of the real world upon a surface, and it becomes a sort of product, an excretion (epiphany) of the real world. To know how to read images becomes a way to understand the real world. This inversion of the relation, by which images are accepted as a product of the world and not of humans, is what can be called *magic*. It is important to stress at this point that the *magical level of consciousness* is not one of a very rich or lively imagination (as one might suppose it to be). Children, or *primitives*, do not have a richer imagination than people with conceptual thinking. On the contrary, imagination is needed to decipher images and thus understand that they are indeed conventional like any other code of communication. Imagination is needed to free us from the belief that images show the *real*. Any tendency to defend imagination against *calculating reason* is a proof of lack of imagination.

Let us try to see how imagination functions, using sketch 2.2.1.a as the image to be deciphered. It is a surface containing information, which can be seen by glancing at the surface. The information is spread out on the surface, as on a platter, available for whoever possesses the key to its code. One may call such a type of information a *synchronizing* message. All its elements are put simultaneously at the disposal of the receiver. One can analyze the message; one can *diachronize its synchronicity*. For instance, one can look first at the *sun*, then the *dog*, and then on the *left man*. This sort of deciphering is called *scanning*, and its technique is known from films. The information will be received more completely the more often the eye travels on the surface of the image and the more intricate are the paths it follows. The information received at first glance is superficial. The more the eye scans the surface, the *deeper* (more meaningful) will become the message.

This is only one aspect of the function of imagination: to scan a surface to render the information ever more meaningful (*diachronize synchronized information*). This is the receiving side of the function of imagination. The corresponding emitting side of it, the one that manifests itself in the making of images, is as follows: it composes symbols within a surface (*synchronizes diachronic information*) to render it even more meaningful. It may be said that imagination is the technique of synchronizing diachronic information for emission and of diachronizing synchronized information at reception.

If one looks closer, it becomes obvious that such a technique involves a very specific time praxis, the one that manipulates time within the frame of a surface. For imagination (and for minds programmed for images), time is a dimension of the surface; it orders the elements of the image within the image; it flows in circles. This is the time of synthesis and analysis, of synchronization and diachronization, the circular time of the eternal recurrence. And for those who believe in images, who have forgotten their conventional character, this is also the *real* time, the time that orders *real situations.*

Time within an image is a stream that holds the elements of the image together. The image is the vessel containing time. It is not itself *temporal* but the place where times gather. This may be articulated by saying that the image means a *scene*, a scene being a place within which times occur (actions and sufferings) in the sense that the elements of the scene change their spatial relations because times that flow within a surface do not order the elements of the image according to temporal categories, such as *earlier* or *later.* They order them according to spatial categories, such as *to the left* and *upward.* There is no sense in saying while deciphering sketch 2.2.1.a that the sun comes *after* the dog: it depends on the scanning eye whether it looks first at the dog, and the eye may reverse the sequence of the two as often as it wants.

The circular time of imagination, the time of planting, reaping and planting, of day, night and day, of birth, death and birth, the time that orders the world according to spatial categories, does not consist of chains composed of links, especially not causal chains. Reaping is just as much the cause of planting as it is its effect, and one may explain day from night just as much as night from day. Events do not form chains but weld their elements together; day cannot be thought of without night, birth without death, night without day, and death without birth. The rising sun and the crowing cock belong together; the sun does not rise if the cock does not crow (*it calls the sun*), and the cock does not crow if the sun does not rise (*the sun calls it*). This complementarity of the elements within a scene is the structure of the world for magical consciousness; it experiences, understands, and evaluates the world as a context of scenes.

Since that level of consciousness is no longer readily accessible, let us try to render it clearer by using sketch 2.2.1.b as an example. The image H-O-H stands within a frame that contains a circular time, and that time orders its elements in spatial relations: *left, right, center.* This *scene* may be transformed into a *process* by rolling the image into a line on both sides of the frame thus: **$2H + O = H_2O$**, and **$H_2O = 2H + O$**. In the first *explanation* oxygen and hydrogen are the causes of water, and in the second *explanation* they are the effects of water. The first *explanation* takes the scene to be the final point of a process, and the second *explanation* takes it to be the starting point of a process. Both these *explanations* are implied in the scene, and they become explicit if the text orders the elements according to temporal categories such as *earlier* and *later.* But by thus *explaining* the image, the two texts change its information: they mean something different, not a scene but a process.

The information contained in the image of sketch 2.2.1.b means a scene that might be called *a molecule of water*, within which time circulates and thus holds the three atoms together. It does not mean the *same* water meant by the two texts that *explain* it: the water meant by the text is a process (analysis or synthesis) within which the *molecule* is a historical event—it *becomes* and it *dissolves.* The two *waters* belong to two different codified worlds; they correspond to two different levels of consciousness and existence.

But this illustration does not grasp the essential difference between the magical and the historical world, between the world of imagination and the world of conception: the fact that the world of magic is *sacred*, and conceptual explanations of it are *profanations.* Let us reconsider the example: The image H-O-H consists of three elements ordered by circular time in what can be called an *absolute order.* The symbol **O** occupies a central position in it, and this position is central in an *absolute* sense: it is *given* by the image. But the text **$H_2O = 2H + O$**, which explains the image, consists of elements ordered in a way that can be called an *order relative to the intent of the explanation.* The group of symbols **H_2O**

comes first because the text has *taken it to be* the point of departure for an explanation. Thus, the linear text renders absolute relations relative to the writer's intent, and this is, in fact, what is meant by the word *profanation*: to render something plain, relative, and indifferent.

The *sacredness* of the world of magic lies in the fact that the *absolute* order that structures it is a *total order.* It has epistemological, aesthetic, and ethical dimensions that can never be separated one from the other. (This was stressed at the beginning of this chapter, when the definition of *image* was under discussion.) Every relation is charged with this absolute, total order. In sketch 2.2.1.a the sun is not only *above* the dog, but it is *superior* to the dog, and it is *splendid.* The man to the right is *right*, and the man to the left is *wrong.* The upper part of the image is *sublime*; the lower one is *infernal.* Each element in the image is in its *just* place. The fact that the sun stands above the dog does *justice* to both, and it would be not only an error but also a crime to put the dog *above* the sun. The *absolute order* of the world (circular time) is true, beautiful, and just; it is *law* in all three meanings—scientific, legal, and formal. It is sacred.

To live in such a world, to live on the level of imagination, is to lead a life both sheltered and terrifying. If we try to intuit it, we can feel, even now, what we have lost and what we were saved from when we achieved *historical consciousness*, when we *profaned* it by our conceptual explanations. The world of imagination is *full of meaning* because every relation in it is charged with the total order. It is *full of gods*; it is a *hierophany* (manifestation of the sacred). Each tree contains a god, each source a nymph, each person a soul because each element of each scene is linked to each other element by the eternal order of circular time, which is a true, just, and beautiful order. Gods, nymphs, and souls are immortal because they are atemporal (spatial) relations. They are links in the structure holding the elements of the world together, which sustains the world. Trees, sources, and humans appear and disappear as time circulates, but their gods, nymphs, and souls remain; they *stand still* because they are the rules along which time circulates; they are the order of the image.

To live in such a world is to be sheltered by it. Because it is a timeless, atemporal, never-changing structure, one can trust it. It cannot disappear into thin air as can the world of conceptual thinking; it is eternal by the very action of time (time goes on within it). But to live in such a world is terrifying because to live is to move about in order to change one's place in the world. But since every place in the world is eternally *adjusted*, to live is to constantly abandon one's just place. To live is to constantly transgress the laws of the world. But of course, time will put everything in its just place again; the transgressions of living will be vindicated. The higher one rises, the lower one will fall, and punishment will follow each crime as a just retribution. The terror of living is that to live is to transgress and then be punished for it. Magic is the vain attempt to escape from the *vengeance of the gods*—to escape justice.

We can still intuit such an existential climate. It lies within our own program, although deeply buried. And it sometimes surfaces in surprising places. We may ask, for instance, whether the trust science had until quite recently in the mathematical structure of the world is not a magical remnant: the specter of the total, sacred order. Or we may ask whether the trust Marxists proclaim in the justice of history (the history of the world is the judge of the world) is not a magical remnant: the specter of divine vengeance. In fact, the whole evaluation of progress may be shown to be magical because it is an absolutization of the relation: *newer* is *better.*

Still, we are no longer as sheltered and as terrified as were our pre-historical ancestors and as are our children. We have learned how to read and write; we can *explain* things. Our world is far less solid and far less meaningful, and our actions are far freer, our sufferings far more absurd. And this shows why and how linear texts were originally invented as a salvation from constant terror, at the price of a life less meaningful and less stable. In sum, it shows that people began to try to explain images into linear texts when imagination became insane hallucination.

2.2.2. Texts

The *second qualitative leap* (A2 in sketch 2.2.) may not have been as radical as the first *leap into existence* (A1). Instead, we can still intuit quite clearly what happened. The *first image makers* are inaccessible, not only in the external sense that we have lost trace of them but in the more important sense that we can no longer intuit how they did it. We can no longer intuit the *first convention*, and it poses the insoluble problem of the connection between the imaginary and the *real*. We have *forgotten* what it means to make a *first* image, although we did it ourselves in earliest childhood.

But we remember quite clearly what happens when one *writes one's first line*. We can very well intuit what was done by the *first* writers, not only because we can observe, on the Mesopotamian tiles, how it happened but also because we remember, from our first year in school, when we learned how to do it. This is so because the *leap* from image into text, the *leap* to escape from hallucination into explanation by daring the abyss of meaninglessness, is one that permits reflection. It is a *stepping back from*—we can see ourselves while writing. In fact, what happens may be illustrated as follows:

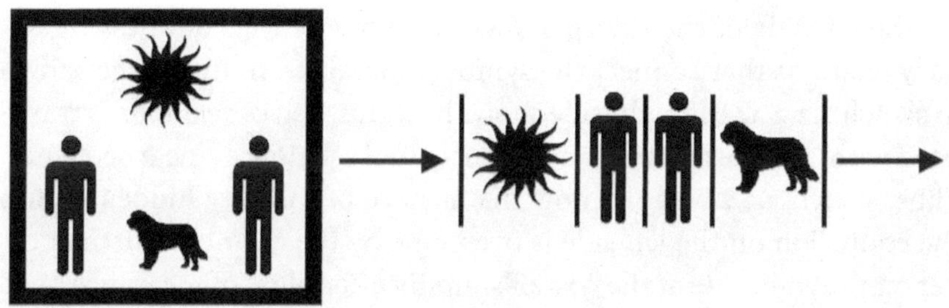

SKETCH 2.2.2.A

This illustration is of childlike (not to say childish) simplicity, not so much because the information it contains is childish and the symbols it contains are childlike. It is childlike and childish because the rules that order the text to the right side of the sketch are childish. These are the rules: tear the symbols contained within the image to your left out of their context, order them in any sequence you like into a line running from left to right, and separate them from each other. Usually, the *orthographic* rules of linear writing are far more complex. Still, the sketch shows what sort of gesture writing is: one of unrolling. It is similar to the gesture that tears a thread out of a knitted woolen pullover: it untangles, stretches out, develops, explains, renders explicit, extends, protrudes (or whatever the verb one chooses to say that it is a gesture that transforms a surface into a line). To write is the gesture by which an image is being exploded into a text—a scene being transformed into a process.

One may object that this is a quite impossible gesture. A surface contains an infinity of lines, and a scene can be transformed into an infinity of processes—no image can ever be described. But linear writing does not aim at *complete* description, at *total* explanation. It is content to lose most of the original information if it can translate part of it into the text it is writing, illustrated thus:

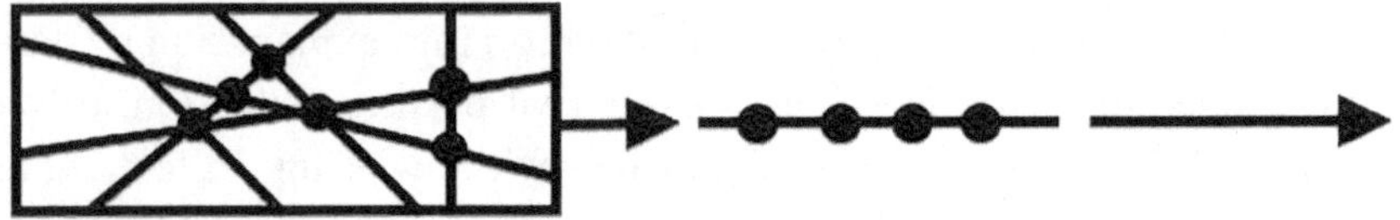

SKETCH 2.2.2.B

The left side of the sketch shows just a few of the countless imaginary relations that connect the symbols contained in the image shown in sketch 2.2.2.a. The right side shows how this web of relations is translated within the text into a single conceptual relation: a linear sequence. Thus, sketch 2.2.2.b shows how the menace of insanity hidden within the confusion on the left side is overcome by the clear and distinct order on the right side at the cost of simplification (loss of meaning). And it suggests that this is a fundamental difference between imaginary and linear codes (between imagination and conception): imaginary codes aim at a *plenitude of meaning*; linear ones, at *clearness and distinction.*

One can see at first glance that linear codes can carry infinitely less information than image codes: there is an infinity of lines within a surface. Linear codes lack one of the dimensions of the surface. This is why pages and pages of printed texts cannot fully describe a small image, and why a single image is able to transmit far more information than a whole book. This has far-reaching consequences in a situation like ours, where photographs are inserted into the pages of magazines and where texts are inserted into images, as in comics.

However, there is another and even more disturbing reason for the relative poverty of conceptual as compared to imaginative thinking. The imaginary relations shown on the left side of sketch 2.2.2.b are (as the previous section argues) *total* relations: *over*, *under*, *between*, *left*, and so on and are charged with aesthetic, ethical, and epistemological meanings. But the conceptual relation shown on the right side of the sketch is a simple relation and then has a single meaning: the rule of linear addition. A code that organizes its symbols according to relations of the first type is called *connotative* (each symbol is surrounded by a dense parameter of meaning). A code that organizes its symbols according to relations of the second type is called *denotative* (each symbol has a single meaning). Thus, translations from image to linear texts imply the loss of all the connotations that surround the image.

This radical loss of meaning one incurs if translating from image to line is, of course, a well-known problem. The fact that the *universe of modern science* is empty if compared to the *universe of imagination* is a structural consequence of the fact that scientific discourse translates images into lines. This became obvious when Descartes proposed analytical geometry: the translation of surface geometry into linear arithmetic. Descartes was fully aware that there is an abyss between surface and line (between the *extended thing* and the *thinking thing*) and that the clarity and distinction of conceptual thinking can never grasp the confusion and plenitude of imagination. Descartes saw clearly that no method could fill the gaps between concepts (not even the later method of mathematical integration) and that if one wants to conceive the world of imagination (which for him meant to translate geometry into arithmetic), one must trust God (*concursus Dei*).

But the radical loss incurred by translating from image to line is rarely as obvious as it is in Descartes (and consequently in modern scientific discourse) because what we do if we describe images is to translate them not into arithmetic codes but into alphabetic codes. Alphabetic codes hide the structural problem of the leap from the surface to the line because they do not seem to mean the image to be described but a spoken language. There seems to be no structural problem: When I describe the image to the left of sketch 2.2.2.a in English, I can use as many words as I need to translate all the connotations hidden in it. For instance, I can say of the relation between *sun* and *dog* that it has to do with superiority and inferiority, with splendor and obscurity, with domination and submission, and I can go on until I am satisfied to have grasped most of the connotations contained within it. It thus seems as if linear, conceptual thinking as articulated in English texts may be just as imaginative (or almost just as imaginative) as is imaginative thinking proper and that this is what *poetry* is all about (at least one of the meanings of the term *poetry*).

The problem here involved (which hides the structural problem) concerns the relation between alphabet and language (and with the pseudo-problem of the relation between speaking and thinking):

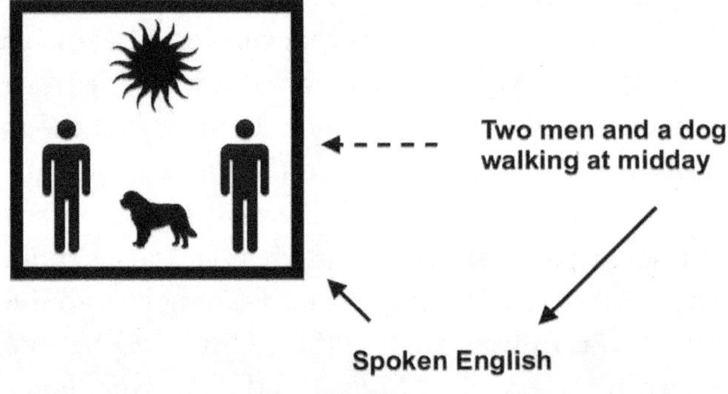

SKETCH 2.2.2.C

At first glance, it looks as if this were the situation: There is an image; it is translated into spoken English (one speaks about it). And then it is written down (one makes a text). And the result is a textual description of the image. But this is not what really happened. Spoken English does not really stand *between* the image and the text; it serves only as a *pretext*. And the written text does not really mean a spoken English sentence; it means an unspoken, although speakable, sentence. Any consideration of the relation between image and speech lies outside the limits, which this book imposed on itself. But it is unnecessary for the present purpose because sketch 2.2.2.c shows that the relation involved in alphabetic descriptions of images is the one between text and image, not the one between speech and image or the one between speech and text. Those two relations are problematic, to be sure, but they lie on a different level of codification. To write alphabetically about an image is structurally unlike the effort to speak about it. (The structure of an alphabetic text is unlike the structure of the spoken language it somehow means.) The problem here involved has to do with the relation between alphabetic text and image. And it is the same problem as in analytical geometry.

This has far-reaching implications. It is impossible to discuss them without going into what is called *formal logic* and *propositional calculus*, which are methods that show how conceptual thinking works. But we need not follow these formal analyses to grasp the fact that *imaginative writing* (a description of images that tries to preserve the imaginary connotations) is no longer *imaginative thinking* in the sense in which image making is. It is conceptual; it conceives imagination (just as much as analytical geometry does) because it orders its symbols according to conceptual rules (*logically*) even if those symbols mean, on a specific level, words of a spoken language. In sum, the intention of sketch 2.2.2.c is to show that all linear texts are structurally clear and distinct and that Romantic poetry is just as much a *calculus* as are the formulae of chemistry and arithmetic equations.

But this does not imply, as it seems to, that the leap from image to text is an abandonment of imagination. Such an interpretation would miss the point altogether. People decided to explain images with texts and thus impoverish the meaning of images through clearness and distinction when meaning became intolerably compact. Conceptual thinking was, and is, the effort to save oneself from the cancerous growth of imagination. Linear codes are methods to escape from the insanity of excessive imagination. Writers, not only Romantic poets but even chemists and mathematicians, do not lack imagination—they suffer from an excess of imagination, and this is why they write: to overcome that excess through clarity and distinction. Linear writing (including purely conceptual writing, such as symbolic logic and pure mathematics) is not an abandonment of imagination but an effort to discipline excessive imagination, which is a way of saying that all linear texts mean images and attempt to explain them: all linear texts, not only those that, like the ones on Mesopotamian tiles, profess openly to be image descriptions. All texts are resolutions of surfaces into lines, even if this resolution is achieved by very indirect methods. The *ultimate meaning* of every text is an image (see sketch 2.2.).

Sketches 2.2.2.a and 2.2.2.b are meant to focus the arrow connecting *text* to *image* in sketch 2.2.—they are meant to suggest that abyss between imagination and conception separating *historical* from *magical* consciousness, which is not only a rupture in history but also one in our own innermost program. However, the two sketches also illustrate how one composes and receives linear texts, how one writes and reads, or how conceptual thinking functions.

Sketch 2.2.2.a shows rather dramatically the difference between imagination and conception by showing the difference between the deciphering of an image and linear writing. While deciphering the image on the left, the eye scans a surface. While deciphering the text on the right, it follows a line as indicated by an arrow. The image spreads its information out, and the text stretches it out. To decipher the image is to analyze the spread-out information (to diachronize its synchronization). To read the text is to synthesize the information at the end of the line (to synchronize its diachronization). One reads as one collects, one by one, stones distributed along a line, and such collecting of stones is called *calculation*. But it is also called *conception* because to *calculate* originally meant to collect little stones and to *conceive* means to take together (to *collect* means to read). Thus, this is the receiving aspect of conception: it is a gathering of elements composed like stones on a line or beads on a string—in other words, calculation.

The emitting aspect of conception was alluded to when sketch 2.2.2.a was first discussed: it is a tearing of elements out of their imaginary context, an untangling of imaginary relations, a counting of the elements along a line, in sum, *telling* (if one remembers that to *tell*, like the French *computer* and the German *erzählen* means to count). The emitting aspect of conception is the recodification of an image into a tale, and to *conceive* means to translate a scene into a story. The abyss between imagination and conception thus becomes somewhat clearer: once an image is explained, told, counted, recounted, and so forth, it can never again be reconstructed because the web of relations connecting its elements has been torn. Once one leaps from the world of magic into history, magic is lost forever, and no amount of nostalgic longing can restore it.

While reading a line, the eye follows it in a specific direction (usually from left to right), which is the direction in which it was produced by a pencil or a typewriter. This is, of course, an inexact description. The eye may *leap* across elements within the line (letters) and even whole lines within a page while reading. There are methods (for instance, *diagonal reading*) that permit the eye to gather the information at the lower right corner of the page without having followed all the lines on the page, and there are methods by which texts are produced without having to compose the letters on the lines (for instance, in computers). Those methods were invented to save time because it takes time to write and read. What time does it take? That is the important question where writing and reading are concerned.

This type of time may be grasped as one that results if the circular time, turning within the surface of an image, is stretched out to form a beam. It is a type of time that orders the eye while reading a text; a time that points to the end of a line; a time with a direction—a time that has not only pierced the frame of the image as in sketch 2.2.2.a but has also done away with it; a time that admits of no framing. It is true that some texts are put in frames (for instance, inscriptions on walls), but they are incapable of stopping the flux of time. Time does not circulate on the surfaces of printed pages; it flows through them in an unmistakable and univocal direction from the past toward the future. Time does not order elements within a surface (as does imaginary time); it carries all the elements within it. Nothing can withstand the flux of time; it comes from eternity and flows forever. Time must be *saved* because salvation is a temporal problem: those who are saved are saved from it.

The type of time just described (*historical* time) is the one we are programmed for, inasmuch as linear writing programs us. We are therefore tempted to believe that this is somehow the *real* time, the time that *prevails in the world* (just as a mind programmed predominantly by images tends to believe that circular time is somehow *real*). But as we now stand on the border of history, we can see that historical time is just as conventional as is the time of eternal recurrence. We do not *experience directly* historical time; whatever we do experience, it is quite unlike the linear time model. For instance, historical time flows from the past toward the future, while we experience time as coming in from the future (from the *opposite direction*). Or historical time flows in a line (in minutes and years), while the time we experience comes in from all directions. Again, historical time passes through the present as if it were a point on its line, while we experience the present as the place where time arrives (*presents itself*). From the distance, we now have with regard to texts (thanks to technical images), we can see that *historical time* is a convention that permits linear codifications.

But this knowledge does not prevent *historical time* from continuing to program all our experiences, actions, and evaluations. That it does so in spite of our *having seen through it* is an aspect of our crisis. We still experience the world as a series of events and not as a context of scenes as does the magical existence. Time for us still runs irrevocably along, and each instant lost is an instant lost forever; nothing repeats itself, and everything is, therefore, unique and irreplaceable. There is no circularity of day and night and day: each day is different from another. Each seed produces a different fruit, each birth a different death, and if there were something like a rebirth, it could in no way dilute the uniqueness and finality of each death, let alone lead to *rebirth* as a repetition of the *first birth*. To live in a world carried away by this type of time, a world with a *beginning and an end*, is to lead a life totally different from the one led by magical existence. Such a world cannot be trusted: it never stands still; it *passes away*. However, it is far less terrifying; it does not expose humans to the inevitable vengeance of the gods; it makes them responsible for their actions—as each person is unique, so is each of a person's actions. Life in a historically structured world is dramatic.

No need to go into the categories of historical consciousness—we know them; they are ours. Suffice it to say that by translating from image to text, from imagination to conception, humans have changed radically their level of existence. They live, experience, understand, and act differently. And the most important aspect of the change is that they can *explain* what they experience and what they are doing. The world they live in is linear, a chain of links. There are causes and effects in it. The past *explains* the present; and the present, the future. Time no longer orders the elements of the world along spatial categories (*above*, *in the middle*) as it does for magical existence. It orders the elements of the world along causal categories (*because*), which means that historical existence *sees through the images*: it can now *explain* them; it has freed itself from terror through reason.

Unfortunately, it no longer works that way for people like ourselves, who stand at the lower right corner of sketch 2.2., who are beginning to alienate themselves from history (A3 in the sketch). It no longer works because the explanations tend to become opaque and do not permit us to see through them. Conceptual thinking may become just as fantastic as imaginative thinking, and reason may become just as insane as imagination. An impenetrable wall of a library can terrify just as much as one of cave paintings. Historical existence at the present stage tends to become just as horrifying as must have been magical existence at the moment of the invention of writing because we no longer believe in the texts that program us.

It may be shown formally that *causal explanations* (on which historical reason rests) are unsustainable (for instance, that they are *grammatical errors*). It may be shown practically that they do not work in extremely refined situations (for instance, in nuclear physics). And there are other methods to show that causality is in a crisis (for instance, the methods of statistics). But this is not what is decisive in the present situation. (Hume showed hundreds of years ago that causal thinking was a myth, but people continued to believe in it.) The new element in our situation is that explanations no longer satisfy us: we are tired of them. We no longer want them because we feel that in a macabre sort of way the relation between humanity and texts has turned around and texts no longer serve humanity in its effort to see through the imaginary world; it is now humanity who serves the texts that surround it. And the symptom of this turning around is that we can no longer imagine the meaning of the enormous mass of explanations with which the texts inundate us. Those explanations are not *for us*; they explain away.

As long as we can imagine what texts mean (as long as their concepts explain images), there will be a link between texts and the world (texts are mediations). The more texts become autonomous of images, the less they mediate and the more they function for their own sake. And when a point is reached where the explanations offered by texts become falsified by any effort of imagination (as is the case of most scientific explanations at present), when it becomes *wrong* to try to translate from the linear code into an image, then it may be said that linear codes will have abandoned the purpose they were originally invented for: to explain images. They will then cease to mediate and will become, in the strict sense of the term, *paranoiac* (*pseudo-knowledge*).

This book has argued that concepts could mean nothing but images, even if they can mean them very indirectly. (To put this in Kantian terminology, the categories of pure reason become meaningful only if they mean forms of perception.) If this were true, no amount of counterargument can hide the fact that unimaginable concepts are *empty*. There are, to be sure, very strong arguments against such a statement. And the strongest of them may be formulated as follows: As texts advance, the concepts become less and less imaginable, but they can be reduced to images at the end of the discourse. For instance, the concept does not have an easily imaginable meaning, but the equations containing it may lead to specific, very much imaginable operations like building bridges. Thus, it is nonsense to believe that equations containing the symbol are devoid of meaning.

Although the argument is strong (it is, in fact, the pragmatic argument in favor of science: scientific explanations may not be *true* in any formal sense, but they permit technical manipulations of the world), it is not as strong as it used to be. To be sure, equations *work*; they lead to more or less successful manipulations. In this sense, they have a *meaning*. But what sort of meaning have those manipulations resulting from such equations? May it not be held that technical progress itself has become *meaningless* and unimaginable, precisely because the texts it is based on have become unimaginable? May it not be held that the best proof for the paranoiac lunacy of current scientific explanations is the meaningless technical progress they lead to? That technical progress is a striking proof of the fact that the relation between humanity and texts has turned around and that *progress* no longer serves humanity but humanity serves progress. It is characteristic of our current crisis that we are condemned to see both sides of the arguments simultaneously: we must admit that science is tending toward paranoia, and that it is the only meaningful discourse, or that progress has become meaningless, and that to progress is the only meaning of life we know of.

But there is a different way to face the problem of the tendency of current texts to become unimaginable and of the current concepts to become empty. One may try to imagine what texts might mean, and one may try to give empty concepts a new sort of meaning. One can, for instance, render imaginable the meaning of the concept. In other words, one can cultivate a new type of imagination and produce a new type of images, ones that imagine concepts. In this book this new type of imagination is being called *technical imagination*, and this new type of image is called *technical image*. And it is precisely this challenge—of texts tending to become devoid of meaning and thus provoking a new type of imagination—that is about to result in a new level of existence: post-linear, post-conceptual, post-historical existence.

It may be held that the tendency of texts toward unimaginable concepts is identical with the tendency of history; that empty concepts (*pure concepts, formal concepts*) and the *fullness of time* (utopia, the Kingdom of Heaven, communist society) are somehow two sides of the same coin; that progress is the advance from *observational* toward ever-more-*theoretical* discourses; and that the horizon toward which history advances is *pure, theoretical reason*. Such a reading of history (of texts) is in agreement both with Plato and with Christian salvation (though possibly not quite with Marxism). But if it is so, utopia, the Kingdom of Heaven, and so forth no longer seduce us. We begin to know what it means to live among unimaginable texts (*pure concepts*): it suffices to open the early-morning paper or watch a TV program. Although we are still being programmed for history (at least as far as the older generation is concerned), we no longer believe in it. This is what sketch 2.2. shows by the arrow A3: our present alienation from history, from political commitment, from scientific explanations, and from technical progress.

2.2.3. Technical Images

We face the difficulty of not yet being able to see through the codes about to be discussed. All of us know how to read and write: we learned it. All of us believe we can decipher images, and in fact, we were in some way programmed for it. But it may be safely said that nobody knows precisely how to decipher the new codes meant here and that those who handle them do not know precisely what they are doing. It is true that we all believe we can understand TV programs and traffic signs; in fact, there is nothing easier than this; every child can do it. We all believe that it is easier to decipher the new codes than even traditional images; it is easier to understand a photograph than a painting. But this is a mistaken belief, and it has consequences that must be called tragic: the new codes program us, although we are not programmed for them. And to be programmed by a code for which one is not programmed implies unconscious servitude.

The mistaken belief that we know how to read technical images is based on the following naïve premise: Technical images are surfaces upon which the phenomenon meant impresses itself somehow; for instance, a photograph of a house is a surface upon which the house somehow impressed itself. It is therefore easy to read a photograph, easier even than to read a painting; if one looks at a photograph, one sees what it means because one sees a trace left by the object it means. This naïve belief may be illustrated thus:

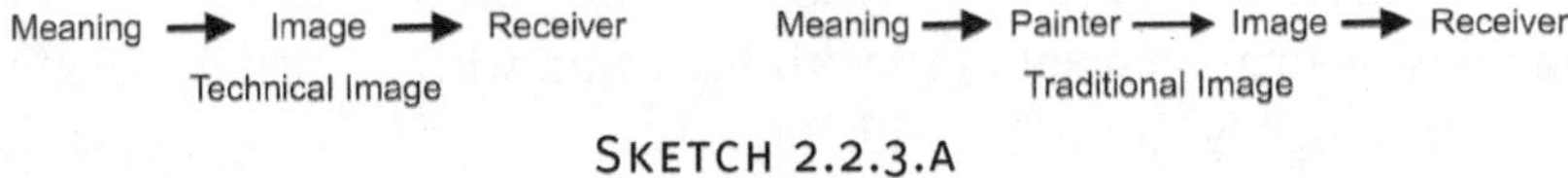

SKETCH 2.2.3.A

Thus, the difference between a technical image and a traditional image is believed to be the absence of human interference in the technical image. Photographs are more *objective* than paintings because the object impresses itself upon the surface, while in the painting there is a *subject* (the painter) who interferes in the image making. Or, to put it differently, between traditional image and what it means stands a painter, and therefore the traditional image is a subjective vision. Nobody stands between a technical image and what it means, and therefore it offers an objective view. The receiver of a traditional image must decipher the painter behind the image before getting at the meaning. The receiver of a technical image can get the meaning directly through the image. It needs no deciphering because it is not symbolic: there is a causal link between a technical image and its meaning. The photograph is the effect of its meaning; it was caused by it. Technical images are not really codified messages at all; they are traces, symptoms of phenomena, like footprints. (Although nobody really believes such a statement, everybody tends to behave as if they do believe it when facing a technical image.) Thus, nobody needs to learn how to decipher technical images: they are not ciphers.

Of course, the moment one articulates the naïve belief as illustrated, it becomes unbelievable, but the fact is that people want to be naïve and refuse to articulate their belief when technical images are concerned. This is why the technical image codes function as they do. They function on the basis of bad faith on the part of both their emitters and receivers, on the belief, not really held, that they are *objective.*

Everybody knows (even if they *forget it* while facing technical images) that this is the situation:

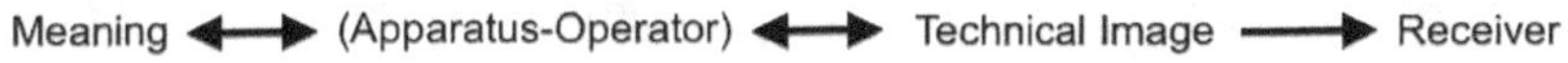

Meaning ⟷ (Apparatus-Operator) ⟷ Technical Image ⟶ Receiver

SKETCH 2.2.3.B

To give an example, there is a photographer holding a camera (*apparatus-operator*). This photographer manipulates the camera within a parameter imposed by the construction of the camera in order to photograph a house (*meaning*). But the photographer also manipulates the house by lighting it, choosing a point of view, and so forth. In the camera, there is a mirror that allows seeing how the photograph might look (*technical image*). There are criteria that allow the photographer with the camera to decide which photograph of all those possible ones seen through the mirror the photographer will produce by pressing on a button. And the result is what the receiver will have to decipher. The *meaning* of the photograph is not correctly received unless the receiver has seen through all these operations.

This is a simplified description of an extremely simple case of technical image production. It suffices to show that there is no causal link between technical image and meaning; that there is a codifying interference between technical image and its meaning; that, if anything, technical images are less objective than are traditional ones, if only because the interference of the *apparatus-operator* complex is far more intricate than is the interference of the painter in the process of image making. Indeed, the fact that there are processes involved in the production of technical images, which are based on causal explanations (chemical processes, for instance), renders the technical image even less objective. All this, and more of the same, is involved in sketch 2.2.3.b as an illustration of the way technical images are produced. But this is not its main purpose. The sketch implies these questions: What, after all, is the meaning of a technical image? What sort of a *house* does a photograph of a house mean? Does it mean the *same house* meant by a painting? Or by a linear description of a painting? And if not, what is the *level of its meaning*?

An attempted definition will stand in provisionally for an answer to this question: Technical images are surfaces covered with symbols meaning concepts. (A photograph of a house is the image of a concept of a house.) The definition proposed is worded in a way that allows it to be read as a special case of *image* as defined in section 2.2.1.—images are surfaces covered with symbols. All the arguments proposed while discussing images must therefore also apply to technical images: They are mediations that have deontological, epistemological, and aesthetic dimensions. For instance, an X-ray photograph of a broken arm is not different from a Lascaux wall painting in that it is true if it shows a given situation, good if it permits change to that situation, and beautiful to the extent to which it is true and good, in other words, to the extent that it *informs*. Or what is now called *video art* is not different from *traditional art* in that it is kitsch if it is not true to something and good for something. In sum, the definition of *technical images* proposes to show that they are images, after all, and not some hitherto unknown form of communication.

Still, there is a catch in the proposed definition. It does not agree at all with what is being called (although quite unsystematically) by the terms *technical image* and *technical imagination* in the texts dealing with the problem. It does not agree with it in three main points: (1) It states that a technical image is different from other images not by the way it is produced (technically) but by its special meaning (concepts); (2) it states that technical images are surfaces (two-dimensional) even if they move and are audible; and (3) it states that technical images are revolutionary not because they are made that way but because they are made in ignorance of their function. This discrepancy of the proposed definition with regard to what can be called the *common use* of the term *technical image* is not the consequence of some caprice but of the conviction that unless one makes a new effort to define the term, one will never grasp what is going on within the codified world at present.

The definition, as proposed, is far wider than the one we are accustomed to. It includes all those technical images considered as such in the usual texts (films, videotapes, holograms, photographs, slides, microfilms, X-ray films, and so forth), but it also includes images not generally considered to be *technical* (blueprints, technical and architectural designs, statistical curves, the sketches contained in this book, and so forth). This is so because the term *technical*, contained in the term *technical image*, is here conceived to mean not the method of production but the meaning of the image. What is *technical* about a photograph of the surface of Mars is not that a complex apparatus produced it but that it is the image of a concept hidden within the apparatus. And the blueprint that made the construction of the apparatus possible is just as much a *technical image* as is the photograph because it means a related concept. The images on TV screens are of the same order as are the statistical curves used in TV programming because they mean related concepts. In sum, the proposed definition tries to give the term *technical* a new meaning, a meaning that has to do with applied theory, not with know-how. In the definition as proposed the term *technical image* will thus mean an image that is the consequence of some theory and thus means some of its terms. Technical images are post-theoretical images, and this is why they are called *technical* in this book.

There are several dangers involved in such a definition, due basically to our ignorance about the essence of this new code. The definition tries to advance toward that essence, but it becomes obvious how difficult it is to grasp it if one begins to try to define it. One of the dangers involved is this: If technical images are said to mean concepts (theoretical terms), are they not a development of ideograms rather than of images? Is not an ideogram defined as being a symbol meaning a concept (an idea)? And in fact, does not the proposed definition include symbols of the type *traffic sign*, which seem quite obviously to be ideographic? One might *feel* that there is an essential difference between a symbol of the type **2** (which may be said to mean the idea of a pair) and a symbol of the type **P** (which may be said to mean the idea of parking permission). One might feel that there is a difference of levels: The number is part of a linear code (the code of arithmetic), and what it means is an imaginary situation (a *pair*). The traffic sign is part of a two-dimensional code (the traffic code), and what it means is a text (a sentence). Still, it is difficult to translate that *feeling* into clear understanding, which is a symptom of the difficulty that technical image codes are posing. Since this example, coming as it does directly from our daily experience with technical images, poses not only a question touching on the essence of the new codes but also a question concerning spoken language in relation to the new codes, we consider this in some detail.

The following sketch illustrates what is being discussed but will be explained later, after a brief excursion:

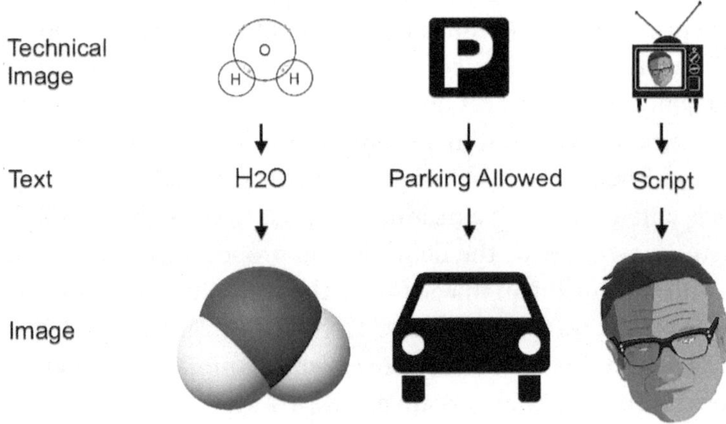

SKETCH 2.2.3.C

2.2.3.1. Literary Languages Overcome

Both the alphabet and ideogram codes are linear, and they run on, so to speak, parallel lines that may (and often do) intermingle. For instance, the text *this costs* $2 contains both letters of the alphabet and ideograms pertaining to two or more different codes. But the parallelism of the two types of codes is not always evident. For example, the text *two plus two is four* seems to be a description of the text 2 + 2 = 4 as if that second text were an image of this type: ⁚⁚ . Of course, this is a mistaken analysis of the situation. Both *two plus two is four* and 2 + 2 = 4 are descriptions of the image just shown, and both translate the imaginary relations prevailing within that image into conceptual relations. Still, we cannot help feeling that the text 2 + 2 = 4 is somehow image-like in spite of our knowledge that the alphabetic and the arithmetic texts mean the same image and do so in the same structure.

The reason for this feeling is that ideographic texts, like images, stand somewhere beyond spoken language. The text $2 + 2 = 4$ and the image ⁘ may both be written alphabetically as *two plus two is four*, as *zwei und zwei sind vier*, and *dois mais dois são quatro*. And this is true not only of traditional images like the one shown but of technical images as well. The sign **P** may be written as *parking allowed*, as *parken erlaubt*, and *permitido estacionar*; and the photograph of a female breast on a poster, as *buy a bra!*, *kauf einen Busenhalter!*, and *compre um sutien!* Thus, in spite our theoretical knowledge to the contrary, traditional images, technical images, and ideographic codes seem to permit a communication beyond spoken language.

Under analysis it may be shown, however, that each of the three extralinguistic codes stands in a different relation with regard to spoken language. Traditional images are independent of spoken language. Ideographic codes are *literary languages* like English, German, and Portuguese and are related to spoken language the same way those other three languages are, although this is not evident. And technical image codes are supralinguistic in a radically new sense. No effort is needed to show that traditional images are independent of spoken language. One can communicate with others through images if both emitter and receiver know the code, and no knowledge of a language common to both is required. But the two other statements require clarification.

Consider the meanings of the ideogram H_2O and of the technical image **P** in relation to alphabetic texts and spoken language, illustrated as follows:

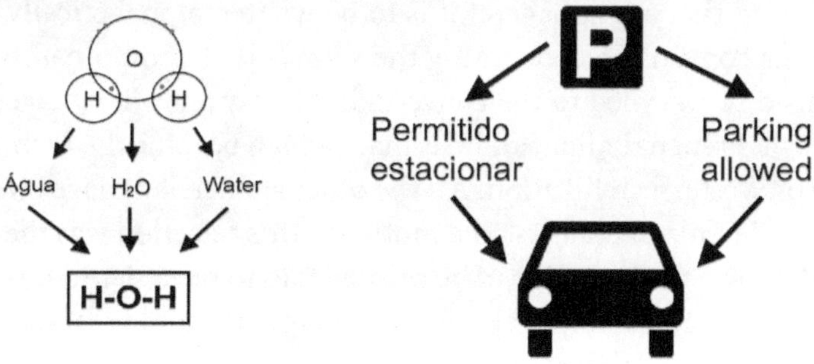

SKETCH 2.2.3.1.A

The sketch consists of three levels. On the upper level stands the technical image. On the middle level stand texts, and on the lower level stand traditional images. The technical image means the text level, and the texts mean the image level. (It does not matter, for this argument, whether H-O-H is indeed a traditional or a technical image; it is here taken to be an image of a *scene*, a molecule of water.) There is no level for spoken language in sketch 2.2.3.1.a because it does not play a role in it. If one wanted to introduce it, one would have to take up the problem of literary languages, as it was briefly discussed in section 1.3.

As long as printing had not been invented, the relation between the alphabets and spoken languages remained hidden. There were several languages that could be written (in the Middle Ages there were four: Latin, Greek, Arabic, and Hebrew), and each of them had a specific alphabet codified for them. There were also a great number of spoken languages that were not written, apparently because no alphabet had been invented for them. It looked, therefore, as if the relation between language and alphabet were of the type as the relation between arithmetic and number: to learn how to write the Latin alphabet, one had to learn the language, and to learn the language, one had to learn the alphabet. It would be absurd to learn the Hebrew alphabet without wanting to learn the language or to learn the use of numbers without wanting to learn arithmetic.

When printing was invented, and letters became prototypes costly to produce, and a single alphabet (the Latin one) had to serve for several languages, then people rediscovered the *original* alphabetic convention: letters meant sounds that may be common to several languages if properly conventionalized for such a purpose. Thus, the invention of printing made all the spoken languages writeable, at least in theory, but it also showed that a language, if it is to be written alphabetically, needs a previous convention concerning the sounds that compose it. In practice, this discovery led to the convention of only a few languages, such as English, French, Italian, and German, which became the *literary languages* of Western civilization. All the other spoken languages were relegated to the role of dialects. The motive of this selection was the sale of printed books: the language to be printed had to be easier to learn than Latin, and it had to be closely related to a great number of dialects to have a sufficiently large number of readers.

The important thing to note is that the literary languages were not originally spoken; they were conventionalized to be printed, not spoken. But as alphabetization went on, especially after the introduction of the daily press, those languages became the common code of speech, and they finally displaced the dialects except for unimportant remnants. Thus, the genesis of literary languages is the opposite of what might be called a *natural* language: they were first conventionalized for alphabetic writing, then they were printed, and finally they were spoken. This *paper quality* adheres to them even now, and everything they produced (nationalism, national culture, national identity, patriotism, imperialism, etc.) has that artificial, deliberate flavor.

This consideration permits insertion of a level corresponding to *spoken language* within the sketch 2.2.3.1.a between the text and the image levels, approximately thus:

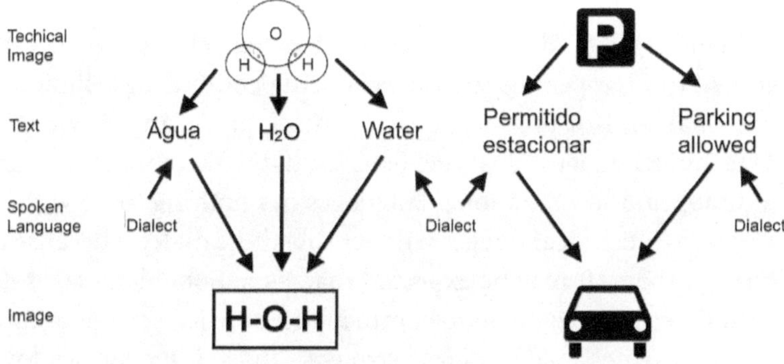

SKETCH 2.2.3.1.B

The purpose of sketch 2.2.3.1.b is to show that ideographic codes such as the code of mathematics, chemistry, and formal logic are on the same level of meaning as are languages of the type English or German: they are codes invented to be written, not spoken, and they mean images. The difference is that languages such as English and German became, secondarily, spoken languages because their symbols (letters) originally meant sounds of spoken languages. But this difference is not essential. Both literary languages such as English and German and ideographic codes such as the code of chemistry pass, so to speak, *through* the level of spoken language and point to the images they mean (they need not be spoken aloud to achieve their meaning). Therefore, the codes of chemistry, mathematics, logic, and so forth are not *international* codes (as many tend to believe); they stand on the same level as do national languages. They can never substitute for national languages because they have the same level of meaning, but from a different angle: H_2O and *water* mean the same image, but each one means it under a different aspect. Alphabetic and ideographic codes can translate into each other and intermingle, but they cannot substitute one for another.

But sketch 2.2.3.1.b shows also that technical image codes are indeed *international* (or better still, *supranational*) in the radical sense that not only do they permit communication independent of national languages, but they also render those languages useless. They are images of printed texts, they mean printed texts, and through the mediation of those texts they mean an image. But since the printed text that the technical images mean is somehow preserved within the technical image, it may be abandoned in future communication. Thus, sketch 2.2.3.1.b shows that national languages (and all their terrible ideological consequences) are condemned to disappear as the world is being codified in technical images: nationalism is a product of the printing press, and it will disappear as technical images substitute letters. But the sketch also shows that such a disappearance of national languages has nothing to do with spoken languages. Technical images will not substitute dialects because they *pass through* them. It may be expected that, as national languages grow weaker and become degraded to commentaries on TV screens and in illustrated magazines, dialects grow stronger. Indeed, tendencies toward such a situation (slang, argot, jargon, etc.) can be observed even at present. In sum, the excursion this section makes into the territory of literary languages concludes with the prognosis that the period of national languages and nationalism is approaching its end because those communications are based on the printing press and because technical images will bring about a *supranational*, universal, *cosmic* (indeed, mass) culture.

It is now possible to return to the discussion in section 2.2.3. and the question that provoked the previous excursion: What is, according to the proposed definition, the essential function of technical image codification? Sketch 2.2.3.c will help approach this admittedly difficult question.

The technical image on the left (which tries to show the interference of electrons within a molecule of water) may be said to belong to the code of *chemical technical imagination*. The technical image in the middle (a traffic sign) may be said to belong to the code of *traffic technical imagination*. The technical image on the right (which is an image on the TV screen) may be said to belong to the code of *television technical imagination*. These technical images mean texts, which may be alphabetic but need not be, and the fact that they mean linear texts is what makes technical images of them according to the proposed definition. And the texts mean images of scenes. The purpose of the technical images is to render the texts imaginable. The text H_2O is so highly conceptual that it no longer permits to be *seen through*. The corresponding image renders the concept H_2O as an image. The same is true, though to a lesser extent, for the text: *Parking Allowed*. The traffic sign makes an image out of a conceptual and almost unimaginable imperative. And the same is true for *TV scripts* (or any other form of fictional literature): one can no longer imagine the meaning of a novel; it has become too *abstract* from the scenes it means. The TV image makes the script imaginable by imagining its concepts.

The three codes, as they are represented on the technical image level of sketch 2.2.3.c, are not usually taken to be of the same type. The first code (*chemical technical imagination*) is usually considered to consist of *models*, and it is being analyzed from the point of view of the theory of knowledge. The second code (*traffic technical imagination*) is usually, and somewhat thoughtlessly, considered to be of the ideographic type. And the third code (*television technical imagination*) is of the type usually considered to be a technical image, but an *audiovisual* one, not a surface. The definition as here proposed lumps the three types of codes together (and some other types as well), and it does so because it suspects that they stand, all of them, on the same level of meaning and that to understand this is an important step toward the understanding of their function.

Sketch 2.2.3.c intends to show that what is here called *technical images* are not images of scenes, as are traditional images and as the technical images often pretend to be, but that they are images of concepts. The image on the left does not mean *a molecule of water* but a concept of an image of a molecule of water. The traffic sign in the middle does not mean a scene of a parking lot but a concept of an image of that lot. The TV image on the right does not mean a monologue scene (although it pretends to mean it) but a concept of an image of a monologue scene. In the same way, a photograph of children playing on a beach does not mean a scene but a concept of an image of a scene. A statistical curve does not mean an economic tendency but a concept of an image of a tendency. Thus, the sketch shows that technical images do not mediate between humanity and some *lost real world* (as do traditional images) but between humanity and their own texts, and that they do so because those texts are beginning to lose their meaning. In sum, sketch 2.2.3.c shows that technical imagination is the result of a step back from conceptual thinking and that it forms a new level of existence. Or it shows that technical imagination does not imagine the world (as it often believes because it ignores its own function) but that it imagines concepts, lest they become empty.

Of course, the purpose of this effort to show what technical images mean is to enable us to decipher their message in order to know what one is seeing if one watches TV or a film, if one looks through an illustrated magazine, if one drives through a red traffic light, or if one considers a sketch in a scientific publication or a photograph of a moonscape. This is a well-known purpose, and every *critic of the current situation* is committed to this: to tear off the mask from the face of those who program us and see what really stands behind the messages that come in through the media. This book does not deny the pertinence of such commitment. Still, it is not exactly the same effort as the one undertaken here. The question posed here is not, In whose interest do the technical images function? but the possibly more radical one, Is the function of technical images inherent in them so that the interests they serve are not their explanation but may themselves be explained by the fact that they are, themselves, programmed by technical images? In other words, the question here posed is, Can one understand technical images by analyzing them, and not by analyzing their economic, social, political, and so forth context? Therefore, cannot the present crisis be approached from the level of communication, and can that level not be taken, at least methodologically, to be its *infrastructure*?

From such a point of view, the next question that arises is, how can technical images program us if very often their meaning is hidden not only for the receivers but also for the emitters? In other words, how is it possible that the world codified by technical images works as it does if the level of consciousness on which it is being codified is of such difficult access? Who are those exceptional geniuses that stand on such a level and program us? Communication specialists? Media owners? Technocrats? So-called *decision-makers*? And how do they succeed in such a miraculous performance?

The answer is surprisingly simple: Technical images function quite differently if they codify information on the level of elite communication than they do within mass communication. An X-ray photograph is deciphered by methods different from those that decipher a photograph on a poster. If one watches an electroencephalogram, one does it in a different way from how one watches TV programs. Statistical curves are read differently than illustrated magazines, and an archaeologist looks at a photograph in a way different from the way one looks at a pornographic photograph. The difference is this: On the elite level both emitters and receivers have somehow learned how to use technical images; they stand on the level of consciousness corresponding to their information. On the mass level, neither emitters nor receivers are fully aware of what they are doing while manipulating the new codes. Those who look at an X-ray photograph know that they see an image of a medical concept because they have learned how to use technical imagination. But neither the producer nor the receiver of a message of a poster fully knows the meaning of it. Nobody believes that an electroencephalogram is an image of the brain but knows that it is an image of a concept concerning brain processes. However, everybody believes that what he or she sees while watching TV is an image of the event it is showing. In short, technical images have somehow slipped from the elite level (where they function consciously as a means to imagine concepts) into the mass level (where they are being almost unconsciously misused).

This difference between *elite technical imagination* and *mass technical imagination* (and the fateful contradiction it involves) will be discussed in the following chapter. But the question demanding immediate attention is this: How did the technical images *slip* into mass communication? How did the photograph *slip* from the laboratory into the poster, and how did the TV change from a cathode tube into the box that stands in the kitchen? A possible way to answer is to compare our situation with the one prevailing shortly after the invention of linear writing, a situation in which the population was widely illiterate, and when those who knew how to write did not know yet all the consequences of what they were doing. The premise is that we ourselves are illiterate with regard to technical images and that those who handle them do not know what they are doing. In sum, let us compare the origin of history with the situation in which history ends: our own situation.

One thing is obvious: The receivers of early linear texts stood on what is here called the *magic* level. They received the messages transmitted by linear codes as if they were imaginary: the *supplex turba* of the end of the Golden Age fell on the ground when the *menacing words appeared on the fixed bronze*, and when Moses descended from the mountain with the tables of the law, the Israelites *saw beams of light* coming out of his forehead. This cannot be called an *appropriate form of reading*, let alone *text criticism*. Those generations at the start of history were being programmed by linear texts without any capacity for deciphering their program. That is, they behaved in the face of the *Lex Duodecim Tabularum* and of the tables of Mosaic Law more or less as we do in the face of posters and TV programs.

But what about the authors of the *Lex Duodecim Tabularum* and of the Ten Commandments, the writers of those early texts, that is, those mythical emitters who, like the present codifiers of radiated messages, programmed the life of Western society for so many generations? Did they really master the codes they were manipulating? The answer of course is difficult, because those authors hide behind magical clouds (*Romulus* and the *Lord*), but it does seem that they believed in the clouds and not in the lines of the text they were writing. They used the code of linear writing, which was to result in historical consciousness and historical action, as a method to sustain imaginary sacredness and a magical, ritual acting. It seems as if those early writers did not know what they were doing (that they were illiterate in spite of their technical skill in producing written texts), and certainly they had no inkling of the revolution they were provoking. In this, very probably, they are not unlike the present programmers.

This situation at the start of history cannot be called one of *bad faith* in the sense of *deliberate mystification*. The Roman legislators and Moses did not intend to mislead the people: they were themselves *misled* in the sense that they were unable to sustain the level of consciousness linear writing demanded of them. But this did not render the situation less dangerous; on the contrary, the incapacity to grasp what was happening on the part of the emitters of the programs rendered the situation even more dangerous. Egypt is proof of the reality of that danger. An elite of scribes unable to overcome the magical level of consciousness used linear writing, not to create a new form of existence corresponding to this new form of communication but to freeze a form of existence rendered meaningless by the new form of communication. For centuries the whole of Egyptian society was transformed into a mummy. Not in spite of but because of the *good faith* of Egyptian scribes and magicians. This is an example of the danger we are facing.

Of course, the comparison between the two situations should not be exaggerated. For instance, it does not look as if we would maintain the level of consciousness previous to that of the new codes while receiving our program, as did the receivers of the *first stories*. We do not seem to maintain historical consciousness in the face of post-historical information, as those generations maintained pre-historical consciousness in the face of historical information. On the contrary, it looks as if we somehow slipped back into pre-historical, magical consciousness in the face of post-historical information. In other words, when we receive technical images, we behave more or less like those generations did when they received their laws: we see beams of light coming out of them. Therefore, the comparison, although it might be helpful for a general understanding of our situation, is useless for the understanding of details.

For instance, the question, How did the new codes *slip* from the elite into the mass level of communication? remains unanswered. In the *first texts* situation very probably the transference of written texts from elite to mass communication had to do with the transference of the writing stylus from the merchants' hands into the priests' hands: the merchants knew what they were doing when writing stock lists, but the priests did not when they were writing laws. But there is no parallel in this with our own situation. The question of how the cathode tube *slipped* into mass communication demands a different approach, one that is suggested in sketch 2.2.3.b, which tries to show the production of a technical image.

2.2.3.2. Apparatus-Operator

The term *apparatus* is here defined as *a tool that produces technical images.*[1] This does not seem to agree with the common use of that term. But if one considers its various uses (for instance, *measuring apparatus, surgical apparatus, party apparatus,* and *administrative apparatus*), one begins to see that the proposed definition aims at what is common to these various uses. The term *operator* here means *a specialist in the handling of apparatus.*

If defined thus, the two terms become intertwined, and one becomes meaningless without the other. In fact, they imply a radically new relation between tool and humans, one for which classical analyses are useless. Classical tools (meant to change the world) either enslave humans or liberate them. The tools enslave a worker in a factory because he or she moves according to the tools' function, and they change the world according to values that are alien to the worker. The worker may be liberated if he or she takes possession of the factory, makes it move according to his or her function, and changes the world in accordance with his or her own values. Such an analysis, so extremely important for the understanding of historical processes, is useless where an apparatus is concerned (a post-historical situation).

It is just as wrong to say that an operator moves according to an apparatus as that an apparatus moves according to an operator: the function is the constant relation, and both apparatus and operator are variables. It is just as true to say that the photographer sees the scene according to his apparatus as that he or she uses the apparatus according

1. In all his English texts Flusser always uses the Latin *apparatus* for both singular and plural. The *Oxford English Dictionary* also accepts *apparatus* as both singular and plural in English. In my translations of his work I have kept this form, so for the sake of consistency, we are keeping it the same here. E.N.

to his or her vision. In fact, the two statements are synonymous. It is nonsense to say that the apparatus *enslaves* the operator (as does a tool that is served by humans), as it is nonsense to say that the apparatus *liberates* the operator (as does a tool that serves humans), because apparatus and operator serve each other. Therefore, the very notion of a *revolution* against an apparatus is nonsense.

The explanation is that an apparatus is a tool in a radically new sense: it is not meant to change the world but to produce technical images, images of concepts indirectly concerning the world. An apparatus is a tool designed to change not what a code means but the code. And also, the operator is human in a radically new sense of that term: he or she is not an *actor* (*homo faber*) but a functionary. The operator does not want to change the world but to have a career. All the classical analyses of *work* no longer apply to the new situation because it is a post-historical situation: it demands a new anthropology and a new definition of *freedom* because the operator is a *new human* and the apparatus is a *new condition*.

This new situation is illustrated as follows:

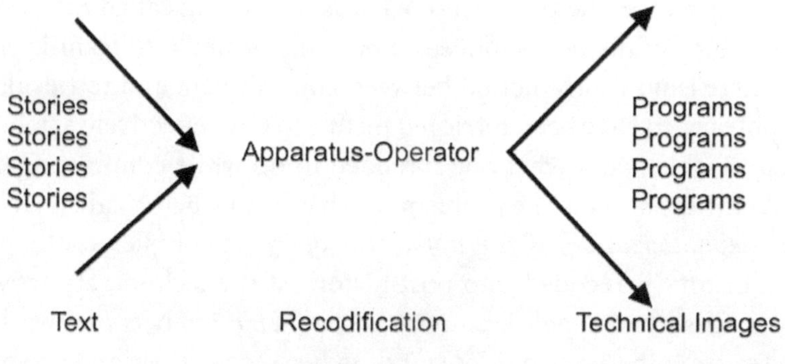

SKETCH 2.2.3.2.A

The sketch shows that the *apparatus-operator* complex is one that devours texts and spits out technical images, one that devours history and spits out post-history. History flows into the complex in the form of texts (scientific, political, and artistic discourses) and is there recodified into post-historical programs (amphitheatrically radiated films, posters, TV programs). But the sketch shows that this transformation of history into post-history is neither *human* nor *inhuman*: the *apparatus-operator* complex is a synthesis of tool and human, and in this sense *transhuman.* This is probably the most revolutionary (and most perturbing) aspect of our crisis: it transgresses human dimensions.

The whole of history flows at present into the *apparatus-operator* complex: every commitment to politics and science, philosophy and the arts is at present a commitment to the *apparatus-operator* complex: the complex sucks it in. Thus, sketch 2.2.3.2. may be read from both sides. If read from left to right, from the point of view of history, the *apparatus-operator* complex is seen as the ultimate aim of history, as the *fullness of time*, as *utopia*, as the *Kingdom of Heaven*, as the *communist society.* If read from right to left, from the point of view of post-history, the *apparatus-operator* complex is seen as the immortal memory of history; it permits Caesar and the landing on the moon to be contemplated over and over again on television. But of course, both readings are fundamentally only one: the ultimate aim of history is to become a TV program.

If one observes sketch 2.2.3.2. somewhat closer (which is good training in technical imagination), one can see several aspects of our situation: for instance, the problem of what is now being called *retrieval.* If the tendency of history is indeed to be transformed into technical images, there is no contradiction between commitment and retrieval. On the contrary, to have been retrieved means to have effectively acted. But of course, this is not what one intended to do while committing oneself. Another aspect is the problem of what is now being called *technocratic depoliticization.* If the *apparatus-operator* complex is the place where history is recoded into post-history, if the technocrats are seen as operators, then *depoliticization* and *politicization* become two sides of the same coin, the two sides standing between history and program. The more politics are at the disposal of the apparatus, the more can the operators depoliticize, which means the better are their programs. But this is not what one intends if one is politically committed. And we could continue to describe such aspects of the sketch.

But the primary purpose of the sketch at this point is not to analyze the Buddhist monks who burn themselves to death in front of TV cameras, the committed philosophers who publish in illustrated magazines, or the *pure scientists* who work at different foundations. The main purpose at this point is to help answer the question, How did technical images *slip* from the elite into mass communication? And this is the now obvious answer: They were sucked into the *apparatus-operator* complex during the process of sucking in technical discourse. Cathode tubes became TV boxes, and photographs became posters, not because the scientists and the artists (the elite) handed them over to the manipulators of mass media but because the scientists and artists (the whole elite) were devoured by the apparatus and became operators. In other words, their own creature devoured them.

It has now become possible to attempt a description of the function of technical images. There is a tendency, inherent in the structure of texts, to become autonomous from the images for the explanation of which they were originally invented. Thus, they tend to become ever more conceptual and less imaginable. They tend toward a critical point when they become meaningless (a series of empty concepts). The world codified by such texts becomes a paranoiac prison. This critical point was reached by part of the Western elite around the mid-nineteenth century, and it is reached individually by each one of us over and over again as soon as we lose faith and interest in explanations, theories, ideologies, in sum, in history and progress. This crisis manifests itself by the fact that, while reading texts, one no longer sees *the world* (the image they mean) but the intention of the author. The texts revolve somehow about their axis in such critical moments; they become opaque for meaning and transparent for their convention. They no longer mediate but obstruct communication. (To see an *ideology* behind the Bible, Marx, Darwin, and Freud implies that those texts are devoid of meaning because what they ought to mean is an image of the world.)

As soon as that critical moment is reached, the danger arises of falling into the abyss of absurdity, of a life without meaning, because the world becomes inaccessible to reason and imagination (Wittgenstein, Kafka). This is so because human communication, which gives the world and life in it a meaning, threatens to fall to pieces. One faces solitude and the void (Heidegger, Sartre). And this point can be reached not only by those who *read too well* (by an elite especially alienated from the world by texts that have become opaque) but equally by those who *read too much* (by the masses who are inundated by the waves of printed matter that becomes meaningless through devaluating inflation). Thus, the feeling that the codes surrounding us no longer mean anything spread, and the climate of absurdity became a social phenomenon in the first half of the twentieth century, especially in Europe.

There are several things one may do in such a crisis. One may burn texts and thus try to open the way toward *magical imagination* (Nazism). One may withdraw into individual and collective solitude, into what can be called *the silent majority* (*whatever cannot be spoken about must be silenced*). One may act as if one still believed in texts and in progress (the *left* between the two world wars). And there are several other methods to try to avoid the crisis. But they are not very good methods for the following reason: What has been done cannot be undone. Nazism is not *good magic*; it is bad faith because one cannot will belief in imagination. The refusal to participate is not *contemplation* but irresponsibility because one cannot will belief in withdrawal. And, most tragically, the commitment to reason, to progress, to the values of humanism is not *revolutionary* but reactionary because one cannot will belief in explanations. In sum, all those methods to avoid the crisis by denying it have proven to be bad methods because it is impossible to reconquer a naïveté once one has lost it.

But there is a different method for overcoming the crisis of texts turned meaningless, explanations turned empty, progress turned automatic and autonomous of human decisions, and life turned senseless. It is the method of stepping back from texts, from history, and of attempting to give it a meaning. It is the method not of deciphering meanings but of deliberately projecting meanings (Husserl's *Sinngebung*). It is an effort to build bridges between the texts (the theories, the ideologies) humans no longer believe in and humanity, which has alienated itself from its own explanations: an effort to produce images that mean the by-now-empty concepts and thus inject meaning into them from outside; an effort to make models; an effort no longer to conceive (to think linearly) but to imagine concepts (to think structurally); an effort not to ask what history means (where it comes from, where it goes, how it may be explained) but to ask what history may be made to mean; an effort, not to change history from within (by action) but from without (by recodification). In sum, it is the method of technical imagination.

All this is very difficult to formulate because it happens on a level of consciousness accessible only in rare moments. Still, since the second half of the nineteenth century one has been able observe unmistakable tendencies in such a direction. Those tendencies (in philosophy and the arts, in politics and the various sciences, and in new disciplines such as cybernetics) indicate that indeed a new level of consciousness is being elaborated. This is, then, the function of technical images; this is what they are essentially made for: to bridge the gap between humans and conceptual thinking, to consolidate a new level of consciousness and of existence, to create a new mode of communication and therefore a new society and a new human. In sum, the function of technical images is to serve technical imagination.

But of course, this is not what they are doing. Although they were born of technical imagination, they function to stifle it and to kill it before it is fully born. Since technical images have begun to pour into our situation, they have been forming a multicolored glittering surface that covers our crisis instead of mediating with concepts. And now, when they dominate the scene, they tend to make second-grade illiterates of us. The explanation for this inversion of the function of technical images lies hidden within the *apparatus-operator* complex, in their method of production. It is this point that needs analysis if one is to grasp why technical images function as they do and not as they were originally meant to; why instead of producing a new level of consciousness, they tend to produce unconsciousness; and instead of producing a *new human*, they produce the operator and the consumer.

But before such an analysis is attempted, it is necessary to insert another sort of consideration because we are not yet fully programmed by technical images; if we were, there would be no crisis. Instead, all the three codes discussed in this chapter coexist in our program. Our consciousness is the result of programs received in technical images, in texts, and in images of the traditional type, and these programs are very often in conflict. This conflict is how we experience the present crisis. Therefore, it is necessary to insert a consideration of the conflict between codes before technical imagination (the motive, aim, and hope of this book) can be meaningfully considered.

2.2.4. Code Synchronization

If *program* is defined as the sum of information stored in a memory and the way that information is stored, then the present crisis may be approached as a conflict in our programs. We are being constantly informed, and we store information to be able to experience, understand, and evaluate the world; to retransmit information to others; and to produce new information during the exchange. Information comes in codes, and each code has a specific decoding method, which implies a special method for the storing of information. At present, most information comes in technical image codes, but many still come in linear codes, and some basic ones come in traditional image codes. Of course, there are a great many other codes that carry our information, but the present study does not consider them because they are not characteristic of the present crisis. Therefore, the question to be asked is, How do the three codes under consideration integrate to form our programs?

This implies three questions: How are images and texts integrated? traditional and technical images? texts and technical images? For instance, how are paintings and printed books integrated? and paintings and photographs? and printed books and photographs? It has become apparent in the course of the preceding analysis that those are not only formal questions, which have to do only with the manipulation of media: How can I insert paintings in printed books or texts in films? They are seen to be existential questions: How can I integrate my imaginary and conceptual experience, my conceptual and my technical imaginary evaluation? Indeed, those are the questions now often called *search for identity.* The point of view assumed here permits approaching this sort of question from an analysis of codes, and not, as usual, from an analysis of the *self,* of psychoanalysis, and so forth.

A few obvious answers to those questions are discussed in the next sections: (2.2.4.1.) Traditional images may *illustrate* texts, and texts may *describe* traditional images (examples are illustrated school books and picture galleries); (2.2.4.2.) traditional images may absorb technical images, and technical images may use traditional ones as elements (examples are *hyperrealism* and TV programs about paintings); and (2.2.4.3.) texts may *prescribe* technical images, they may *describe* them, they may use them, they may be incorporated in them, and there are several combinations of text and technical image that have not yet been fully explored (examples are film scripts, film critiques, sketches in scientific texts, texts on the TV screen, and surface projections of arithmetic equations).

It becomes obvious if one contemplates those examples that what is here involved has to do with existential levels: where a film critic stands in relation to a scriptwriter, or a designer of comic strips in relation to a writer of explanatory texts on a photographic exhibition. This is not, let it be repeated, only a technical question: What has a museum director to do in the present situation, or how can an art gallery compete with the shop windows that surround it, or what relation is there between a cover and the contents of a best-seller? On the contrary, those technical questions arise because the conflict between the three types of codes is unresolved and because it is an existential conflict.

2.2.4.1. Traditional Image/Text

The dialectical tension between image and concept, magical and historical action is, as previously argued, the basic theme of history in the strict sense of the term. Linear texts were originally invented to describe images, and thus served as a function of images, but the relation of this function proved to be reversible, and images were soon used according to texts. The drama of this sometimes-violent tension between image and text, the iconoclastic fanaticism of Byzantine scribes and Protestant preachers, and the incineration of books by second-degree magicians like the Nazis can still be felt even now when both traditional images and texts are being overshadowed by the new codes. And it can be felt in the program within each of us. In a sense, each one of us is programmed for idolatry and iconoclasm. The conflict is unresolved even now when it is no longer very *operative* because traditional images have become marginal.

The oscillation of the relation between text and image (texts explaining images on Mesopotamian tiles, and images explaining texts on medieval manuscripts) provides an avenue of access to the understanding of historical periods. Church windows are a symptom of the effort to render texts imaginary (to translate the Bible into a magical, ritual context), while the illustrations in nineteenth-century school primers are symptoms of the effort of alphabetization (to translate images into writing). The image at the service of texts (for instance, *committed art*) and the text at the service of images (for instance, prayer books) can be taken as examples of the historical conflict: the image *sacrificing* itself for reason, and reason as the handmaid of imagination.

But for us, the same oscillation goes on against the background of omnipresent technical images and thus has changed its impact. In fact, we can no longer distinguish very well between *illustration* and *description* because traditional images are being *reproduced* by technical images and thus no longer mean what they did before the revolution in communication. A reproduction of a church window in an illustrated book no longer means what the window meant, an effort to translate the Bible into the world of magic. It now means an *imaginary museum*, the concept of a church window. And if we do get at *original images* (which are traditional in the sense here employed precisely because they are avant-garde), the problem of *originality* overshadows the problem of the conflict between imagination and conceptual thinking. The *aesthetic* aspect of images predominates in a situation where images are no longer important codes of communication and where imagination has degenerated.

This does not imply that the conflict has become of secondary importance. It implies only that it has changed: as technical images push traditional images into hidden corners of the codified world and our programs (as they now hang on the walls of forgotten galleries and forgotten tunnels of our consciousness, like the world of dreams), the conflict between imagination and conception becomes one between two *alienations*. Since images have become opaque for the *world* (hallucinations) and texts have become opaque for *images* (empty concepts), the conflict between them has become a mirroring of mirrors. A beautiful example of this is the analysis of dreams by Freudian and related texts: imagination at the service of conception at the service of imagination at the service of conception. The further such a mirroring goes on, the less the concepts *mean* (the concepts of psychoanalysis may be taken to be examples of unimaginable concepts) but also the less the images *mean* (analyzed dreams are dreams emptied of their meaning). The same may be said of art criticism, and the opposite may be said of surrealism and similar battlegrounds between imaginary and conceptual thinking. Art criticism, like psychoanalysis, is a destruction of the meaning of images by empty concepts. And surrealism and similar methods are a destruction of meanings of concepts by hallucinatory images. In short, the conflict between image and text, between imagination and theory, as it goes on at present against the background of a world codified by technical images, has a surrealistic flavor: it goes on somewhere in the *depth* of our program.

This rather ominous change in the climate of the historical conflict can be grasped if we compare Leonardo da Vinci with science fiction. At the point when printing was invented and the victory of concept over image became a real possibility, Leonardo tried to save imagination by establishing a balance between image and concept in what he called *fantasia essata*. He projected a science in which acoustics would not be an analysis of concepts like wavelength but of images like birds singing, and still be *exact* in the sense of linearly progressive and measurable by scales. Leonardo failed and Galileo won because *mental experiments* are far easier to codify in print than is *fantasia essata*. Present-day science fiction—which is an effort to *imagine the future of scientific discourse* and which occurs at the point when the victory of the technical image over concept becomes a real possibility—is the very opposite of Leonardo's project. Science-fiction images are not *technically imaginative*; they do not mean concepts; rather, they are conceptualizations of empty images: *fantasia inessata*. The machines of Jules Verne are the opposite of those projected by Leonardo: texts, not images, and aiming at past images, not future texts. They show the hallucinatory side of the image/text conflict.

2.2.4.2. Traditional Image/Technical Image

When photography was invented, it looked like the end of the traditional image. Technical images seemed to be better than traditional ones (more *objective*) and easier to make (an apparatus did it). Later, it looked as if technical images would *liberate* traditional ones from their slavery: they no longer *served to transmit information* (technical images did that better) but to *create information* (they could become *aesthetic*, *pure*, *abstract*, and so forth). Later still, when it was discovered that technical images could be as free as traditional ones and that they are not less *subjective*, it looked like a competition between the two types of image: photography, film, and video became *art forms*.

Of course, it looked like that only for those who did not know what technical images are made for, that they are made to mean concepts, not scenes, as traditional images are. Those who knew this, the specialists in branches of the scientific discourse (physicists and archaeologists, astronomers and biologists), used technical images without any reference to traditional ones to imagine concepts. And if they used traditional images (drawings of specimens seen under the microscope, of geological or geographical forms seen through the telescope), they never had any doubt about what they were doing: using imagination in the service of technical imagination, making an image of a technical image. In other words, elitist technical images have always been accepted to stand on a different level from that of traditional images, and there was no conflict of consciousness, no confusion between imagination and technical imagination.

On the level of mass communication, however, the conflict may be said to assume grotesque forms. The incapacity to distinguish between imagination as the capacity to grasp the world through images, and technical imagination as the capacity to grasp concepts through images, is at the bottom of what is being called very commonly *the crisis of the arts*, and it would be ridiculous, were it not so fateful. It is fateful, not only because it covers up the true impact of the present revolution (as long as there are video artists, and as long as there is an *art department* in advertising businesses, the meaning of the technical image codes will remain obscure) but even more so because it leads to a confusion of codes in relation to the medium that carries it (of film and cinema, of video and television).

One gets the impression, if one becomes a victim of such confusion, that the present amphitheaters (mass media) were made for technical images and that technical images were made to be radiated. However, one knows better. There are textual mass media (such as the press) and technical images that are not being radiated (such as electroencephalograms). Also, one gets the wrong impression that traditional imagination is in a crisis because traditional images cannot be radiated but are condemned to be published in archaic structures.

What is so fateful about this confusion is not that it asks the wrong questions but that it cannot ask the right questions. For instance, one asks whether an artist should commit himself or herself to the mass media, whether one can make *artistic TV programs*, whether one can organize *cultural activities* with the help of or against mass media, what may be done to detour mass media from their sinister purpose (for instance, project films onto buildings or make video exhibitions), and how the *town furniture* such as advertising posters, traffic signs, and shop windows may be rendered more human. These sorts of questions (which can be continued ad nauseam) are wrong not because they lack interest but because they conceal what is essential. No doubt, those who ask such questions are not only motivated by ideology (*fight the system*) but also existentially (if they do not penetrate the media, they will stay unemployed), but their questions leave the *masses* unconcerned, which is proof that they are indeed the wrong questions because they do not concern the present crisis.

The fateful aspect of all of this is that the good questions cannot be formulated as long as one confuses imagination with technical imagination, and traditional image with technical image. Here are some of the good questions as they appear the moment the distinction is made conscious: What are the changes required in TV to render the technical images effective, as they are in university closed circuits? How can a cinema be changed into a school by conscious use of technical images? Can politics be lifted from the conceptual to the technical image level by rendering amphitheaters dialogical? Can traditional images and technical images clash (not formally as in reproductions but existentially like a photograph and a drawing of the structure of a crystal)? What can be done to do away with the distinction between *art*, *science*, and *politics* by consciously employing technical images in theatrical structures like schools and traditional images in amphitheatrical structures like political meetings? Those are only rudimentary questions, and they can be endlessly continued.

In sum, as long as mass technical images are given over to *artists* and *programmers*, and as long as elite technical images are given over to specialists, one cannot begin to ask the good questions about the relation between image and technical image. A *theory of technical imagination* is needed, but before such a theory is elaborated, we must be content with the tragicomic conflict between *artists* and with tragicomic events such as film festivals and video-art exhibitions.

2.2.4.3. Text/Technical Image

The *apparatus-operator* complex, which transforms texts into technical images, is at the core of the conscious discussion on the relation between text and technical image at the elite level. It is often analyzed from the epistemological approach, however. The belief that knowledge is a meeting between the knower and the known (between an astronomer and a star within a telescope) has long been challenged. Most are inclined to believe instead that the *observation* within the apparatus is the primary factor (*knowledge*) and that the astronomer becomes a *knower* and the star a *known* only after the observation. No doubt, such a belief is a symptom of a radically new form of consciousness; it makes of *subject* and *object* (the knower and the known) an abstraction of a concrete relation (knowledge) and places them at the extreme limits of such a relation (it turns them into *borderline situations*). *Subject* and *object* become almost empty concepts, and the traditional dichotomy *realism-idealism* (who comes first, the star or the astronomer?) becomes an empty quarrel. In sum, the meaning of the concepts *knower* and *known* (astronomer and star) becomes dependent on their relation (the telescope).

If one broadens the epistemological approach to include other, for instance, communicological, aspects, the radicalness of the change in thinking becomes even more apparent. For instance, the question, Where is the star I observe through the telescope? then becomes meaningless. Since the star is concrete only as part of a relation and is an empty concept outside it, the star is *within the relation*, which means *within the telescope* (although the term *within* now acquires a different meaning from the one it has in traditional discourse). And the same applies to the question, Where and what am I while observing a star? I am an astronomer if and only if I enter into the concrete relation of *star observation*, and outside that relation I am somewhere else and something different, depending on the relation I participate in. And an *absolute I*, one outside all relations, is an empty concept, which implies, of course, that I am an *astronomer* within the telescope, a *man* within society, a *father* within the family, a *consumer* within the economy, and outside these relations, these *apparatus* show that *I* is an empty concept, a mental construction, a theoretical point of coincidence of all those concrete relations.

It now becomes clearer why this definition of *apparatus* is being proposed: a tool for technical image production. A photograph of a star made in a telescope is a *technical image* in the sense that it injects meaning into the empty concept *star*, and by doing this, it gives the empty concept *I* a related meaning; that photograph does not mean a *scene* (as did Ptolemaic drawings) but a concept, and every astronomer knows it. In fact, it is because the astronomer knows so that he is an astronomer. The astronomer is a functionary of the telescope because he is what he is due to the technical images he produces within the apparatus. And this is true for telescopes and for the film industry, for banks and for political parties, in sum, for every apparatus. With this qualification, it is only on the level of elite communication, on the level of scientific apparatus, that the functionary is aware of this.

Still, the apparatus has been built for a purpose. The telescope is an apparatus for star observations. It was built in the belief that there are stars to be observed, which is true for all apparatus; they were constructed in the belief that they are useful *for* something, not in the belief that everything is *their* function. Somehow, and in a way that is still obscure, apparatus have escaped their original purpose, turned it around, destroyed the belief they were based on and made for, and created a new belief, which is a way of saying that apparatus somehow turned history around and recodified it. They are products of history and produce post-history: technical images, which seem to be a myth until one remembers that apparatus are not a god-like invasion of history from without but a complex that contains human operators and is a human product. It may be *transhuman* in the sense that it is *more than an assembly of humans*, but it may also be *subhuman* in the sense that it is *less than human*.

To say that apparatus are a product of history is to say that they are a product of texts (mostly scientific ones). And to say that they produce technical images is to say that they project meanings into texts. Thus, it would seem that apparatus have circular functions; they devour texts to give them meaning, and they give meaning to texts in order to devour them. A circular time seems to structure the function of apparatus, similar to the time that structures images. And in fact, technical images are a species of the class *image*, and the time experience within the apparatus is a species of the class *eternal recurrence*, but there is a difference. The circularity of apparatus is one of reinforcing feedback, and as long as there are texts not yet devoured (history not yet recodified), they will continue to grow stronger. This circularity is not of a wheel but of a whirlpool.

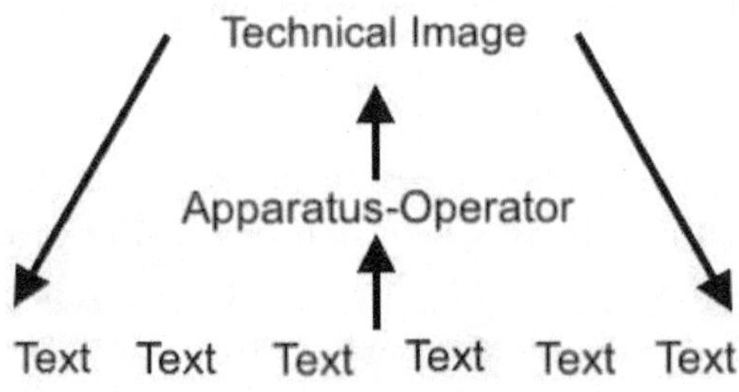

SKETCH 2.2.4.3

This sketch can be interpreted thus: Specific texts have resulted in telescopes and astronomers. That complex makes photographs of stars. Those photographs produce further texts, they give the life of the photographer a meaning, and they attract other texts in their surroundings. This leads to an improvement of telescopes, of photographs, and of the functions of the *apparatus-operator* complex. Second interpretation: Specific texts have resulted in film cameras and film operators. That complex makes films. Those films produce further texts (film critiques), they give the life of the operator a meaning, and they attract other texts in their surroundings (film scripts). This leads to an improvement of cameras, films, and the *apparatus-operator* complex. The difference between the two interpretations is that astronomers are operators who are conscious of their functions, while film operators (such as technocrats, party apparatchiks, and so forth) believe that they are committed to history, to texts, and thus are unconscious of their function.

The sketch illustrates the relation between text and technical image as one of circular progress. The apparatus sucks in texts in order to be progressively translated into technical images, which produce new texts. Or concepts are being progressively translated into technical images in order to produce new concepts. This is a radically new concept (and technical image) of *progress*, which is no longer linear: no longer does history advance toward the future but is being sucked into a vortex to become a program that again will provoke history to be sucked in. As long as people do not become conscious of their function within that vortex, the two concepts of *progress*, the historical and the post-historical, will not be distinguished. People will serve *progress* in the new sense while believing that they serve *progress* in the old sense, which, of course, renders *progress* in the new sense even more rapid. Sketch 2.2.4.3. serves as a technical image of *progress* in the new sense.

This circular progress, which may be defined as the tendency of texts toward translation into technical images, or as the tendency of history toward a new code, results in the progressive reinforcement of apparatus and the progressive transformation of humans into operators. Since the progress is circular, it does not matter whether texts are intended for technical images or technical images for texts (what the *commitment* of the participants in progress is); it will always result in apparatus reinforcement. There is, of course, a theoretical limit to this progress: a situation in which all available texts have been devoured, all of humankind has become operators, all of history has been digested, and a perfect universal and autonomous apparatus has been established. Such an ultimate situation of eternal repetition of the same programs on TV screens, of a life of pure contemplation (because to *operate* will then mean to *consume*), such a *society of saints* can be avoided only if people become aware of what they are doing, if they learn the new code.

It does not seem to be so difficult to understand the relation between text and technical image, and thus distinguish between the two meanings of *progress*. Astronomers know how to do it; an astronomer looking at the photograph of a star does not see an image of a star but a spot on a chemical surface. He knows the texts that permitted the surface to be produced and the texts that *expect* the spot he sees if certain conditions are present. He *interprets* the spot he sees as follows: This is an image that gives meaning to the concept *star* in some texts, and it gives this concept a very specific meaning. Other technical images, for instance, spectral analyses, will give the same concept *star* a different meaning. Thus, the concept becomes meaningful within the technical image; it *aims* at the image. However, the spot on the chemical surface means a different concept in different texts (for instance, it may mean the concept *chemical transformation*). The meaning of the spot depends on the text to which it is applied. In this sense, the meaning *aims* at the text. *Progress* is not linear but a sort of oscillation between levels of meanings and is dependent on interpretation.

If the astronomer stands so firmly on the level of consciousness corresponding to technical imagination, why should it be so difficult for us to climb to it every time we are exposed to technical image programming? The reason is simple: the astronomer (and other such specialists) is an operator of a very specific apparatus, one that produces technical images for *inner consumption*. In fact, he receives the photograph he is emitting; he decodes what he himself has been codifying. Elite technical images are inserted within the specialized dialogues that make up the scientific and technological discourse. They are part of the hermetic codes that serve for elitist communication. Astronomers are on the level of consciousness of technical imagination only in regard to their specialty because they were programmed for that very special sort of technical imagination. They are just as unable as the rest of us to decipher other types of technical images (X-ray photographs of broken arms, economic statistics, etc.), and they behave in cinemas and in front of TV sets exactly as we do. Their hold on technical imagination is slippery: the moment they leave their telescope, they slip back into linear thinking and become mass human beings.

It would look as if we could escape from utopia if we were able to transfer technical imagination from the elite level (where the technical images are being produced) into the mass level (where they program us). But such a transfer would involve much more than an *epistemological effort*. The astronomer may dispose of technical imagination in his specialty, but it is technical imagination with regard to knowledge only. What is involved, however, is *total technical imagination*, imagination not only of scientific texts but also of all the concepts of all the texts that make up history and *progress* in the old sense. Utopia could be avoided if we were able to develop technical imagination in what is now called the scientific, the political, and the aesthetic realms, in short, if we could develop it in our daily lives and if it became our level of existence. It is this the students of May 1968 had in mind when exclaiming *l'imagination au pouvoir!*, and if it was not this, it should have been. And that is, of course, not easy.

This is then the relation between texts and technical images in our programs at present: On the level of elite communication texts and technical images complete each other; they *aim* at each other. Technical images give texts very specific meanings, and they provoke new texts. It is not a question of technical images *illustrating* texts, and texts *describing* technical images, as is the case in traditional image-text relations: there is feedback between the two codes that lifts texts to the level of technical imagination. But this works as it does only within the closed circuits of hermetic dialogues in technology and science.

On the level of mass communication, apparatus are progressively devouring all the texts in order to be recoded as technical images. This is a case of absorption of conceptual thought by technical image codes to be radiated and to program receivers that have no technical imagination: a case of progressive destruction of conceptual thought, of historical reason, of linear consciousness, and of passive reception of opaque yet effective programs. The result is a progressive strengthening of the *apparatus-operator* complexes that radiate the programs.

The final part of the book considers technical imagination somewhat closer. But it may be concluded even at this stage of the discussion of our crisis that if the present tendency continues as it does currently, all texts will continue to be sucked into the apparatus vortex, linear codes will be *overcome*, and humanity will fall into functioning. And if technical imagination develops into a consciousness that gives meaning to empty concepts by recodifying them, which gives a new meaning to history, we stand on the threshold of a situation that cannot be as yet either conceived or imagined. We are facing either second-degree illiteracy or a new level of consciousness: this seems to be the challenge our situation poses.

3
WHAT IS TECHNICAL IMAGINATION?

• • • In the course of this book, an attempt has been made to define the term *technical image* and thus, implicitly, the term *technical imagination*. If one considers, however, the almost incredible variety of multicolored surfaces that have surrounded us since the Second World War, any attempt at a unifying definition seems misplaced. The multitude of colored symbols that press upon us from street posters and shop windows, from the walls of buildings and public places, from books and TV sets, from textiles and beverages, from tools and gadgets appear to have nothing in common. No doubt, in comparison with the gray uniformity of industrial societies ours has a *style* the powerful breadth of which may be felt in all those manifestations, and nineteenth-century thinkers used to call this *the spirit of the time*. It may be said that this *style* (the first true style in Western civilization since Gothic) is what is common to all the otherwise heterogeneous elements of our codified world. Yet that is an insufficient common denominator: the moment we try to grasp the style common to a plastic bag containing a hot dog and a photograph of the trace left by a particle within the Wilson chamber, we lose it.

There are various possibilities to *define* what is happening in our surroundings and thus grasp what is at the bottom of the apparently bewildering chaos. For instance, one may say that we are in a process of *Americanization* or that we have reached a point where the products of culture conceal nature and thus tend to become a second-degree nature (trash). Again, ours is a mass civilization, and the *style* of the objects surrounding us proves this. And other such generalizations may be advanced to permit a more penetrating view of the explosion we are in, a view of the core of the explosion.

Each of such tentative generalizations has its justification. Indeed, we are *Americanizing* if we decide to call the consumption of colorful ice creams and plastic pens *American* and if we decide that the relative drab uniformity of the *socialist* countries is a symptom of their backwardness due to resistance to Americanization. But then we will have used the term *America* as meaning *the place where the present revolution started*, and we will not have advanced very far toward the essence of that revolution. Indeed, we may say that civilization is becoming pollution if we decide to consider the colorful heaps of cars and station wagons a sort of eczema on the skin of beaches. But then we will not have grasped the essence but one of the effects of the present revolution. Indeed, we may call our lifestyle *Pop* and say that such is the style of mass people, as the Renaissance is the style of the bourgeoisie, and Gothic the style of the clergy. But if we call Manhattan *Pop*, as we call Florence *Renascent* and Toledo *Gothic*, we will have grasped a manifestation of the present revolution (albeit an important one), not what propels it. Such generalizations each have their truth, and they are necessary if we are to understand what is going on, but they are not sufficient.

This book is advancing yet another, but quite different, sort of generalization. It proposes to look at the explosion of gadgets and public happenings of programs and cosmic consumption, not as if it were primarily a politico-economic phenomenon (*Americanization*), or primarily an economic phenomenon with biological and psychological disastrous effects (*ecological pollution*), or primarily a socio-aesthetic phenomenon (*Pop* lifestyle), but as a radical change in the codes that inform us. It considers the multicolored surfaces of buildings and traffic signs, posters and Coke bottles, socks and pajamas to be messages just as much as are the maps in atlases and the statistical curves in scientific publications. And it suggests that what is essential to the present explosion around us is that the surfaces, and no longer the lines, as before the

First World War, inform us and program us; that we experience, know, and evaluate the world we live in through messages received through surface codes instead of written or printed texts; and that this is the fundamental reason we are now immersed in a sea of colors and gadgets—because we are no longer being programmed by texts printed in black on white pages but by technical images that beam in Technicolor.

This is not to claim the approach here proposed is *better* than any other. It is only to suggest it may be worthwhile to follow the direction in which it is pointing. Even if no claim about the superiority of the method proposed over any other is made, it cannot be denied that the preceding chapters have tried to show that an approach to the current crisis from the perspective of communication may reveal very characteristic aspects. Thus, if the method here proposed is not *better* than any other, it certainly is not *worse* than any other.

There is no need to stress the radicalness of the thesis here submitted. If seen as a crisis in communication (and especially one of recodification), our situation does not appear as *merely* an economic, social, political, cultural, epistemological, or religious revolution; it appears as the *end of history* in the strict sense of that term. Not *merely* all the traditional categories of knowledge, evaluation, and experience are being questioned but also human existence in its traditional form; not *merely* science, the arts, politics, and religion are in a turmoil but also the very meaning of these terms and their distinction from each other; not *only* is there a generalized mental confusion, but an entire mental level is being abandoned. In sum, if one approaches the present crisis from the point of view of communication, it does not appear as *merely* a revolution but as a mutation.

This implies, among other things, that most of the problems confronting us in everyday life (in newspapers and books, in dialogues and in our activities, not only in the evidently alienating mass media) are somehow *false* problems. They concern situations that are about to radically change and are thus strictly no longer valid. However, we are having difficulty seeing the *true* problems, those concerning imminent new situations, and thus posing the really important questions. Thus, the hypothesis here advanced may be seen as an effort to hesitantly formulate some really important questions.

Such radicalness is intolerable and looks suspiciously like the numerous irresponsible apocalyptic prophecies that abound at present, as they do in every critical situation. But it does not look apocalyptic at all if compared with what is called *futurology.* According to those projections of the present into the future, radioactive clouds and a poisonous atmosphere hang above our heads while we walk on earth—the mineralogical, biological, and energy reserves we are about to exhaust. Futurology has become far more apocalyptic than prophecy; if we all shall either starve to death, or choke to death, or burn to death in a not-too-distant future, why should we bother about the prophecies of doom (or of heaven on earth) about *ideological projects*?

Ideology and futurology cancel each other out; they produce apathetic indifference. One does not believe in either of them (be they Club of Rome or political party programs), because one tends to trust either the permanence of the prevailing situation or the human capacity to adjust to changing situations. But there is yet another reason for our lack of interest in prophecies and projections: we no longer seem to be able to believe in explanations.

It is against this background of generalized apathy and lack of interest in explanations that the radicalness of the present hypothesis should be seen. If it wants to avoid the barrenness inherent in current ideology and futurology, it must become responsible, capable of being responded to in a way that may change its prognostics. The radicalness here proposed is thus meant as a challenge: What can we do about our situation if it is seen the way the radical analysis sees it? It is in this sense, as a proposal for future dialogue and not as a prognostication, that the following considerations about *technical imagination* should be read.

3.1. SOME TECHNICAL IMAGES DECIPHERED

Nobody is really aware of the fact that, while watching a film or television, while looking through an illustrated magazine or at a poster, while trying to follow traffic signs or instructions on a tin of pineapples, one is deciphering technical images, that what one is doing is comparable to deciphering X-ray images, economic graphs, or industrial blueprints. Everybody believes (in a rather confusing way) they are receiving messages that pose no problem for decoding. Most people, and not only naïve teenagers, believe that they can *read* a film as if it were a novel or watch it as if it were a theatrical play; or that they can *read* an illustrated magazine as if it were a book printed in a linear code or contemplate it as if it were an exhibition of paintings. People tend to approach chicken soup tins as if they were either chicken or cookbooks. Drivers tend to regard traffic signs as if they were like the names of streets (inscriptions) or like road maps. Nobody is aware of the fact that what these codes demand of their receivers is a new method of decoding, here called *technical imagination*.

This lack of awareness on the part of the receivers is responsible for the curious *pseudo-magical* climate in our codified world. It is clear neither how the symbols composing it were produced nor what they mean, and still they program us. The climate is curious because the symbols are *incomprehensible* even if we produce them (if we make photographs or videotapes), and the more they are *incomprehensible*, the more they program us. This shows that our difficulty in understanding those symbols is not a technical one but has other causes. And the climate is *pseudo-magical* because the symbols program us in spite of our ignorance of their meaning, but such ignorance of ours is not a clue to some *mysteriousness* of the symbols but to our tendency to permit them to program us. In short, our codified world is curiously *pseudo-magical* because we normally lack the will to master the codes that compose it.

There seems to be a very simple method to break through the magic circle within which we are being hypnotized by technical images: call in the specialists. Is not this what we always do when facing a problem? The operators of TV and the film industry, the manufacturers of tins, and the codifiers of traffic signs should have no trouble teaching us how to decipher their codes correctly, just as specialists in linear writing (primary schoolteachers) do with regard to their code. Unfortunately, this method does not work in practice; the specialists cannot teach us because they themselves do not know what they are doing. Very impressive proofs of the failure of such a method are *video exhibitions* in which the public is invited to *participate*, but less impressive proofs of the incapacity of operators to understand their own codes, let alone teach their receivers, can be observed everywhere: at film festivals, at international symposia, and, more dramatically, in the schools that are supposed to teach *media research* or *communication*. The following sketch illustrates how to understand this failure on the part of specialists:

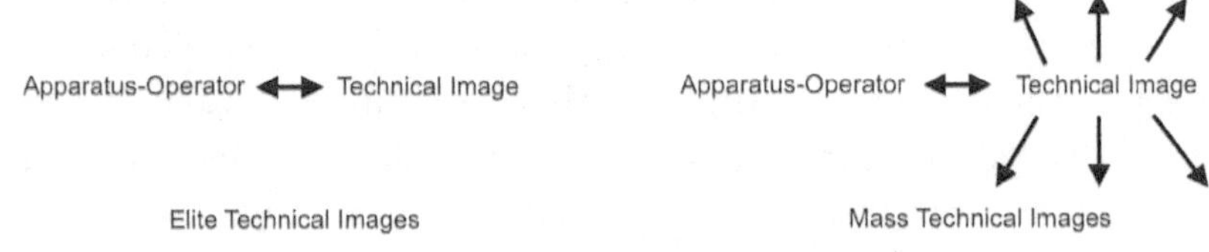

SKETCH 3.1

The specialists involved in the production of elite technical images are also their receivers, but those involved in the production of mass technical images radiate them. Or technical images on the elite level are meant for the dialogues that form the closed circuits of a tree discourse, and the technical images on the mass level are products of tree discourses meant for amphitheatrical radiation.

This implies a different relation between the specialist and the technical image on both levels of communication. Both know, of course, the apparatus within which they operate (if *to know* is to know how to handle). But the operators on the elite level also know how to use the technical image they produce, while operators on the mass level are supposed to *stand above* technical images. The nuclear physicist knows the meaning of an electronic photograph in the sense that he made that photograph for himself to have an image of a previously unimaginable concept. But the producer of a TV program or of an illustrated magazine is not supposed to *believe* in his own message (he *knows too much about it*). He is only supposed to make others believe in it. In reality, however, to *know too much* implies ignorance because it is only after reception that a message acquires meaning. In other words, operators of technical images on the elite level of communication have technical imagination, while those on the mass level do not.

Specialists cannot teach us how to decipher technical images because they do not themselves have the necessary technical imagination if they produce on the mass level, and they cannot translate their technical imagination from their restricted specialty if they produce on the elite level. Thus, we must look for a different method to break through the magic circle because we cannot accept that circle. It is intolerable to be programmed in a state of lack of awareness by operators who themselves lack awareness of what they are doing. This is intolerable, not only because such programming works very well but because it works progressively better. There is no hope that the circle will somehow crack open by itself because the lack of awareness on the part of emitters and receivers will render it absurd. On the contrary, the longer the circle gyrates, the better it functions. People were more aware of the meaning of films at the time of the Lumière brothers than they are at present.

One method to try to demythologize technical images is to observe somewhat more carefully what happens during their production. One may hope that such an observation will reveal the level of consciousness demanded of such a production. Another method is to observe what happens during reception. One may hope that such an observation will reveal how technical images program in the absence of a level of consciousness adequate for them. Both methods will be rudimentarily applied in what follows. The first method will use three examples: the production of photographs, films, and videotapes. The other will use two examples: the TV set and the cinema. Two factors must be stressed, however: What follows is a suggestion of future analyses, not an investigation. And what follows is not aimed at an understanding of the phenomena considered but at an approach to what is essential for technical images in general.

3.1.1. Photographs

Photographs are, historically, the oldest technical images. They are not exclusively *mass technical images*, in the sense of being destined for radiation in amphitheaters like magazines and posters; they can be stored in more archaic structures like albums. One may observe easily how they are being produced: it happens all over and in the open. And most of us know how to handle a photographic camera and how to make photographic pictures. The *apparatus-operator* complex, which, according to the thesis here defended so fatefully translates history into program, can be observed with ease in the case of photography: the tourist with a camera dangling against his belly. Those are some of the reasons that photographs are considered here as the first example.

The first thing that strikes an observer is that to photograph is to look for a point of view. Let us suppose that a tourist wants to take a picture of his wife standing against a cathedral. His gestures (which may be taken as motions of the *apparatus-operator* complex) show that he is looking for a position from which to take the picture. Those gestures are questions of this type: Where shall I stand and for how long shall I expose the frame if I am to fix what I am seeing on a surface prepared for that purpose? That is, of course, a question concerning the four dimensions of space-time. The photographer looks for a position within the frame of the four dimensions.

His decision with regard to such a position will depend on the following factors: on what he is seeing (the scene), on the construction of his camera (the apparatus), and on his intention (on the photograph as a symbol of communication). For instance, if the tourist wants to show how his wife smiles because he wants his children to know that their mother is happy, he will have a specific parameter of points of view at his disposal, which is different from the parameters he can choose from if he wants his children to see the cathedral behind his wife and thus educate them. If to take a picture of the smile is the purpose, the choice of the point of view will depend on factors such as the brightness of his wife's teeth, the atmospheric condition, the time of day, but also on factors such as the quality of the camera, the type of film, and filters at his disposal. Of course, the tourist will say, *smile!* to his wife and thus interfere in the *scene* he is fixing, but the wife may react and move an arm, which then becomes a possible center of interest for the photographer's intentions. And this enumeration of conflicting and interfering factors is far from exhaustive.

But it suffices to show that such a conflict is quite unrelated to the dialectics between *subject* and *object* of traditional, linear thinking. The brightness of the teeth is an *objective* factor in a sense quite different from the one in which the quality of the film is *objective*. The manipulation of the wife by the tourist when he says *smile!* is *subjective* in a sense quite different from the one in which his intention to produce an *educational* photograph is *subjective*. To ask whether a photograph is an *objective* or a *subjective* image of what it means, and to what degree it is *subjective* and *objective*, is to ask a question quite inadequate to the level of its production. It is an irrelevant question because it belongs to a level of consciousness that does not correspond to the level of image production.

The questions the photographer asks have to do with his vision of a scene, with the apparatus he is operating, with the photograph he intends to take, and with the receivers of the photograph with whom he intends to communicate. And these questions are specific motions within the four dimensions of space-time. In one of those dimensions, the photographer approaches the scene he is looking at and steps back from it. In the second dimension, he dances around the scene to experiment with various horizontal angles. In the third dimension, he leaps up and down and climbs steps or lies flat on the ground to experiment with various vertical angles. And in the fourth dimension, he manipulates the camera to experiment with various durations of exposures of the film to light rays. Of course, these four dimensions imply each other and cannot be concretely separated one from the other.

The important thing to note, however, is that they do not form a *space-time* continuum and that the *space-time* characteristic of photography is not the one we are told of in physics. The photographic *space-time* is subdivided by barriers into compartments; the photographer leaps over hedges while looking for his point of view, and he does not swim in a continuous ocean. Photographic space-time is ordered by categories quite unrelated to Kantian categories: they are specifically photographic. There is, within photographic space-time, a region for bird's-eye views and one for frog perspective; there is a region for frontal staring with wide-open archaic eyes and one for the sideways furtive glance of bad faith; there is a region for lightning-like surprise attacks and one for the patient repose of contemplation. Each such category is a specific *form of perception*, each will result in a specific existential climate on the photograph to be produced, and each is determined by the view the photographer has, by his camera, by his intention with regard to the future photograph and future receptors. It is the sum total of such regions that make up the universe in which the photographer moves to make his decisions. To ask what sort of *ideological world vision* this universe is, is to ask a quite irrelevant question: it is proof of lack of technical imagination.

This photographic world vision manifests itself in the motions of photographing; the photographer leaps from conclusion to conclusion; his movements are abrupt; they have a *quantic* structure. The camera does not permit the photographer to *travel*, to swim, and to float as do the film and video cameras; he cannot *suspend decision*. He is conditioned by his apparatus to leap from one point to the next while searching, and he cannot, like a film or video operator, *suspend* (which means *doubt*) all the possible points of view before deciding. The mechanism of the photographic camera demands of its operator a series of provisional decisions before the final decision is taken, the one that will result in a photograph. The same structure can be observed in the photographic code: Although the film within the camera is a tape, the photographs produced are *clearly distinct* from each other. Every single photograph is a *clear and distinct perception*. The universe of photography has an arithmetical structure: it is quantic. Or technical imagination is, in the case of photography, an arithmetical imagination.

The function of the *apparatus-operator* complex can be observed while watching the photographer's gestures. It can be called one of *functional decisions*. It is a miniature of *technocracy* if by that term is meant the functioning of operators within gigantic apparatus. While looking for a point of view, the photographer moves his camera according to his search, but he searches according to the mechanism of the camera he is handling. He uses his apparatus for his decisions, but he decides regarding his apparatus. He does not move with the apparatus or against it; he does not *motivate* the apparatus, nor is he *motivated* by it. All those distinctions are categories of a level of consciousness irrelevant to the level of photographic technical imagination. On the contrary, there is a complex motion of which camera and photographer are aspects. It is neither a *human* nor a *mechanical* decision: it is a complex decision. If *freedom* should mean the capacity for effective decision-making, then the photographer is free, not through or within or in spite or against the apparatus, not due to the apparatus, which is a new level of the meaning for *freedom*.

This implies a new political level, if *politics* is still the correct term to describe this new type of search for a point of view. The historical categories of politics can no longer grasp it. The fundamental reason for this mutation is that the production in which the photographer is engaged can no longer be called *work* in any meaningful sense of the term. The photographer does not move his camera in order to change the world, as a blacksmith does by moving his hammer. He is interested in changing a code, which means, very indirectly, the world, in other words, in the production of a photograph (a symbol meaning indirectly the world). The camera is not a historical tool, one that changes the world. It is a post-historical tool, one that changes the meaning of the world. Politics as sets of values meant to change the world (as discourses saying how the world should be) are meaningless on the level of technical imagination. And so are *revolutions* in the historical sense of that term: it is meaningless to want to take *possession* of an apparatus because it is not an *object* in the sense a traditional tool is.

Still, the gesture of photographing does imply a change of the world. When the photographer tells his wife to *smile!*, when he uses filters, even when he waits for a cloud to pass before pressing his button, he may be said to be changing the world. But this cannot be called *working* in the historical sense of the term. To work, historically, means to act in a way that changes what is into what it ought to be: it is the materialization of a value. But the photographer acts in a way that changes what is into what is meant by a symbol: he is not interested in how the world is, or how it ought to be, but in making a photograph of it. Historical human beings use images and text for changing the world. The photographer changes the world in order to make a technical image of it. Technical imagination is an inversion of the historical relation between symbol and meaning. No longer does it *explain* the world in order to change it; it changes the world in order to *explain* it. Technical imagination is not *value-free* (as nineteenth-century scientism thought it would be), nor is it *beyond good and evil*, but it stands on a level that is different from historical, political, and ethical evaluation: it aims at *good* photographs of the world.

The search for a point of view and the act of changing the world are two aspects of the same motion. To search is to change the world, and to change it is to research it. If a photographer moves a curtain, he does so because he looks for a point of view behind it; and if he moves a curtain, he suddenly discovers points of view he did not look for. The fact that research changes the world it aims at is an obvious datum on the level of technical imagination. The enormous difficulty in accepting this fact on the level of conceptual thinking disappears on the new level. For conceptual, historical reasons, *discovery* is progressive in the sense that new regions of the world are continuously being penetrated by research. And this implies a specific concept of *truth*: a statement is *true* if it reflects what the researcher has found. Thus, progressively the amount of truth is increased by research. All this is meaningless on the level of technical imagination. The photographer does not *progress*; he goes around the scene in his search for a point of view. A photograph is not *true* if it reflects what he has found because what he finds is a point from which to make it reflect, not something to be reflected. *Truth* is not an *equalization* of knower to known but a manipulation of the thing to be known. And if research results in an increase of knowledge, it does so not because it *progresses into the world* but because it provides ever-new points of view of the same scene.

But this revolution in political and epistemological categories (in values and in the meaning of *knowledge*) cannot be appreciated without this additional observation: The true motive of the photographer's motions is to produce an image to be looked at by others. It is the future receiver of the photograph who motivates him. He looks for a point of view that might be shared with him by those who will look at his picture. His is not a search for *objective* truth and *transcendent* value; those are meaningless terms on his level. *Objectivity* is meaningless because he functions in an *apparatus-operator* complex. And *transcendence* is meaningless because, wherever he might step in his search for a point of view, and however far he might step back from the scene he is photographing, he will still be always within the world. What he looks for is *intersubjective* truth and *intersubjective* value: a point of view to be shared with him by others. Photographs are points of view meant to be shared with others, and the more they are thus shared, the *truer* they are and the *better* they are. Intersubjectivity provides radically new criteria for *knowledge* and *value* on the level of technical imagination.

Of course, if the tourist reads what has just been written, he will first stare unbelievingly, and then he will deny that it is this he is doing while photographing his wife standing in front of a cathedral. He is totally unaware of what he is doing, destroying the traditional categories of politics and science, doing away with the traditional categories of truth and goodness. If pressed to state what he is doing, he might say that all he is trying to do is to take a few pretty pictures. The lack of consciousness on the part of the operators who produce technical images is a basic problem of our crisis. But here it is more important to take seriously the claim that the motive for technical image making is aesthetic. The photographer claims in fact, if he states that his motive is pretty pictures, that the revolution in political and scientific categories that manifests itself in his motions is somehow fundamentally an aesthetic, *artistic* revolution, that in photography science and politics have somehow become artistic dimensions. Such a claim demands attention.

What does the tourist mean by *trying to make pretty pictures*? His camera disposes of a mirror. If the tourist looks into it, he sees how a picture would look if he were to press the button. He will press the button if he likes what he sees, if he thinks it is *pretty*. What he sees in the mirror is a reflection of a scene as viewed from a specific point: it is an *aspect*. But it is also a *project*: it is how future photographs might be. Therefore, it is an *aspect of the future*. The sum of all the possible mirror reflections is the universe of all possible photographs, and what the photographer sees while looking for a point of view is a specific section of the future. This is *futurology*, not prophecy, because it projects the present into the future and thus preempts the future. Prophecy is the opposite motion: it projects the future into the present and thus preempts the present. In other words, the decision of the photographer to press the button is a decision in favor of a future aspect he likes.

It has been argued in the previous chapters that what the photographer sees while looking into the mirror are images of concepts: each reflection he sees is an image of a specific concept of the image of a scene he sees if looking directly at it. Thus, the reflections in the mirror are images of a conceived future. This is what makes them *pretty*: that they are reflexive, speculative, and that they preempt the future, put it out of action. This is the beauty of technical imagination: it is the beauty of conception made image, like the beauty of a Maxwellian equation made image, or the beauty of the Declaration of Human Rights made image. In this sense, it may be said that the tourist is right; technical imagination is indeed a synthesis of science and politics on an aesthetic level. Politics and science become *art*, albeit in a radically new sense of the term.

The observation of photographing has here been restricted to very few aspects, and the whole complex of producing the material photograph has been excluded. Still, it is hoped that some categories of what is here called *technical imagination* have become more apparent and also how unaware we are of what we are doing while producing technical images, how we lack technical imagination.

3.1.2. Films

If one compares film and photographic codes, many differences are obvious: photographs are still and films move, photographs are silent and films talk, and so forth. But there is one difference that is more radical: photographs are based on manipulations of scenes, and films are based on manipulations of events; it is this difference that might explain all the others.

In a movie, pictures seem to move (and one sees that the motion is a *trompe l'oeil* if the apparatus works badly and they start leaping) because what they mean is a *story*. And the pictures *talk* (one does not only sit opposite them but is also surrounded by sound waves) because they mean an *action*. This has caused various problems for the analysis of films. How many dimensions does a film have? The two dimensions of the screen and the three dimensions of the sound waves? The time dimension of the story it tells and the time dimension of its action? No doubt, these are important questions for deciphering films. But they are not the fundamental questions.

Fundamentally, the film has two dimensions: it is a tape, a band, that contains images and traces of sounds and is thus a *technical image code*—all the other dimensions are not only *trompe l'oeil* but also *trompe l'imagination*. They are problems during reception, not directly during production, and are better dealt with when the cinema (reception of films) is under discussion. Here the production of the tape, of the band to be later projected in cinemas, is under consideration. The question here is, What characterizes this production?

It was suggested during the discussion of making photographs that it is characterized by a search for a point of view, that it is *deideologization*.

Ideology is to assume and defend a point of view; photography is to leap from one point of view to another. Photographic technical imagination is essentially post-ideological, in the sense of using and adding ideologies and thus *standing above them*. Something similar may be observed in filmmaking. Although the cameraman need not leap from conclusion to conclusion as the photographer does (his apparatus permits him to *travel*, to *zoom*, to float without any commitment to any point of view), he still uses points of view for his floating: he *doubts* all possible points of view by melting them into a fluid. The tape he produces may be considered doubt materialized, or methodical indecision, and in this sense film technical imagination, like the photographic one, stands beyond ideology, though in a slightly different direction beyond it.

But this is not what is characteristic of filmmaking: The cameraman is not the producer of films. He supplies only what can be called the *raw material* of films, tapes covered with images and sound tracks. The true film producer is an operator who stands above that tape with scissors and glue, who cuts the tape into strips and then glues them together again, in sum, an operator who transforms the tape into a film. Thus, the film producer stands on a level that permits him to look at the tape as if it were the raw material for history production and to manipulate that material in order to make a history of it. This can be called a *transhistorical* level in the strict sense of that term, and it is this level that is characteristic of film technical imagination.

While cutting and gluing the film tape, the film producer may be said to hold *linear, historical* time in his hands. The tape is a *text*, a linear code, a chain composed of distinct symbols (photographs), which are arranged like pearls on a string and may thus be *calculated* and *recounted*. But it is not a true text; it is a *pretext*. It is not meant to be read but to be fed into an apparatus that will project it. It is a pretext for technical imagination, not (like alphabetic texts) information for conceptual thinking. The film producer uses the text (historical linearity), not for action within it (as does a writer and reader) but for action upon it from without (as raw material for technical imagination).

It may be held, of course, that the place where the film producer stands is the one where *God* stands for historical, linear reason: he sees the beginning and the end of time (of the tape) and can make them coincide by sticking them together and thus transform the tape into a collar, history into a circle. But this is not a good description: The film producer makes things that the *God* of historical thinking is incapable of doing. He can repeat events, have them unroll from the future to the past; he can leap back and forth in time; he can manipulate the duration of events; in short, he can *compose time*, which is to show that the *God* of linear thinking (the Judeo-Christian one, the unmoved mover of Aristotelian philosophy, and so forth) is a historical concept, quite inadequate for grasping the technical imaginary level. The film producer, the operator within the film apparatus, is much closer to Kafka's *God* than to historical concepts of *transcendence*.

The purpose of the film producer is to compose linear time into a different one that may be projected on screens. In this he is similar to a music composer: he makes scenic harmonies, like the musical composer makes tonal harmonies. His flashbacks, slow motions, close-ups, repetitions, and so forth are methods to produce a two-dimensional time, one that does not flow in a line but informs like circles, spirals, and ellipses. This is not circular time as in magic: it is not the eternal recurrence of birth, death, and rebirth. On the contrary, it is a time when circularity is one among various possible structures. Thus, the film producer is not a sort of magician but one who shows that magic and historicity, circle and straight line, stand on the same level if seen from technical imagination. The film producer can use them both; line and circle. He can use magic for history and history for magic. And he can do so because he stands *beyond* both of them; time is out of joint for him.

This is a position that has never before been practically accessible (although, of course, as a mental exercise it begins to articulate itself in philosophy and in scientific thought as early as the late eighteenth century, in Kant, for instance). Time is out of joint for a film producer because it is a sort of time that permits acting on two different levels. There are those who act within linear time, not only the film *actors* in the strict sense but the camera operators, the scriptwriters, the whole complex of makeup specialists, designers, lighting technicians, and all the other operators who make up the film apparatus. And then there are those who act upon those actions from without with glue and scissors. And it is they who are the true film producers.

Before advancing to the obvious conclusion that the film operator is a model for post-historical operators in general (not only Adolf Eichmann, but Henry Kissinger and Siad Barre, Latin American generals, and East European apparatchiks as well), it is appropriate to ask how that operation that transforms history into raw material functions. The answer is surprisingly simple: It consists of cutting history and gluing it together again in a way that produces a *trompe l'imagination* (a movie) in the receivers. It consists of transforming history into a movie story. But nothing is achieved by calling this *bad faith* on the part of the operators. By transforming *true story* into *trompe-histoire*, this sort of recodification shows that *true history* is just as fictitious as is a *movie story* and that to commit oneself to history is pure folly. *Bad faith* with regard to history may be *good faith* with regard to human existence. And this is characteristic of film technical imagination.

This is an attempt to formulate it: For historical thinking, *to be* is *to become*, and consequently *to live* is *to act* or *to suffer*. For film technical imagination, *to become* is an illusion created by a rapid projection of distinct images upon a screen, and *to act* and *to suffer* are a result of that illusion. But this loss of faith in the *reality of the process* is not a return to the magic faith in the *reality of the situation*. A single photograph projected upon a screen is not less illusionary for technical imagination than is the whole movie. *Still frames* are just as fictitious as are *close-ups*. Technical imagination stands beyond the contradiction between situation and process.

In fact, since pre-Socratic speculations only two possible world structures (structures of the *real*) have been conceived: The real is *wave-like* (everything flows), or the real is *atom-like* (motion is an illusion). Of course, it has always been admitted that a great number of atoms may look like a wave (dunes look like waves although they are composed of sand grains) and that if one stops a wave, it looks like something fixed (the electronic waves look solid like a sand dune). But the question remained: What is *real*, the particle or the wave, the situation or the process? And Judeo-Christian historicity decided in favor of the process.

For film technical imagination the question has lost all meaning. If a series of situations is projected, they look like processes, and if a process is arrested, it looks like a situation, but neither one is *real* in any meaningful sense of that term. *History* is an unfolding of situations, and *magic* is a freezing of processes, and both are equivalent methods in film production. Anybody committed to history (an actor, a *hero*) can be made to stand still (become an idol, a god), just as anybody in a situation (an idol, a totem) can be made to move (become an actor).

One may begin to understand the function of a film operator only after having said that. He does not use actors as *puppets*; he does not use *committed idealists* for his *unconfessed purposes*: actors interest him only as raw material, but as a raw material he intends to make meaningful. He intends to inject new meaning into action by including it in a new time structure. It is a mistake to believe that the operators within the gigantic apparatus manipulate us in their own interest: they have no interest of their own at the historical level. They manipulate us to give our actions a meaning that is not ours because for them *to live* is not *to act* but *to function*.

Of course, this is a dangerous situation, more dangerous indeed than if the operators acted in *bad faith*. The only way to face it is to try to grasp it, which means to make an effort at being capable of technical imagination. And this consideration of filmmaking has intended to show that it is a very difficult effort.

3.1.3. Video

Compared with photography and film, video is a relatively new code, and the apparatus that produce it (camera, player, and monitor) are relatively expensive. Thus, a fascination emanates from the video image that has spent itself as far as photography and film are concerned. Habit has not yet made the essence of video invisible by its gray and trivializing cover.

New apparatus are fascinating for two reasons: they are unpredictable and therefore dangerous (like computers and laser beams), and they may be turned away from their original purpose. This second reason contradicts the first one in a way, but in another way it reinforces it: as the uses of new apparatus are unpredictable, one may discover unsuspected uses in them and thus turn them around (*revolution*). Motorcars used for making out are dangerous in a different and revolutionary sense from the danger they represent if used for transportation. In sum, a new apparatus is fascinating because it holds both oppressive and liberating virtualities.

The video equipment is an apparatus meant to serve television. It serves to preregister programs to be radiated and thus permit previous censorship, and it serves to register radiated programs and thus permit repetitions of broadcasts. Thus, it is meant and widely used as a medium of the TV apparatus. But there are virtualities in video equipment that permit it to be used independently of TV, and against TV, and these virtualities are slowly being discovered. Video is a fascinating apparatus because it holds a promise for revolution.

The videotape is a memory that stores information in a code that is superficially similar to the film code. But the film tape is a series of photographs manipulated by an operator to become a movie. Videotape does not permit such a manipulation; it unfolds the way it was registered in the first place. Its time dimension is quite different from film time: it is not the result of a manipulation of historical time (of *editing*), but it is a new form of repetition of history (the present is superimposed upon the past, which thus becomes background).

There is a curious similarity between videotape and sculpture. Both may be said to have three dimensions; sculpture the well-known dimension of space, and video the two dimensions of a surface, and a third one in which *depth* is a temporal sequence. Both sculpture and video are codes that somehow *freeze* the flux of time, but each in its own way: in sculpture time freezes to become space (magic), and in video it freezes to become the background of a surface (technical imagination).

There is another, even more curious, similarity: the one between video and medieval manuscripts. In medieval parchments two linear texts may be registered, the second one between the lines of the first one. Such palimpsests may provoke a dialectic tension between the two linear texts contained in them. If videotapes are used like palimpsests, the second register will be impressed upon the first one, and the scene first registered will thus become a sort of shadow of the scene that follows it. If the *same* scene is registered twice, one register *on top* of the other, historical time (which is a concept) becomes an image. And it becomes equally correct to say that on such tapes the past is *presented* or that the present is *perfected*.

Although historical time may be rendered an image on videotape, it cannot be manipulated as on film tapes. However, the videotape permits erasures, like a blackboard covered with chalk texts. There are techniques that permit the erasure of a specific layer if various layers were registered on the same tape. This amounts to an analysis of time stored, a *memory* analysis like psychoanalysis, archaeology, and geology, and it permits layers that were covered up to *emerge*. But of course, the analytical disciplines mentioned are conceptual, while the videotape as technical imaginary and *emergence* is no longer a concept but the image of a concept.

This is a typically dialogical structure: the operator does not manipulate the apparatus in search of his own point of view only (as do photographer and film cameraman) but in search of a point of view common to those who are present. Therefore, those who are present are neither part of the scene (as in photography) nor actors in an event (as in film) but partners of the operator in the same operation. The monitor is a tool for dialogues, it makes *brothers and sisters* of everyone within the operation, and it is therefore not surprising (although it may be horrifying) that the current use of monitors is one that makes spies of them in supermarkets and in traffic (*big brothers*).

The monitor is not a classical mirror. It does not invert the right and the left sides; it is not a *reflection*. Those who are not accustomed to monitors are very much upset by this; we are programmed to conceive of *reflection* as being synonymous with *speculation* and to conceive both as inversions. The monitor is a speculation, not a reflection; it is an image of non-dialectical opposition for which we have no concept.

The monitor is no classical mirror for a different reason as well: it does not reflect rays emitted by the objects mirrored, but it emits cathode rays. This is one of the extremely rare forms of light that do not issue, indirectly, from the sun, and this is a reason that the monitor appears in a fascinating, even hypnotizing, light (in a very literal sense of that term).

Monitors look like TV sets, and, in fact, most TV sets may be used as monitors within video equipment. But if this is done, the functional difference between the two becomes apparent: The TV set works like a window through which images may be seen that were radiated from beyond the horizon. The monitor works like a mirror of events present (if linked to the camera) and events past (if linked to the tape). The common confusion between monitor and TV set, and between the two functions of the monitor, is a beautiful example of our lack of technical imagination.

But there is an even more fateful confusion, the one between video and film (the *cinema at home* thing). There are superficial similarities between video and filming techniques (traveling, close-up, zooming, and so forth), videocassettes may register movies, and it is possible to buy a film and watch it on television. But these technical and functional similarities conceal a profound structural difference. In film, technical images are projected against a surface; in video, they emanate from a glass lens. This difference can be genetically illustrated thus: *the genealogical tree of the film*: cave wall—church wall—framed painting—photograph—film; *the genealogical tree of video*: the surface of a pond—mirror—telescope—microscope—video. No doubt, the two trees do converge, and both are technical image codes. But, *essentially*, film is an art form (a projection), while video is a form of perception (a way of knowing). *Video art* is a misunderstanding.

This is not meant to quarrel with the obvious fact that *art* is a way of knowing, and perception is always artificial; or with the obvious fact that films may be used for perception (*documentary films*) and, therefore, videotapes as *artistic phenomena* (whatever that may mean). What is meant is that the virtualities hidden within video are being concealed if video is taken to be a kind of film and that it is necessary to liberate video from film oppression.

The original purpose of video was to serve television, which means to serve the synchronization between mass media and public opinion. Somewhat later it was discovered that monitors might be used for spying. Thus, the purpose of video is to serve the totalitarian state, and this servitude is much more apparent in video than it is in photography and film because the video apparatus is more recent. This is why any effort to deviate video from its original purpose presupposes that the essential characteristics (the virtualities dormant in it) be discovered.

Video artists are committed to such a deviation. They want to extract monitor and tape from their apparatus context, they want to tear them from the hands of totalitarian operators, and they want to use them against *mass culture* and for *counterculture*. But they cannot succeed unless they become aware of its essence: that it renders historical time imaginable, that it permits memory analysis, that it speculates without reflecting, but, most of all, that it permits dialogical communication in a revolutionary sense of that term.

The monitor shows all those present as the operator sees them. (It is a revolutionary experience to see oneself from behind and thus to imagine, not only to conceive, the concept of *being for another*.) Those who are registered on it may watch tapes immediately after their registration, and thus the tape may serve for immediate dialogical reuse. Articulations during the dialogue may be *withdrawn* (erased from the tape), and as on musical records, an ever-more-perfect dialogue can be aimed at. And there are several other dialogical virtualities in video that may be suspected. Many more are certainly not yet discovered.

3.1.4. Television

Television looks like this, if seen from the point of view of the receiver of its message: There is a box that stands among the furniture. It has a window-like glass and various buttons. If those buttons are appropriately manipulated, movie-like images come out of the window, and cinema-like sounds come out of not easily visible loudspeakers. The manipulation of the buttons is simple, but the reasons why it works are so complex as to be impenetrable. Such systems are called *functionally simple and structurally complex*. Their opposites are *functionally complex and structurally simple* systems, like the game of chess. The TV set is the opposite of chess in the sense that anybody can play it, even if one does not understand it. One seems to master the game but is, in reality, a pawn.

The inhabitants of a room sit in a semicircle around the TV set in order to receive the images and sounds emanating from it. Some analysts believe that the set thus occupies the spot previously occupied by the mother, the teacher, the concert player, the lecturer, and the theater actor. This is, however, a mistake. The set is not an emitter (like mother or teacher) but is the last link in a chain that radiates from an invisible center. And the semicircle occupied by the inhabitants of the room is a segment of a gigantic, invisible circle around the invisible center of radiation.

The receivers decipher the images and sound as if they were traditional symbols. They mean *events over there*, and the TV set thus becomes a periscope through which the world *above the surface* can be observed. The receivers know, of course, that this is not so, but they repress that knowledge. The receivers know there is an apparatus behind the TV set, an apparatus within which operators manipulate information to codify it into the images and sounds emanating from the TV. But they do not want to know it. They cooperate with the emitter in this deception.

There is one type of image among those that emanate from the TV that provides the key for the code: the *announcer*. This image indicates whether the following images are *factual* (whether they mean *real events* as in the news), whether they are *fictitious* (as in TV shows), or whether they are imperatives (as in commercials). The images themselves do not permit that distinction. The *announcer* may be fictitious (an actor representing an announcer), but this does not matter as much as it seems to. The receiver is not interested in such distinctions and does not want to know the meaning of the information being received.

The receiver is willing to accept that the TV emits information concerning the *world* and does not care whether that world is factual, imperative, or fictitious. He or she wants it to be *interesting*, which means provoking ever-changing and ever-more-intense sensations. The receiver controls the TV, can switch it on and off, and can choose among a number of programs (*channels*). But to switch the TV off implies severing the most important (and often the only) link between the receiver and society (the world). And the receiver may choose among a limited number of programs, but they all mean the same information because the apparatus radiating them is synchronized. Thus, the *freedom* the box offers its receiver is just as illusory as is the meaning of the information.

The receiver takes the TV to be a mediation between him or her and society and thus to be a tool for politicization. The opposite is the truth. *Politics* means *the public*, and to participate in politics is to publish. It is to leave the private space and enter the wide space of the public. The box reverses that direction. It makes the so-called *politicians* and *public figures* invade the receiver's private space. *Politics* means also *dialogical exchange of information*, responsible participation. The TV excludes any possibility to dialogue with those *public persons* who penetrate the receiver's private space. This has a powerful depoliticizing effect.

The images and sounds that emanate from the TV function like drugs: they are habit forming. The more they supply the receiver with sensations, the more they condition him or her for further consumption. This is why the TV emits exclusively imperative information: models for passive consumption behavior. All the apparently factual and fictitious information it emits (be it of a scientific or artistic nature) is in reality of the type *commercials*.

The TV set glass looks like a window, but it is a false one. True windows are holes in walls that permit the inhabitant of the walls to see the world before leaving. They are meaningless if there is not another hole called *door* that permits the inhabitants to go into the world. True windows and doors are synchronized: the window serves as a map for action after egress through the door, or the window is the theory for door-praxis. But the TV set has no door. It permits no action. In this sense, it provides *false theory*: a wrong, because impractical, vision. The information received through the glass is existentially wrong because the glass is a false window.

The term *television* (which wants to connote the term *telephone*) is misleading, just as misleading as the term *network* if applied to TV broadcasting systems, because the TV set is a one-way medium: it does not permit emission. This limitation is not due to technical but to ideological reasons. The receivers are programmed not to want to use television for dialogues, as they do with telephones.

This becomes evident if one looks at a modern city from a bird's-eye view: one then sees the countless antennae the city advances into the electromagnetic ocean, within which it knows to be submerged, but which it is unable to imagine. Those antennae are the materialized desire of the city to consume the unimaginable; they are open mouths ready to devour unimaginable concepts. And the result of this consumption, of this devouring, of this uninterrupted sucking in of unimaginable concepts, as it emanates from the TV set, is inconceivable images, TV programs. If seen in such a way, the whole city appears to be an immense apparatus feeding on unimaginable concepts (the electromagnetic field) and recodifying it into inconceivable images (TV programs). This shows that the inhabitants of the city (the operators of the gigantic apparatus that recodes history into programs) are in no way interested in changing the situation. They are satisfied with it: it works perfectly well, and it works better and better. Why should anybody want to change the structure of TV? It is a near-perfect form of communication.

If there were a will to change the situation, there would also be methods to become aware of the *true* character of television. But in such a case it would no longer satisfy its receivers. They would then discover hitherto hidden virtualities in television codes, unsuspected possibilities in changing the present radiating structure, and even the almost utopian fact that McLuhan's *cosmic village* is perfectly feasible if only people refused to participate in the *cosmic circus* that the current TV situation has erected around us. They would discover that TV is not necessarily a tool for the construction of technocratic totalitarianism (as now) but may become a tool for a cosmic democracy in a sense that cannot yet be imagined.

There is no such will to change the situation. The receivers cooperate with the operators in their effort to program illusion, to foster alienation. The effort to switch off the TV set and, instead of letting oneself be programmed, begin to use technical imagination, is apparently too demanding. TV programs work because everybody wants them to work, and TV images program without having been deciphered by the receivers because the receivers do not want to decipher: they are programmed to be programmed.

3.1.5. Cinema

It is easy to compare the cinema with the *archetypical Great Mother*, that black uterus, that windowless cave that means birth and death.

The similarity between the cinema and Plato's cave is indeed compelling, and Plato's myth cannot but be read as if it were the first film criticism. But the purpose of this consideration is not to analyze the cinema as such; it is to analyze what happens during the reception of movie pictures. And this implies that the cinema must be seen in its context, which is the context of our codified world: it must be seen as one of the centers of the world of technical images that surround us at present.

It must then be admitted that the cinema is one of the rare places in our surroundings where silence and darkness prevail before the screen begins to glare and the loudspeakers begin to howl. Within the colorful multitude of the technical images that inundate us ubiquitously to divert us, the cinema is one of the rare places where we can convert diversion into concentration. This is the true reason why film is the predominant art form of the present: because it happens in one of the rare places of possible concentration, of *contemplation*, not because there is some inherent aesthetic superiority in film codes over traditional ones but because traditional codes cannot be received in silence and darkness and thus do not permit concentration.

This is also why cinemas are considered to be a sort of theater, although their structure is, in reality, quite different because cinemas permit *contemplation* (in Greek, *theoria*), and the *theatron* is the place of *theoria*. In fact, the role cinema plays within our codified world cannot be compared to the theater in classical times but to the church during the Middle Ages: they are places of concentration on the reception of a religious message. Films are received in a way comparable to the reception of the Mass by medieval receivers.

The architecture of the cinema is a late descendant of the Roman basilica (not of the theater or the circus). It is an empty vaulted hall. The Roman basilica (like the Pantheon) had various uses. One was to serve as a covered market; the other (and subsequent one) was to serve as a church. Both these basilica forms are still with us: the supermarket is the basilica in its profane form; the cinema is the basilica in its sacred form. But both are still basilicas and therefore must be regarded as forming a whole if one is to grasp the essence of technical image reception.

The supermarket is a labyrinth of technical images into which the receiver is swallowed. The entrances into that labyrinth are wide open, which creates the illusion of free access and of public space (the marketplace in a village or the *agora* of a *polis*). Of course, this is a deception, not only because no *political dialogue* is possible in a supermarket as it is in a true market—there is too much *noise*, too many whispered and screamed solicitations by sound and image—but also because the supermarket is a trap: it has no free exit. If you want to escape from it, you stand in a queue and pay a ransom. The supermarket is the exact opposite of a true market; it does not serve the exchange of goods and information but imposes consumption, and it is not a public space (a *republic*) but a prison (which is the most private of all places). That it is a mockery of a true market is what makes it *super.*

The cinema is the complement to the supermarket. It is true that the cinema entrance is glaring and colorful, it solicits and invites, but it is not an open entrance. It is a narrow slit, and if you want to penetrate the cinema and partake in its mystery, you have to stand and wait (and in that sense *also serve*). The queues that form in front of the cinema mouths are the complementary phenomena of the queues that form in the supermarket bellies, and the *obolus* you pay to escape from the supermarket trap is the other side of the coin you pay to get into the cinema in order to become programmed. However, once the program is over, the cinema exits open wide, and they vomit the faithful mass into the street and to the buses, the parked cars, and the subways; they *evacuate* what the narrow entrance had sucked in.

This synchronization of supermarket and cinema (which only a few years ago was a characteristic of the towns all over the world but now has invaded the countryside of all the continents under the form of *shopping malls*) must be understood as an important aspect of mass-culture metabolism. Supermarket and cinema are loose ends of radiating cosmic amphitheaters. One sucks in the mass that has been vomited by the other. The cinema evacuates the programmed mass, and the supermarket sucks it in to transform that program into consumption. And the supermarket expels the mass drop by drop and sand grain by sand grain so that it may be remassified in wave and dune at the entrances of the cinemas and reprogrammed for further consumption. The cash registers at cinema entrances and supermarket exits propel the cosmic amphitheater: they make the merry-go-round of mass culture turn. Of course, this is only one among the numerous cycles on which the gigantic apparatus of technical image culture gyrates, but it is a very instructive one: it shows the pseudo-magical character of mass civilization.

Within the cave of the cinema, there are seats geometrically ordered and arithmetically numbered (Cartesian-extended things put there by Cartesian-thinking things). The faithful sit motionlessly upon those chairs (extended things they are) and contemplate gigantic Technicolor shadows on a gleaming silver screen, while sound waves oscillate to and from within the walls of the cave, which has a structure appropriate for sound wave reflection. High above the heads of the faithful, and far behind their backs, there is an apparatus with an operator projecting the shadowy gods against the screen to make them seem to move. The receivers know about the apparatus, and they know how to operate it because they possess miniature apparatus of a similar construction: domestic projector, slide projector, magic lantern, and so forth. But they never turn their heads to look at the apparatus and thus demythologize the program, as did the Platonic prisoners in their thirst for truth and wisdom. Or, more exactly, they turn their heads to face the apparatus only if it does not work well, and then they do it in anger at the bad performance.

This is, strictly speaking, unbelievable behavior: How can people cooperate to such an extent with their own domination by an apparatus? There are some explanations. The faithful know that the apparatus above their heads is not a true emitter: it is only the last link in a chain radiated from an invisible center. Thus, if the receivers were to turn against it, they could not influence the program they are receiving; they can only interrupt it (which is not a good form of revolution). The faithful know that if they destroyed the film within the apparatus, they would not have destroyed the *original program* that determines them but only a copy of a prototype that may be easily substituted. And they have other such knowledge.

But this is not the true explanation of their behavior, of their cooperation with the totalitarian apparatus that programs them: that any revolution is useless. The true explanation is that they want to be dominated. They pay to go to the cinema in order to get the illusion. This is a pseudo-magical situation. The cinema is unlike a Malay shadow theater in that the mass people do not believe that the shadows they see are gods or spirits. They make believe that they believe it. They make themselves believe what the apparatus wants them to believe. The faith of mass people is bad faith. They know better, but they want to forget it. It would be easy for them to turn their heads and face the apparatus: they might then see that the cinema may be used for purposes quite different from the ones it is being used for currently, and some of those purposes might be revolutionary. For instance, the cinema might solve the present crisis in teaching, especially the university crisis. But this is precisely what they did not go to the cinema for: to see *truth* or *wisdom*. They went there, not to acquire technical imagination but to be programmed by technical images for illusions.

Observation of the production and reception of technical images shows the following: The producers are not fully aware of what they are doing, and the receivers do not want to know the meaning of their program. This is why technical images work as they do: toward totalitarian alienation. This tendency can be inverted only if technical imagination becomes a conscious way of thinking and existing. Therefore, technical imagination will now be considered.

3.2. HOW TECHNICAL IMAGES MIGHT WORK

Technical imagination, as here defined, is the capacity for the imagining of concepts and the corresponding capacity to decipher images of concepts. Whoever disposes of such capacity thinks, evaluates, experiences, in sum, exists in a very specific manner. But before the attempt is made to consider this new manner of existence, it is wise to remind oneself of how and why technical imagination came into being.

This book defends a thesis according to which humans are alienated animals that try, over and over again, to regain contact with the world they lost after having stepped outside it, after having begun their *existence*. These human efforts at reintegration result in ever-new codes that are systems of symbols. The purpose of the codes is to allow mediation between humanity and the world; they *mean* the world, which is to say that they give human life (which is, after all, life within the world) a meaning. Human life is meaningless, in a sense applicable only to humans and to no other animal; humans *exist*, which implies that they know they are going to die. This knowledge of death is knowledge of the ultimate meaninglessness of living. The purpose of codes is to make life meaningful in spite of such knowledge.

Codes can achieve this purpose because the symbols they are composed of are based on conventions between humans. They *have* the meaning humans agreed upon, a meaning common to all those who use the symbol. As a consequence, the codified worlds humans built to serve as mediations between themselves and the world they live in mean such a world for all those who participate in that codified world. In fact, the codified worlds mean the *concrete, natural world* because they were agreed upon to mean it. Which is a way of saying that human life has a meaning as long as it participates in the agreement concerning that meaning. Or that the meaning of life, of action and passion, of experience, value, and knowledge, is founded on an agreement, a communion with others. Again, that communication with others gives life a meaning in spite of one's knowledge of one's death (and of the deaths of all the others) because in some way the others one communicates with are the immortality (the memory) that renders death harmless. In short, the only possible meaning of life in the face of the knowledge of death is in communication with others, in code convention and utilization.

This then is the thesis from which this book has attempted to approach the present crisis. And as it did so, several consequences became ever-more apparent. And the most important consequence is that the dialectics inherent in mediation defeats, over and over again, human efforts to give their lives meaning. Symbols do not only point at what they mean but also hide their meaning. A codified world not only signifies the world it means, but it also replaces it. To live within a codified world, to commit oneself to culture, to communication, to others (or however one wants to state this) does not imply necessarily leading a meaningful life in spite of one's knowledge of death. It may imply, on the contrary, a life comparable to one in an impenetrable and inescapable prison. And this happens whenever the symbols surrounding humanity become opaque and then mean nothing but themselves. If such a situation emerges (as it seems to do at present), one may call it a *crisis*, not only of all the aspects of the culture one participates in but an existential crisis.

This book distinguishes three such crises in the past of humanity (among others that were not considered), and of each present human, and three attempts to overcome such crises: the *first* crisis, when humans became human (stepped out of the world into existence), which they tried to overcome through imagination (by the construction of an imaginary world); the *second* crisis, when the images with which humans had surrounded themselves became hallucinatory, which they tried to overcome through conceptual, rational thinking (by the construction of a conceptual world of progressive explanations); and the *third* crisis (ours), when the texts with which humans have surrounded themselves become paranoid (especially those of the sciences and of technology), which they are now trying to overcome through technical imagination (by the construction of a world of images intended to mean the by-now-empty concepts and explanations).

Of course, this is only one among many possible approaches to our crisis. And it is interesting only in as far as it allows us to see how it may be overcome. It is different from many other attempts to understand our situation by the fact that it takes the communication structure to be the *infrastructure*, not in any dogmatic way but in the sense that it suggests that our situation may be changed by a transformation of the codes and of the means of communication. This is, however, a radical, even a revolutionary, suggestion because it involves a mutation of human relations (of society) and of human existence (a *new human*). What follows is an attempt to describe such a mutation as it begins to condense from the fogs that surround us.

3.2.1. Points of View

The linear world of history is codified in concepts. Concepts are symbols that mean images. They mean images by pointing at them from a specific point of view, one that stands *outside* and *above* the image. It can be called the *objective viewpoint.* For instance, a tumbler is conceived to be circular because the text that describes it stands (looks at it from) above and from a point located in the center of the circle.

This objective point of view that concepts assume with regard to the imaginary world is extraordinarily characteristic of the linear world. It renders that world dynamic (historical). The aim of history is to conceive the whole imaginary world objectively, that is, to grasp it from the point of view of concepts. In the early stages of history, that aim revealed what can be called its *transcendental* aspects: the *objective viewpoint* was the point where God stands, and the aim of history was *salvation* (the way leading to God); or the *objective viewpoint* was the point where the eternal ideas stand, and the aim of history was *theory* (the way leading to the ideas). But as history advanced, more aspects of *objectivity* showed themselves, and the one that now prevails is this: the *objective viewpoint* is *value-free* (scientific, honest, uncommitted, fair, neutral), and the aim of history is to overcome all *subjective ideologies* by *objective knowledge.* In a sense, of course, all those various aspects of objectivity have a common core: *progress* is the method (be it religious, philosophical, scientific, or political) to lift humanity up from the level of images to the level of concepts.

For technical imagination the *objective point of view* is nonsense and a nuisance. It is nonsense because there is no criterion to distinguish between the position of various points with regard to what they point to: it is just as valid to call a tumbler *circular* as it is to call it *oval* or any other shape it shows when looked at. Every phenomenon is surrounded by an infinity of points of view, and each one of them is just as valid as is any other. And the *objective point of view* is a nuisance because one can never step *above* or *outside* the thing one means; one is always together with it (*interested* in it) because however far one might step back, one is always inside the world within which the thing meant is. The fact that objectivity is both nonsense and a nuisance became obvious when photography, film, and video were under discussion, but it is equally obvious in any other technical image production. The problem is not to find a preferential viewpoint from which to imagine a concept but to find as many viewpoints as possible. Objectivity is revealed to pose a false problem.

This revelation will have consequences that we cannot begin to imagine. One of them is that *progress* on the level of technical imagination has a totally different structure from the one it has on the level of historical reason. It no longer means a linear tendency toward objectivity but now means a *peripheral* tendency (a circling of what is meant) in the search of ever-different points of view. But such a change in the meaning of *progress*, this mutation from linearity into a spreading motion, involves unimaginable transformations.

For instance, what sort of science will there be if *objective knowledge* is both an impossible and an undesirable ideal? Or what sort of politics will there be if to be *progressive* is no longer to stand on a point of view nearer to objectivity than are most the others, but to be progressive now means to be able to change points of view in steady progression? Or how is one to distinguish between science and art if the criterion of distinction between objectivity and subjectivity is abandoned? If science is just as *non-objective* as art is, is it a sort of art, is art a sort of science, or are both forms of politics (searches of points of view for future action)?

This kind of questioning can be continued indefinitely, and none of the questions can now be answered. But there is, even at this point, a way to at least intuit the direction of future answers. It is clear that as soon as technical imagination empties the concept *objectivity* of all meaning, the concept *truth* must be imagined from various new angles. For linear, historical reason truth is a process; it is either the progressive unveiling of the unknown by the knower (Greek truth), the progressive revelation of the unknown to the knower (Jewish truth), or a combination of both. And *total truth* is the happy end of history: absolute objective knowledge.

For technical imagination the search for truth is a sort of circling of a problem, a dance from point of view to point of view, and the purpose of the search is not to unveil or reveal the problem but to solve it. A problem cannot be unveiled or revealed because it is a problem only in the sense that it is being circled. It is the investigation that makes it a problem, an *object*, and there is no sense in speaking of a problem outside such a circling. And a problem is *solved* if all those who circle it share the same points of view, if the problem becomes an *intersubjective problem*. (See the discussion on photography.) The solution of a problem is in the agreement about its meaning. And this involves an image of the concept *truth*; the more people share a point of view, the truer it is. Intersubjectivity, not objectivity, thus becomes a criterion for truth.

Although we are familiar with such a vision of truth (since the neopositivists, on the one hand, and the phenomenologists, on the other), and although we apply it while photographing, filming, videoing, and so forth, it is difficult to hold on to it. No longer is the search for truth an advance in the direction of an *objective world*; no longer is it a *discovery.* It has become a stretching out of arms in the direction of others who are here with me, an invitation to an agreement. Truth is no longer a pursuit for the sake of knowing and dominating the world, and even less for its own sake. It is now a pursuit for the sake of living together with others by agreeing with them in regard to the world we live in.

If one tries to hold on to such an image of truth, one may begin to see that on the level of technical imagination the present distinction between science, technology, art, and politics will become nonsense. This will be so because *truth* on that level will not be a category of knowledge but of concrete living together with others. *Truth* will no longer be a category parallel to such other categories like *goodness* or *beauty.* It will become a *total* category, and *search for truth* will become a *religious* search in a sense we cannot yet fully intuit because we are programmed only for magical or salvational (historical) religion.

Still, we may vaguely guess at what may happen if we consider the following: There were moments in history when the *equivalence of all possible viewpoints* was being asserted, and the eighteenth century is an example. This implied a tolerant indifference. In this sense it was anti-ideological: to defend a point of view is nonsense because all of the possible points of view are equally wrong. This attitude can be called *skeptical* or *irreligious.* But intersubjectivity is the exact opposite of tolerance and indifference. It states that every point of view shows a *value* specific to it and is *true* in this sense. That *equivalence* does not mean *indifference* but *equality of value.* It does not state, as enlightened tolerance or classical *skepsis* did, that the quest for truth is a lost endeavor but, on the contrary, that truth increases if viewpoints are welded together. In short, it does not state, as historical indifference did, that *objectivity* is unfortunately impossible. It states that *objectivity* is an undesirable, even criminal attitude, precisely because it claims to be value-free. This is not being irreligious but being religious on a new level.

To weld viewpoints together (as, for instance, optics does when it regards light to be quantic and undulatory) is only a step toward this new attitude toward truth. Welding Marxist and Freudian viewpoints shows better what is *religious* about it. But we may vaguely guess at what will happen if we consider the possibility of simultaneously evaluating Marxism from a Freudian viewpoint, Freudism from a Marxist viewpoint, and both such evaluations from a Catholic viewpoint. Such a *welding is not a synthesis* but a circling because it remains possible to evaluate Catholicism both from a Marxist and a Freudian viewpoint. To be able to imagine this overlap of viewpoints, and to be able to transfer this image into science, the arts, politics, and action, is to have technical imagination.

3.2.2. Time

For a consciousness programmed by linear codes time is a stream that flows from the past toward the future and carries everything with it. This is *historical* time, the time of the irrevocable uniqueness of every event, the time of causal chains. For technical imagination, such a concept of time is insane because it inverts the direction of time as it is experienced. Time is experienced as the arrival of the future, not of the past (what *comes* is not yesterday but tomorrow). But it is even more insane because it reduces the present to a point on a line, while the present is being experienced as the place where time flows.

If one tries to imagine time, this is what might happen:

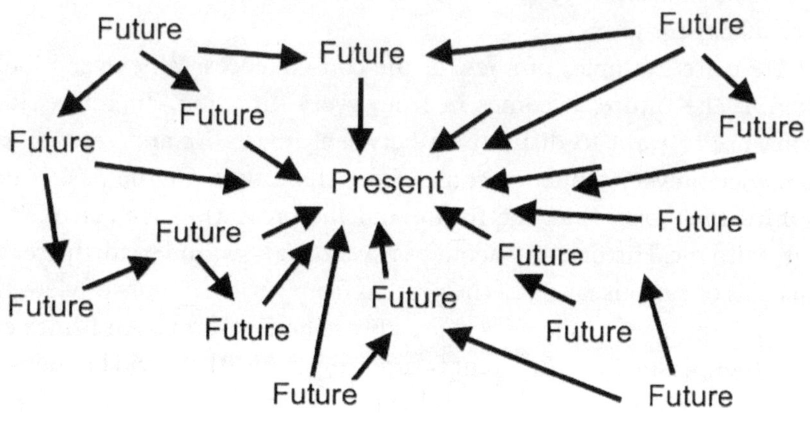

SKETCH 3.2.2

The sketch shows that as soon as we try to imagine the concept *time*, and as soon as we try to bring it in some relation with the experience of time on what was here called the *imaginary level*, it becomes obvious that the present occupies the central position. To conceive of the present as a point (the instant the present is, it is no longer) is paranoia because, as the sketch shows, the present is where everything happens; for something to happen is to *present itself.*

But this is not the main purpose of the sketch. It shows that the ontology fundamental to historical thinking (to be is to become) acquires a revolutionary, new connotation on the level of technical imagination. The arrows symbolize tendencies toward realization (*becoming*): the future *becomes*, in the sense that it tends to present itself, to emerge from the realm of *possible events* into the realm of *effective events.* But once it presents itself, the event no longer *becomes*; it *happens.* It is *the case* (as Wittgenstein puts it). The present is the end of *becoming.*

To have grasped this is only the first step toward having grasped the earthquake now happening in our time experience and time evaluation. The definition of *present* cannot be an *objective* one, as historical reason desperately tries to formulate; it is simple: where I am, there is the present. Or the other way around: I am always present. This is a simple and obvious statement. But it involves, if taken in its full impact, consequences that shatter all the categories of historical existence. They may be summed up like this: I do not *become*; I stand always still; it is the world that comes toward me; it *becomes me.* Or I do not happen; the world happens to me.

Here are examples of a few of the consequences: Wherever I look, there is the future. It comes in from every direction. Therefore, it is nonsense to want to distinguish between *progressive* and *reactionary* tendencies: every tendency comes from the future. Or the past is not a third *time form* (like the future and the present); it is present. It is here with me. History, archaeology, psychoanalysis, and so forth are the analysis of various layers of the present from various points of view. Or again, I am never alone; others are always here with me. And since every other person has a different future from mine (the world happens to them differently from the way it happens to me), to *open up the future* (increase the parameter of possible events) is not to make projects but to open myself up in the direction of those present with me. Or once again, it is nonsense to want to explain the present from the past (by *causal chains*) because what comes in is the future. It is an error to say birds build nests *because* their genetic information programs them that way or that the French Revolution is a cause of the Russian Revolution. The correct way to speak is this: the genetic information manifests itself in nest building, or the Russian Revolution shows what the French revolutionaries wanted. It is the present that *explains* the past, as the future will *explain* the present.

The moment one begins to enumerate such consequences (and the enumeration may go on), they sound, all of them, convincing to a point where one asks oneself why, for heaven's sake, one did not always see them. Yet, curiously, such an enumeration cannot, by itself, do away with historical reason. We may agree, for instance, that the concept of *avant-garde* is an empty one and still be unable not to distinguish it from academicism. We may admit that the past is synonymous with the present and that the difference between *ancient past* and *recent past* is a difference in depth of layers (of *memory*) and still be unable to deny an *objective* meaning of statements like *before Jesus*. We may admit that the presence of others with us is an increase in time dimensions and still be unable to abandon *absolute* time scales like centuries and minutes. We may admit that historical explanations are nonsense (because there is no *first cause* and because the future will show what has happened) and still be unable to deny that scientific explanations (which are historical explanations) can predict what will happen. And so forth. In short, we may have an image of the historical time concept that renders that concept untenable and still be unable to abandon such a concept because it is deeply inscribed within our program.

But this may change in the near future. Technical imagination invades historical reason. This is obvious in the realm of natural sciences, for instance, in the critique of causal explanations, but it is even more effective in other, and quite unrelated, regions. For instance, in the *new novel*, in certain films, in the use of drugs, in the attitude toward historical explanations and the teaching of history, a radically non-historical, post-historical consciousness is forming. And it cannot be done away with by catchwords such as *structuralism* or *new left*. This goes far deeper.

Any attempt to continue and describe the new experience of time and the paradox that results from it—that to be *progressive* now begins to mean that one is on a level of consciousness no longer valid—must fail if one is not to consider, simultaneously, the new experience of space that goes along with it.

3.2.3. Space

The fact is that any image of the concept *time* must necessarily be spatial. Historical reason, thinking programmed by linear codes, possesses two distinct *forms of perception*, time and space, but those are in reality concepts of images and thus a translation from surface to line: both time and space are fundamentally a projection of space upon a surface. This is the structural reason that it is impossible, on the level of linear thinking, to establish a satisfactory relation between space and time: either space is conceived of as somehow containing time, or time is conceived of as somehow carrying space away in its current. This explains why there are various *times* for such a way of thinking: physical time, biological time, psychological time, in short, why the well-known dichotomy *time and duration* obscures the issue.

For technical imagination the opposite is the case: the instant an image of the concept *time* is produced, it automatically implies an image of the concept *space*. Time and space are unimaginable one without the other. This must be put in stronger terms: the concepts *time* and *space* must be imagined as one, or they become empty concepts. Thus, while for linear reason the problem is how to relate time and space, for technical imagination the distinction between the two becomes problematic. This provides a beautiful example for the emergence of a new level of thinking: When the concept *four-dimensional space continuum* was first proposed, it was considered to be a difficult, because unimaginable, concept. But now, for those who have even rudimentary technical imagination, it is the space concept of classical physics that has become unimaginable.

Care should be taken, however, in believing that the revolution in space and time experience is due to scientific *advances*, illustrated thus:

Far
Far Far Far Far
Far Far Near Far Far Far
Far Near Near Near Far
Far Far Near Near Near Far Far
Far Near Near Near Near Far
Far Near Near Here Near Near Far
Far Near
Far Near Near Far Far
Far Far Near Near Near Near Far
Far Near Near Near Far Far
Far Far Near Far Far Far
Far Far Far

SKETCH 3.2.3

It should be obvious that sketch 3.2.3. is in no way different from sketch 3.2.2. and that it is the same sketch. The word *present* in sketch 3.2.2. is synonymous with the word *here* in sketch 3.2.3., and the word *future* in sketch 3.2.2., together with its various arrows, is synonymous with the words *near* and *far* in 3.2.3.. It is a concession to conceptual thinking if one were to call sketch 3.2.2. an *image of the time concept* and 3.2.3. an *image of the space concept*: they are the same image.

The source of the two sketches has nothing to do with the concepts in modern physics, with the *four dimensions* of space-time. The question is not at all, how is space related to time? But, when does "here" mean a space concept, and when does it mean a time concept? A way to state this is that from one point of view *time* is imagined as space melting into a flux, and from another point of view *space* is imagined as time freezing into a block, and only if the two points of view are welded together can one imagine the meaning of the two concepts. Again, the concept *space* can be imagined as a synchronization of time, and the concept *time*, as a diachronization of space. The scientific *advance* cannot be the cause of this type of technical imagination; on the contrary, it is the result of technical imagination.

Where I am, there is *here*: I stand always in the center of the Cartesian system of coordinates. The center of space cannot be chosen at will, as it is in classical physics: it is given by my position. But there is no way to measure space by absolute scales. All measurements are relative to me, as it is my position that must be the point of departure for all scales. Objects surround me by what is called *the objective world*. Those objects press on me from all sides, as they tend to present themselves *here*. They are *objects* because they obstruct (*ob-jacere*) my view of the horizon. They come ever nearer, and they do not permit me to see far. The measure of the objective world is the nearness and farness of objects from where I stand.

The horizon the objects do not permit me to see is my future. The objects come in from the future. The nearer they come, the more they obstruct my view: they become ever-more objective. If I try to glance over and above the objects, if I stand on futurological tiptoes to glace at the future, I can see how the objects become ever sparser and ever less objective toward the horizon. They are too far to constitute objects. This then is the structure of space: it is dense and objective where I stand; it gets ever more scattered and nebulous as I approach the horizon; and it dissolves itself into nothingness in the far, distant, inaccessible future. This does not imply that space is *limited*: there is no limit; there is nothing *outside*; and the farther toward the future my glance advances, the farther the horizon of space recedes. But it does imply that there is *nothing* outside space and that I can see such *nothing* in the form of an ever-receding horizon.

Such a space cannot be measured in kilometers or in light-years, or in seconds and billions of years, or even in a combination of the two scales. The distance of an object is relative to my existence. It is the closer the more it approaches me and the more it becomes involved with me. It is the closer the more I become *interested* in it (*interest = to be involved*). The only scale of measurement such a space admits is a scale that measures my interest in the objective world. Such a scale may become as exact as are the scales of classical physics. If one accepts that the *mathesis* of the objective world is my interest in it, my interest becomes just as quantifiable as are centimeters and seconds. Still, it cannot be denied that a disciplined application of such scales in the immediate future will have consequences that exceed, by far, our imagination.

It is true that there are, even now, methods of measurement that try to apply scales of the type just mentioned, for instance, the so-called *proxemics*. But consider this: If all possible scales take their departure from *here*, they cannot be infinite in the sense we are accustomed to by linear thinking. They cannot have *negative* values, marks that advance from zero toward the left: they stop where I stand. But even to the right, in the direction of the future, they cannot go on forever and disappear from sight in the abyss of billions of kilometers, of tons, of years, as do the traditional scales. Neither can they disappear in that curious abyss of nanometers and milliseconds that has transformed the scientific discourse universe into the bottomless pit of paranoia. They must stop where my interest stops because it is such interest they measure. Again, this shrinking of the scales as they approach the horizon of the future (that region where space gets less and less objective) must have a counterpart where the measurement of the past is concerned. Although the past is an aspect of the present that shows itself from various points of view, it is still measurable according to my interest in it. Not only will the new scales measure the recent past before the ancient one (today comes before yesterday, and Charles V before Charlemagne), but the twentieth century will occupy a far larger span on such scales than will the geological period of the fishes. And again, such scales, which expand from *here* toward the horizon of nothingness like fans, will not work like passive, wooden rulers, as do the scales of linear thinking. They will fan interest as they advance; they will *bring nearer* the objects they measure. They will change what they measure by rendering it measured (more objective). They will not be wooden but living.

This *science fiction* (which is nothing but an exercise in technical imagination) intends to suggest that the new space and time experience will necessarily result in a revolution of all historical categories, not only of those that have to do with knowledge. For instance, if the world is experienced as *beginning* here and now and *ending* where my interest in it ends, then the question of *transcendence* is posed in a context that cannot be conceived by historical reason, by a consciousness programmed by texts that aim at *objective* knowledge, because it will become obvious that to *transcend* means to overcome the subjectivity of existence. The world is *transcended* on the side *here-now* by the inclusion of others who are here and now with me: the more others there are with me, the more have I transcended the world of my existence and the more have I penetrated a world of intersubjectivity, of *coexistence*. And the world is *transcended* on the side *horizon* by the amplification of my interests, which I achieve by including the interests of others (including those who will come *after me*). In fact, the horizon of my interests is my death, and the world *ends* when I die, because it then no longer has any *here-now* center. By amplifying my interests beyond my death, by rendering them intersubjective, I have *transcended* my interests and therefore the world.

This example of how all the historical categories will be exploded by time and space technical imagination (an example that can easily be multiplied) opens a sort of window onto the possible future. If *transcendence* is passing from subjectivity into intersubjectivity, then the transcendence of the world implies penetration into a new one, which is to say that expeditions into the abysses of traditional space and time (such as spaceships and nuclear research) are no longer meaningful because they do not effectively expand experience, knowledge, and values. It is the trips that expand interest and increase the number of people who can share my points of view that really matter. For the time being, these trips are pursued mostly through two methods: drugs and pointless violence, but this is due to immature technical imagination. No doubt, as the traditional *adventures*, such as expeditions to Mars, will become less and less interesting and more and more sensationalized by mass media, far more refined methods than drugs and violence will be found to expand true interest and to *transcend* the world by intersubjective commitment.

The transgression of history by the explosion of traditional categories of thinking may perhaps be grasped if one considers the fundamental categories of technical imagination, as they begin to crystallize from the previous description. Those categories are *here*, *now*, *near*, *far*, and so forth (or similar *time-space* and *points-of-view* aspects). It was argued that the fundamental category of historical, linear thinking is *and then* (or *if-then*). History is transgressed if the causal category is replaced by the new categories, not only in theoretical thinking but also in everyday experience and acting. And this will happen when *proximity* will substitute *reason* by imagining the meaning of *reason*.

The explosiveness of such a translation from reason into an image of reason can be felt if one considers that *proximity* (that technical image of causality) is charged with political, even religious connotations, while causality is not. If I translate the causal chain into the *far-near* relation, I have translated from clear and distinct calculation into highly connotative technical imagination. The fateful sentence *love thy neighbor* acquires a new meaning because *the nearer, the more interesting. Love* and *hatred* become integrated within knowledge as they never were during history; one knows what one loves and hates because it is near, and the less something interests, the less one knows it. This is, of course, far more *human* than the cold, objective attitude of calculating scientific reason. But it is not *humane* or *humanistic*: I am far more interested in the fly that bothers me here and now than I am in the future of eight hundred million Chinese, and I love my dog more than I love the suffering masses.

All the categories of historical reason, including the most profound ones such as the so-called *Christian* or *humanistic* values, are certain to be rendered inoperative by technical imagination. This is why the *new human* and *new society*, as they begin to form around us and within us, are so terrifying. We cling to the historical categories because we cannot imagine the post-historical ones and thus are terrified by them. The leap from history into post-history, which is for us a leap from well-known, although empty categories into the unknown, is a critical experience in the full sense of that term. And this is best seen in the example just offered: if *proximity* (intersubjectivity) substitutes *causality* (objectivity), this will be the end of *humanism*, which has been the ideal of history since the Jewish prophets and Greek philosophers up to Marxism.

The first section of this chapter examines production and consumption of a few technical images. The second section proposes some daring generalizations from this examination. They may be summarized as follows: If one considers how specialists manipulate technical images, both on the elite and mass-media levels, one can observe the formation of a new form of consciousness and action. They are new in the sense that they are no longer linearly programmed. Categories such as *sooner-later*, *if-then*, *true-false*, or *real-unreal* do not apply to it. Other, non-dialectical categories, such as *proximity*, *point of view*, or *the other*, form the structure of this way of experiencing, knowing, and evaluating. And this may be observed in action: how video cameras are handled, how photographs of stars are made, but also how gigantic apparatus are being operated.

One of the obvious consequences of this revolution is that the concept *progress* has become devoid of meaning. Another is that the traditional distinctions between science, technology, art, and politics have become inoperative. A third one is that *doubt* has become a method of living: it consists of changing one's point of view so that it may be multiplied and that others may share it. And there are several other consequences, already obvious by now, of this change in level of thinking and acting. Many more consequences can only be guessed at, and there will be consequences, no doubt, that we cannot even suspect, let alone imagine. In sum, one may observe how a *new human* is about to be born.

However, if one considers how technical images are being received through mass media, one gets the opposite impression. It then appears that a gigantic, and ever-more-autonomous, process of loss of consciousness is going on, one that will lead to total alienation and to the establishment of technocratic totalitarianism. And since consumers seem to cooperate with their programmers in this process of massification, it seems that the *new human* who is about to be born is the unconscious mass human being.

This contradiction is inherent in our crisis. It may be said that a new level of existence, one of technical imagination, is about to be formed but that it is so terrifying that most of us (and all of us most of the time) prefer to sink into unconsciousness instead of facing it and trying to integrate it. This contradiction is, of course, what makes of our situation a *crisis*: that it holds conflicting virtualities, all of which terrify us, and that we are unable to choose, let alone predict, what will happen. The last section of this book attempts to describe this.

3.3. THE PRESENT SITUATION

The present mutation in human communication appears, if looked at superficially, as a change in communication structures. A gigantic and ever-increasing mass of people all over the world is being annexed to a mass-media apparatus (to radiated amphitheatrical discourses) in order to be programmed by it. All the surviving structures for a true dialogue are in dissolution. The empty chatter of network dialogue, which transforms information received from mass media into public opinion, quenches every effort at creative intervention in the communication process. The explosively progressive discourses of science and technology spout an ever-increasing flow of information over the heads of a massified humanity, but this information does not nurture a true dialogical communication and feeds instead the apparatus that programs the masses. Those who participate actively in the production of information (the specialists) are themselves being programmed by the mass-media meat choppers for information production. The better the apparatus works, the more autonomous of independent opinion and decision it becomes, and the feedback between radiated information and public opinion reinforces its ever-more-automatic programming. The tendency appears to be in the direction of a totalitarian mass society within which life will become ever lonelier and more senseless.

This sort of analysis of our present situation has been, for some years now, one of the more usual approaches to our crisis. It is no doubt justified to a large extent and must be undertaken. But this book suggests that it is insufficient. After having considered a few of its aspects in the first chapter, it concludes that one cannot grasp the essence of the current revolution if one does not consider the change in the type of predominant codes in our situation. Therefore, the second and third chapters present a tentative (and admittedly preliminary and insufficient) analysis of some codes through which we receive our programs.

The result of that investigation may be summarized this way: *decline and fall of linear codes and rise of a new type of code, composed of a new type of images.* It would seem that this is not a very efficient method to analyze our crisis. The fact that the alphabet is less important as a code carrying information than it used to be (if indeed this is a fact) does not seem to be of the same importance as the fact that mass media program us. And the fact that we are exposed to a greater number of images than were previous generations does not seem comparable in importance to the fact that we can no longer undertake dialogue as significantly as did our parents. One might be tempted to say that, to be sure, such an analysis of codes is interesting, but it can be used at best as a supplement to the analysis of communication structures if what one is interested in is an understanding of our crisis.

This book argues that this is a mistake. It suggests that the change in codes implies a profound mutation, and, in fact, that we are at present witnesses to and participants in a transformation that can be compared, in its radicalness, with no other except the one that brought about history and historical existence, that the passage from linear to the new type of codes is a *reprogramming* comparable only to the one that occurred by the invention of writing; indeed, that if one concentrates one's attention on the more obvious changes in our communication situation only, one might miss what is going on altogether; in short, that it is hopeless to want to do anything about the present communication structures (TV, the press, schools, political institutions, etc.) before having understood what sorts of programs any such action of ours is founded upon (what sort of information we have at our disposal).

Of course, it is far easier to claim that our program is radically different from any previous ones; that we think, feel, evaluate, and consequently act in a way radically different from any previous form of existence than it is to prove such an extravagant claim. Is it indeed true that a *new human* and a *new society* are in the making? Are we indeed approaching the *end of history* in the sense this book has suggested? Is there indeed a tendency toward the abandonment of such ancient categories as *science*, *the arts*, *technique*, *politics*, and may one indeed observe that people begin to give their lives a new meaning? This book, especially Chapter 3, tries to render such a claim somewhat less extravagant by advancing a few observations taken from the current situation. And this has resulted in a view of our present situation that may be stated as follows.

The crisis we are in may be looked at from two points of view: one that looks at it from where we are and one that looks through it at where we are. It may be seen as an *external* crisis, a change in our surroundings, or as an *internal* crisis, a change in our way of being within our surroundings. No doubt, those two points of view imply each other: to say that civilization is a product of humanity implies that human beings are a product of civilization, and to say that the threads of the net of communication connect humans implies that humans are knots in the net of communication. Still, if we take our crisis to be an internal one that grips each of us in its very bowels, we might gain more immediate access to understanding it.

If we assume such a point of view, we find that we are not conveniently programmed for the world we find ourselves in at present. We do not understand this world because we are programmed to understand by conceiving. But most of the symbols that surround us are not conceivable. But a great amount of information at our disposal has come into our memories via those inconceivable codes that program us to understand by imagining. And as a result, much of what we know through conception has become unimaginable. In sum, we have two programs, one linearly coded that permits us to conceive the world and the other coded in technical images that permits us to imagine we do not really know what. This conflict within our program renders the world we find ourselves in both inconceivable and unimaginable, and it does so on two different levels: what we conceive, we cannot imagine; and what we imagine, we do not believe in. Thus, our crisis is a sort of civil war within our program.

If we now project this inner aspect upon the outer situation, we find that it is a mirror of our inner disruption. And then we find an explanation for a series of curious behaviors we observe in others and ourselves. For instance, why do we behave so differently in front of a TV set than in a chemical laboratory? Or why do we behave at the entrance of a cinema so differently from the way we behave during a committee meeting? The explanation is this: There are situations for which we are programmed by linear codes, and we behave according to linear, conceptual, historical reason. And there are situations for which we are not yet correctly programmed, as the technical images that correspond to them have not yet formed what can be called a *technical image reason*. And in those situations, we behave *unreasonably*. If seen thus, our crisis is the fact that our world consists of two types of situations.

But this is not what is essential. The core of our crisis is that in those situations for which we are not adequately programmed we behave in a way that prevents us from understanding them, and we do so because we do not want to understand them. Mass media manipulate us, not so much because some *hidden* interests use them against us by some superhuman cunning but because we want to be manipulated. And we want to be manipulated because we fear that if we grasped the situation, we would lose the *other side* of our program, our historical, conceptual way of being. We allow the media to manipulate us for fear of loss of *reason*. We do not dare make the leap from linear thinking to technical imaginary thinking for fear of disintegration. Thus, we are, of course, easy prey to those who are interested in manipulating us: we collaborate with them.

No use blaming those *hidden forces* for the situation we are in, not only because they are themselves victims of the same context we are in—they manipulate us because they were programmed for manipulation—but principally because the problem is not one of the classical *master/slave* human relation but of a new type of relation. We cannot *liberate* ourselves from apparatus *manipulation* (the classical political categories no longer apply) because we have no *after-apparatus program* and cannot have one. And we can no longer believe in the programs we do have. This becomes obvious if we consider what might be the situation after the hypothetical destruction of current structures.

There is no difficulty in changing and even destroying those structures, neither technical nor even political or economic ones: the structures we find ourselves in are flexible and relatively inexpensive. No technical difficulties prevent the TV set becoming a two-way channel like a telephone, and there is very little opposition to such a change in most countries. And if thus changed, it would become a powerful tool for *democracy* and thus be far more revolutionary than are public meetings (let alone political elections). But such a change would require a new vision of politics, of decision-making, of action; it would involve the abandonment of concepts such as *nation* or *class*, and it would involve the abandonment of the present, highly satisfactory use of television. It would require a technical imagination that nobody is willing and able to mobilize, neither those who manipulate current TV nor those who are its victims. For this reason, not because of some technical, political, or economic difficulties, the current TV structures work as they do, as radiating amphitheaters.

There is no technical, economic, or political difficulty involved in changing primary schools into what can be called *dialogical cinemas* (where tapes permit feedback). There are probably more cinemas than school buildings all over the world, the reproduction of dialogical films is cheaper than training teachers, and the computers that could reprogram the tapes are already in existence. Such a synthesis of school and cinema would not only serve as a powerful tool of true cosmic politicization but would form a network of artistic worldwide collaboration on all levels. But it would involve the abandonment of traditional categories of education, of *sovereignty*, of the distinction between *art* and *science*, and a whole series of similar categories of historical thinking. It is not because it is in the interest of *neoimperialists* or *international communism*, or against such an interest, that such a change is not even envisaged but because nobody has at their disposal sufficient technical imagination to contemplate it.

Those are two very obvious examples of the flexibility of current communication structures. Many more equally obvious examples, and an even greater number of slightly less obvious ones, may be easily enumerated. They mean to show that the difficulty is in daring to leap from historical into post-historical thinking and not in the resistance of the apparatus to our *liberating* efforts.

The flexibility of current communication structures is almost hidden from view by our incapacity to dare and imagine what may be done about them. This is why they appear to be so rigid. The generalized infantilization (not to say idiotization) produced by the reinforcing feedback between radiated information and network dialogue (by the synchronization of TV and public opinion) prevents us from seeing how relatively easy it would be to do away with the barrier between elite and mass culture. And those specialists who know about such flexibility because they operate the various apparatus, those who know that the current communication structures allow entirely different communication than that being used at present, are unable to translate knowledge from their specialty into a wider context. Photographers know that there are potentialities hidden in their code that have not yet been taken advantage of, but they are unable to see that those potentialities may be applied in the field of politics or in science; and film operators know that their code has not yet begun to be effectively manipulated, but they are unable to see the possible applications in the field of philosophy or education. This is so because specialization is a sort of idiotization in the strict sense of that term: a limitation to a single *idiom* (hermetic code).

This general tendency toward infantilism and idiotization both on the elite and the mass level of communication, which prevents us from grasping the situation we are in (and which manifests itself as the tendency to blame *others* for it), is a tendency *willed* by all of us most of the time, because infantilism and idiotization (*consumer culture*) are evasions from the responsibility to embrace technical imagination. It is preferable to behave as if one did not know of the countless openings that our situation offers us and continue to let oneself be programmed (and at the same time complain about *lack of freedom and meaningful communication*) than to dare to face those openings and give up cherished categories (*linear programs*).

If this is a correct description of our situation, it may drive a naïve observer to desperation. All the necessary conditions are given to transform human relations to allow the establishment of a new form of society and a new form of civilization. Creative cosmic dialogue is possible, one that could result in such a wealth of information that everything previously produced must appear to be mere preparation. We stand on the threshold of a new level of existence on which human life would attain a radically new meaning: the conscious pursuit of immortality in the memory of others through the production of information together with them. And as we stand on that threshold, all we do is watch TV and talk idly about it or continue to think on a level no longer valid in categories that have become devoid of meaning, such as *Third World*, *class struggle*, or *energy crisis*. In sum, the very moment a *new human* is about to be born, all we see around us is either the *silent consuming majority* or a minority of *progressives* who behave as if the nineteenth century had never ended.

Such naïve desperation is obviously in error, just as much as its counterpart, naïve utopianism. There are no openings within our situation as long as we do not have at our disposal sufficient technical imagination to use them. We stand on no threshold as long as we do not dare to leap over it. Or as long as we have not mastered the new codes we invented, the possibilities contained in them are not available to us. A metaphor illustrates what is meant here.

Suppose that medieval alchemy has resulted in the construction of a modern chemistry laboratory together with all the apparatus that equips it. And suppose that there is an alchemist who inhabits it and intends to use it. He will use it for his magic formulae because he cannot decipher the chemical formulae he finds in the texts in the laboratory. The magical recitations will somehow, and vaguely, conflict with the laboratory equipment. The alchemist will be in a *crisis* because he will feel that the laboratory (the *world* he helped produce) has no meaning. As long as he does not learn the formulae of modern chemistry, it will indeed have no meaning. All the alchemist can do is give up and allow himself to be narcotized by the fumes coming out of the various bottles (*consume*) or continue to search for the *quintessence* or the *fountain of youth* and the *philosopher's stone* (be *progressive*). The metaphor would be incomplete if the laboratory did not contain highly efficient employees (functionaries, operators, etc.) who make the laboratory work and produce ever-new chemical products without being able to decipher a single formula, and if the alchemist did not blame those employees for the fact that the laboratory produces chemicals instead of gold. Such a laboratory would exclude both utopian optimism and desperation. It would depend on the alchemist, on his capacity to learn chemistry, and on his willpower not to inhale fumes whether and how the laboratory will ever be used on its appropriate level.

As is the case of every critical situation, ours holds two extreme possibilities between which it oscillates: to either freeze into automatic totalitarianism or explode into technical imagination. And, as is the case of every crisis overcome, none of the two possibilities will become fully effective. Should the first alternative prevail over the second, we may imagine the future: humans will become functionaries, society will become an apparatus, and *history* in the strict sense will be over. Should the second alternative prevail over the first one, we cannot imagine the future. Technocracy is imaginable; technical imagination is not.

We are, all of us, committed to communication, which means committed to the future. We are committed to it even if we allow ourselves to be willingly alienated by radiated programs because it is this commitment that allows us to live: there is death in isolation. But of course, how can we commit ourselves to communication if it either isolates (technocratic totalitarianism) or is indecipherable (technical imagination)? How can we commit ourselves to a future (a culture, a codified world) if it is either meaningless or dreadful? This is the situation we are in.

The purpose of this book is to contribute to the understanding of this situation by proposing the point of view of codification. It will then be seen as a radical mutation of human relations, a radical change of the agreement between humans concerning the meaning of life in the world. No attempt has been or will be made to minimize the difficulty of our crisis, as if it were easy to decide between the omnipresent apparatus and the *new human*, between semiconscious or unconscious functioning and fully awake technical imagination, between *order and progress* and *creative freedom*. It is no easy decision because although totalitarian apparatus are certainly a horrible prospect, so is the *new human*. Like everything new he is dreadful, and that is why he is being called a *terrorist* whenever he begins to show his unshaven face and his despicable manners. The *new human* is dreadful because, whatever else he may be, he cannot be *humane* in the historical sense (neither Christian nor Marxist). It is difficult to choose between Adolf Eichmann and Baader-Meinhof, between technocracy and technical imagination. The difficulty is in no way *objectively given*. It is our difficulty, to the extent to which we are still committed to historical freedom and the dignity of human action and passion, to the extent to which we are *old humans*.

This book attempts to open up a few aspects of the *new human* by analyzing what it called *technical imagination* and the origins of such capacity to think and act beyond concepts. These attempts are both unsatisfactory and incomplete and are far too sketchy. Others must come and do it better and continue it in a possibly quite different direction from the one here taken. But is this not *commitment to communication*: to ask others for help?

... **Sensing Media**

Aesthetics, Philosophy, and Cultures of Media

EDITED BY WENDY HUI KYONG CHUN AND SHANE DENSON

What does it mean to think, feel, and sense with and through media? In this cross-disciplinary series we present books and authors exploring this and related questions: How do media technologies, broadly defined, transform artistic practices and aesthetic sensibilities? How are practices, encounters, and affects entangled with the deep infrastructures and visible surfaces of the media environment? How do we "make sense"—cognitively, perceptually, and culturally—of media?

We are especially interested in contributions that open our understanding of media aesthetics beyond the narrow confines of Western art and aesthetic values. We seek works that reestablish the environmental connections between art and technology as well as between the aesthetic, the sensible, and the philosophical. We invite alternative epistemologies and phenomenologies of media rooted in the practices and subjectivities of Black, Indigenous, queer, trans, and other communities that have been unjustly marginalized in these discussions. Ultimately, we aim to sense the many possible worlds that media disclose.

—

Mark Amerika, *My Life as an Artificial Creative Intelligence*

The authorized representative in the EU for product safety and compliance is:
Mare Nostrum Group
B.V Doelen 72
4831 GR Breda
The Netherlands

www.ingramcontent.com/pod-product-compliance
Lightning Source LLC
LaVergne TN
LVHW091132080826
845145LV00008B/2127

* 9 7 8 1 5 0 3 6 3 4 4 8 0 *